The Official Microsoft®

Microsoft® Windows™ 3.1

Step by Step

PUBLISHED BY
Microsoft Press
A Division of Microsoft Corporation
One Microsoft Way
Redmond, Washington 98052-6399

Library of Congress Cataloging-in-Publication Data
Microsoft Windows 3.1 step by step / Catapult, Inc.
p. cm.
Includes index.
ISBN 1-55615-501-8
1. Microsoft Windows (Computer program) I. Catapult, Inc.
QA76.76.W56M524 1992
005.4'3--dc20 92-10824
CIP

Printed and bound in the United States of America.

6 7 8 9 MLML 7 6 5 4

Distributed to the book trade in Canada by Macmillan of Canada, a division of Canada Publishing Corporation.

Distributed to the book trade outside the United States and Canada by Penguin Books Ltd.

Penguin Books Ltd., Harmondsworth, Middlesex, England
Penguin Books Australia Ltd., Ringwood, Victoria, Australia
Penguin Books N.Z. Ltd., 182-190 Wairau Road, Auckland 10, New Zealand

British Cataloging-in-Publication Data available.

The Catapult, Inc. Curriculum Development Group
Editor: Gregory G. Schultz
Writers: Donald Elman, Stephen J. Matlock

Contents

Part 2 Application Management

Part 3 File Management

Lesson 6 Managing Disks, Directories, and Files 76

Part 4 Accessories for Windows

Lesson 7 Using Accessories for Windows 97

About This Book

Microsoft Windows 3.1 helps you use the full power of your computer. Its graphical interface helps you organize your applications and files, run several applications at once, move and copy information between documents, and switch between applications on your desktop. Microsoft Windows 3.1 also includes accessories to make your work more efficient, such as Windows Write, a word processor, Windows Paintbrush, a color painting and drawing application, and Windows Calendar, a scheduling application.

Microsoft Windows 3.1 Step by Step shows you how to take advantage of the features of Microsoft Windows 3.1. The book contains information on both the Windows graphical interface and the accessories that come with Windows 3.1. *Microsoft Windows 3.1 Step by Step* is designed as a tutorial, to be used at your own pace and convenience. Each lesson should take between 30 to 45 minutes, including exercises.

Finding the Best Starting Point

This book is designed to help both new users who are learning to use Microsoft Windows for the first time and experienced users who want to learn the new features in Microsoft Windows version 3.1. If you have used a previous version of Windows, you'll have a head start on the basics, but be sure to review the revised File Manager, covered in Lessons 5 and 6. Other major new features are scalable TrueType fonts, improved support for non-Windows applications, and enhanced object linking and embedding.

This book is separated into six parts, each containing lessons on similar topics;

- Part 1 introduces the fundamental skills needed to manage the mouse, windows, and the menus and commands which operate Windows and its accessory programs.
- Part 2 explores the Program Manager, the "home base" from which you operate and organize programs.
- Part 3 introduces the greatly enhanced File Manager. You also learn how to manage your disks, directories and files.
- Part 4 includes five chapters. Together, they cover all the major applications and accessories furnished with Windows.
- Part 5 tells you how to customize your Windows environment. Topics include how to use the Control Panel, fonts and printing, including the new TrueType fonts.
- Part 6 shows you techniques for using MS-DOS–based applications from Windows.

To decide if you need to work through a lesson, look at the summary at its end. If you are unsure about any of the summary topics, work through that section of the lesson. You can work through the lessons in any order, skip lessons that you do not need, or repeat lessons to brush up on particular skills.

The following table recommends starting points depending on your Windows experience.

If you are	Follow these steps
New to Windows	Read "If You Are New to Windows" in "Getting Ready" later in this book. Next, work through lessons 1-2 in order. Work through the other lessons in any order.
New to the Mouse	Read "Getting Comfortable with the Mouse" in "Lesson 1" of this book.
An experienced Windows user	Read the summaries at the end of lessons 1 and 2. Work through the other lessons in any order. Note the changes in File Manager. You may also be interested in Appendix B on using OLE.

Using this Book as a Classroom Aid

Microsoft Windows 3.1 Step by Step can be used for teaching novice users and for teaching new features of Windows 3.1 to experienced users. You can choose from the lessons to tailor your classes to the needs of your students.

If you plan to teach the entire book, you should allocate approximately two days of classroom time to allow for questions, discussion and any extra practices that you create. Lessons 1 through 6 cover fundamental Windows skills. Lessons 7 through 14 focus on Windows-based applications and intermediate skills.

Conventions

Keyboard Conventions

- Names of keys appear in small capital letters; for example, TAB and SHIFT.
- A plus sign (+) between two or more key names indicates that you should press the keys at the same time. For example, "Press ALT+TAB" means that you should hold down the ALT key while pressing the TAB key.
- A comma (,) between two or more key names indicates that you should press each of the keys consecutively, not together. For example, "Press ALT, F, X" means that you should press and release each key in sequence.

Notes

Notes appear throughout the lessons, between two horizontal lines.

- Notes marked **Tip** contain explanations of possible results or alternative methods.
- Notes marked **Important** are things that you should check before completing an action.
- Notes marked **Note** contain supplementary information.
- Notes marked **Caution** contain warnings about possible data loss.
- Notes marked **Warning** warn of possible hardware damage.

Other Features of this Book

- Text in the left margin will give you additional notes and help or point you to other chapters or sections in this book or in your Microsoft Windows 3.1 documentation.
- One Step Further sections, at the end of every lesson, give you the opportunity to develop the skills you have learned in that lesson. These exercises allow you to explore additional techniques related to the lesson topic.
- Lesson summaries list the skills you have learned in each section and give a brief review of how to accomplish particular tasks.

Cross-references to Microsoft Windows Documentation

Microsoft Windows 3.1 Step by Step helps guide you in using your Windows documentation. At the end of every lesson is a table listing the topics covered and where to find them in your Microsoft Windows documentation. Marginal notes in the text of the lesson will also direct you to more information in your documentation. You'll find references to the following Windows documentation:

Microsoft Windows Getting Started Includes basic setup and installation procedures plus enough information to get you started with Windows 3.1. This volume also contains a brief introduction to Windows and a section on troubleshooting.

Microsoft Windows User's Guide Includes information about using Windows 3.1. Your basic reference book, it contains instructions and explanations for all user levels.

Online Lessons An online tutorial covering mouse procedures and basic Windows tasks.

Online Help An online reference to procedures and commands with context-sensitive help for specific information about applications.

Getting Ready

By following the lessons in this book, you can learn how to use the features of Microsoft Windows version 3.1 to organize and expedite your daily work. The structure of the book allows learning to take place in two steps. First, you follow the detailed exercises to carry out specific action sequences related to each skill. Second, you reinforce and extend your newly learned skills by trying the tasks described in the "One Step Further" sections.

Before you begin the lessons, there are a few thing you need to do. This section of the book shows you how to install the practice files on your computer's hard disk and how to start the Windows program. You must have Windows 3.1 installed in your computer system to carry out the lesson exercises. If you need instructions on installing Windows, see Appendix A, "Installing Windows 3.1," or refer to your Windows 3.1 documentation.

Installing the Step by Step Practice Files

To learn the skills necessary to use Windows effectively, it is important to practice tasks similar to those you are likely to perform in your actual work. For most of the lessons, sample files have been developed to simulate real-life situations. Inside the back cover is a disk of practice files for this Microsoft Windows 3.1 Step by Step book. Before you start your first lesson, run a special program on the practice files disk that copies the files onto your hard disk, by following these steps:

Set up the practice files on your hard disk

1. Turn on your computer.
2. Insert the practice files disk into the floppy disk drive of your computer (usually drive A or B).
3. At the MS-DOS command prompt, type either **A:INSTALL** or **B:INSTALL** depending on the drive you use, and then press ENTER.

   Do not type a space between the colon and "INSTALL."
4. Follow the instructions on the screen.

MS-DOS stands for Microsoft Disk Operating System, which is the software that controls how your computer transfers and stores electronic data.

The Step by Step setup program displays a message asking where you want to install the practice files. It suggests the C:\WINDOWS directory, where Windows files usually are stored. Then it copies the files from the floppy disk into a subdirectory called WIN31SBS. As you work through the exercises that use practice files, be sure to follow any instructions for renaming a file before saving it, so that you can use the original files again if you choose to do so.

A directory on the practice disk called FINAL contains finished example files that are similar to those you create in some of the lessons. If you want to compare a file you create with the corresponding example file, you can open the example file from the FINAL directory after you have completed the lesson. If you have questions while creating an exercise file, you can look at the example in the FINAL directory to help guide your work.

Starting Windows

*If you have not yet installed Windows in your computer, refer to Appendix A of this book, and to **Microsoft Windows Getting Started,** which is included in your Windows 3.1 package.*

The most direct way to start Windows is from the MS-DOS command prompt, as described below. If you have a menu system, you can set up a selection that starts Windows from the menu screen.

Start Windows from the MS-DOS command prompt

1 At the MS-DOS prompt, type **WIN**

2 Press ENTER.

Loading the Windows program may take a short time.

After the initial startup, your Windows screen looks similar to the following.

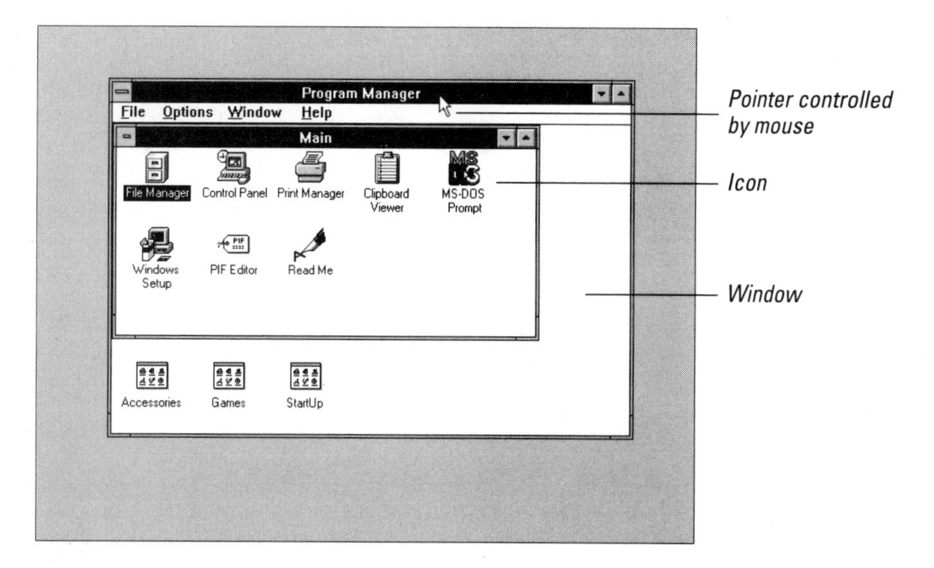

This picture illustrates some of the visual elements that constitute the building blocks of any Windows screen. A *window* is a rectangular work area that is framed by a border and has a title at the top. An *icon* is a small, named picture that can represent a program or a document. The *pointer* is a small arrow or other symbol that moves around the screen whenever you move the mouse on your desk.

Quitting Windows

If you have started Windows and would like to quit, here is a simple way to exit the program.

Quit Windows

1 Hold down the ALT key and press F4.
2 When you see a box with the message "This will end your Windows session," press ENTER.

Later you will learn some other ways to quit Windows using the mouse.

If You Are New to Windows

What benefits can you expect to receive from using Windows? The Windows graphical environment helps you handle virtually all daily work that you carry out with your computer. It is designed for both ease of use and sophistication of function. First, you can use Windows to organize and start your application programs—in many cases running multiple programs at the same time. Second, you can use Windows to manage the multitude of electronic files stored on your computer's hard disk and on floppy disks. Third, Windows-based applications are designed with many characteristics in common—both in the way they share data and in the way you control their operations. After you become familiar with the basic skills for interacting with Windows, you can apply them to learn and use many types of applications such as word processors, graphics programs, or spreadsheets.

Managing Programs

An operating system provides a single point from which any application can be started. In the MS-DOS environment, the command prompt (C:\>) serves this purpose. In the Windows environment, the Program Manager window is the launching platform for all application programs. Several applications—called *accessories*—are included with the basic Windows package. Other Windows-based applications that you can purchase separately, such as Microsoft Word for Windows or Microsoft Excel, become accessible from the Program Manager after you install them.

Program Manager allows flexibility in displaying and grouping icons that are associated with programs. The initial arrangement of the Program Manager window includes several icons organized into groups. You can easily add new groups, and move or copy icons from one group to another. For example, you might create a group that contains all the icons associated with a specific project.

A major advantage of Windows is its ability to run more than one Windows-based application at the same time. For example, while working on a word-processor document, you can quickly switch to a spreadsheet or graphics program without shutting down the word processor. This capability, known as *multitasking*, allows you to switch instantly among several active applications. With the right hardware,

Windows can also multitask non-Windows-based applications (those that can run directly under MS-DOS without Windows).

Managing Files

A typical computer system stores hundreds, or even thousands, of individual electronic files on one or more disks. Some of these are *program files* that are necessary to run applications and other system functions. Others are *data files* that constitute the work you have completed using application programs. Every time you create and save a document with a word processor, for example, you add a new data file to the disk storage area.

The programs that run on your computer, including Windows, are based on the MS-DOS operating system. This operating system allows you to organize files into *directories* that provide a convenient way of grouping files together. File Manager is a built-in Windows-based application that provides quick access to information about directories and files on any disk, and displays a clear, visual representation of a disk's file structure. The improved File Manager in Windows 3.1 is faster and more convenient to use than the previous version. File Manager also helps you carry out all common MS-DOS maintenance operations such as copying, moving, renaming and deleting files, creating and removing directories, and formatting disks.

Integrating Applications

Windows makes it possible for different types of applications to be integrated in two ways. First, Windows-based applications have many similarities in their visual elements and basic operations. The skills you learn through this book will give you a head start in learning any new Windows-based application. You'll be able to switch among various Windows-based applications without having to reorient yourself to a new interface each time.

A second aspect of application integration is the ability to share data between documents created with different Windows-based applications. For example, you can place a spreadsheet chart into a word processor document by a simple copy-and-paste operation. With some Windows-based applications, you can create an active, dynamic link that automatically updates the copy whenever you modify the original. Also, you can embed an object—such as a picture created by a graphics application—into a document that was created by another application such as a word processor. When you want to revise the embedded object, it retains a direct link to the application you used to create it.

Part 1

Basic Skills

Working with Windows

An essential skill in the Windows graphical environment is using the mouse to select, move, and activate the elements that appear on your screen. It is also important to become familiar with the standard types of control features that are part of every window. In this lesson, you learn how to use the mouse and screen pointer to select special objects called icons and to control window elements. At the end of the lesson, you will be able to modify the elements on your screen so that they look similar to the following:

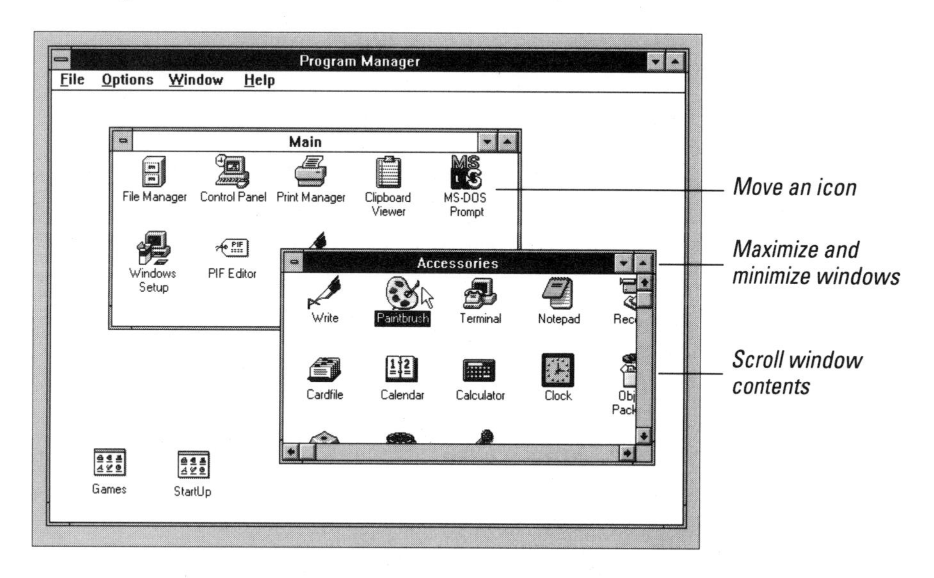

This lesson explains how to do the following:

- Use the mouse and on-screen pointer to control window elements
- Open a window from an icon
- Move and resize a window
- Scroll to find items that seem to have disappeared
- Manage multiple windows in the display area

Estimated lesson time: 35 minutes

Getting Comfortable with the Mouse

Windows is designed to be used with a *mouse,* a hand-held input device with buttons. When you move the mouse on a flat surface, an on-screen object called the *pointer* moves a corresponding distance and direction. Although most operations can also be carried out from the keyboard, the mouse provides a more direct way to select and move screen elements.

You can run the online Windows Tutorial to get additional guided practice in basic skills. For instructions on starting the tutorial, see the summary section at the end of this lesson.

Mouse Actions

All mouse operations involve some combination of the following basic actions:

For this action	Do this
Point	Move the pointer (arrow or other shape) to a specific place on the screen by moving the mouse.
Click	Press and release a mouse button.
Drag	Hold down a mouse button, move the mouse to a different location, and then release the button.
Double-click	Press and release a mouse button two times in rapid succession.

Windows is designed for a two-button mouse. (If you have a three-button mouse, ignore the middle button.) The *primary button* is used for most mouse actions. Initially, the left mouse button is set as the primary button and the right button as secondary, but you can reverse them through the Windows Control Panel if you want (see Lesson 12). Throughout this book, any reference to a mouse button means the primary button unless otherwise specified.

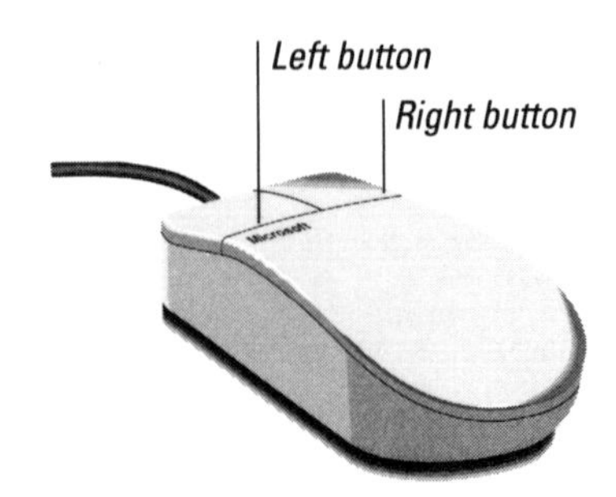

Pointer Shapes

Standard pointer

Pointer at window border

The pointer appears in different shapes depending on where it is placed in relation to other screen objects. For example, it usually looks like an arrow pointing up and slightly to the left. When you place the pointer near the edge of a *window*—a movable, rectangular area defined by borders—it changes to a two-headed arrow. In a text area, such as a word processor document, the pointer looks like a vertical I-beam. When a program is busy, the pointer looks like an hourglass.

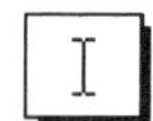

Text pointer

Appearance of pointer when program is busy

Point at screen objects by moving the mouse

If you have no previous experience with a mouse, try this exercise to practice the necessary hand-eye coordination.

1 Move the mouse so that the pointer goes to an open area in the lower-right corner of the screen.

  Your screen looks similar to the following:

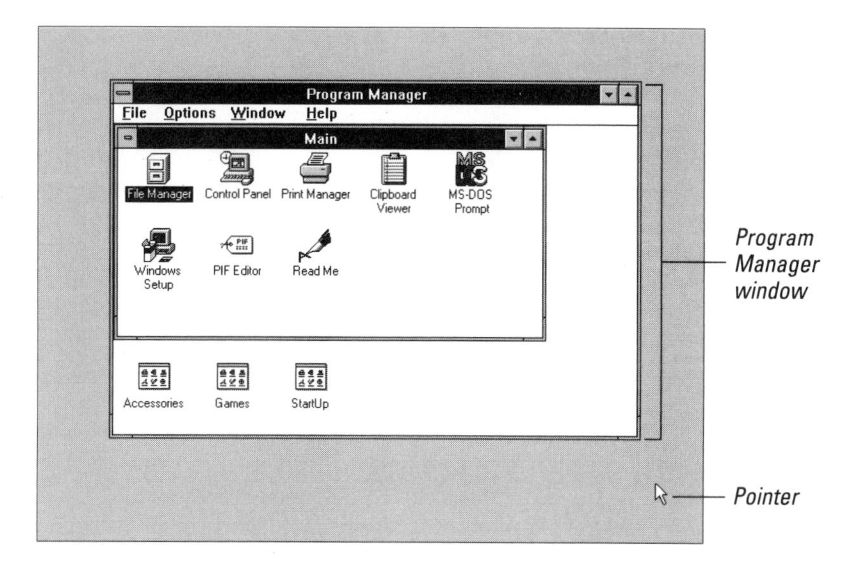

If you have not yet started Windows, follow the instructions in Getting Ready, earlier in this book.

2 Point to the word "File" near the upper left corner of the Program Manager window.

  "Point" means to move the mouse until the tip of the pointer arrow is on the specified object—in this case the word "File."

3 Click the left button once.

  A list of commands drops down.

4 Point to the background area and click once.

  The command list disappears.

5 Point to the graphic object labeled "Read Me," and click once.

  The label area changes color to show that the object has been selected.

6 With the pointer on the Read Me object, press and hold the left mouse button, and move it about one inch to the right. Finally, release the mouse button.

  Step 6 tells you to drag an icon. In later exercises, the word *drag* is used to mean all three actions combined: pressing and holding the button, moving the mouse, and then releasing the button.

Your screen should now look similar to the following:

Depending upon how Windows is set up, Program Manager might display additional group icons such as "Applications."

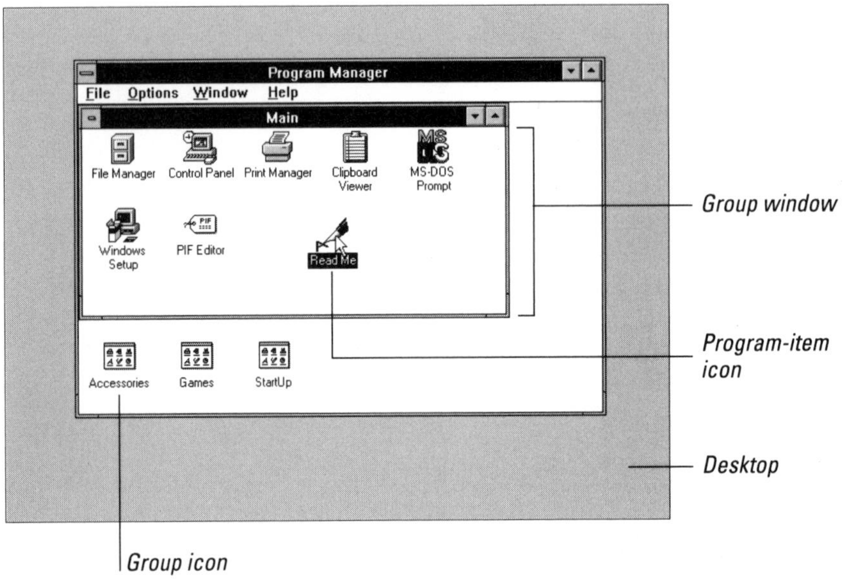

Group window

Program-item icon

Desktop

Group icon

Selecting and Moving Icons

On the screen is a combination of windows and small graphic objects called *icons*. These are all arranged against a background called the *desktop*. Each window has a title at the top and is surrounded by a border frame. Each icon consists of two parts: a graphic symbol and a name.

Within the Program Manager window, you can see a smaller type of window that is called a *group window* because it contains a group of icons. For example, the screen picture above shows a group window called Main. Within the Main window are several *program-item* icons representing applications that are part of Windows 3.1.

Another type of item in the Program Manager window is a *group icon*. You can open a group icon into a group window, as described in the next section. Your screen shows three group icons, called Accessories, Startup, and Games.

The following exercise provides practice in selecting individual icons and moving them around the screen with the mouse. As you gain experience with these basic Windows skills, the terms and concepts described here will become more familiar.

Select and move an icon

1 Point to the Games group icon.

2 Pressing the mouse button, drag the icon as far to the right as possible.

The pointer does not move beyond the border because you can't drag a group icon outside of the Program Manager window.

3 Move the Games icon back to its original position and release the mouse button.

4 In the Main group window, point to the Read Me program-item icon.

5 Try to drag the Read Me icon out of the Main group window.

When you move the icon, it changes to a black-and-white outline. If you drag it to where it can be moved no further, it becomes a circle with a slash. Windows does not let you move the icon to the Program Manager window or to the desktop.

6 Drag the Read Me icon to the Games group icon and release the mouse button.

While a program-item icon can only be located in a group window, it can be moved into a different group window or group icon. You can't see the Read Me icon until you open the Games group window in the next section.

Activating Icons and Windows

Keeping two principles in mind helps in understanding the Windows environment. First, all work is carried out within a window. Second, each window can be reduced to an icon and each icon can be opened to a window.

Although it is possible to have several different windows on the screen at the same time, too many open windows can make the desktop appear cluttered and disorganized. Both group icons and program-item icons help to keep applications organized and easily available when they are not in use. A group icon can hold a number of program-item icons. Whenever you are ready to use a program, you can quickly open its program-item icon to a window.

A typical window includes some or all of the following elements:

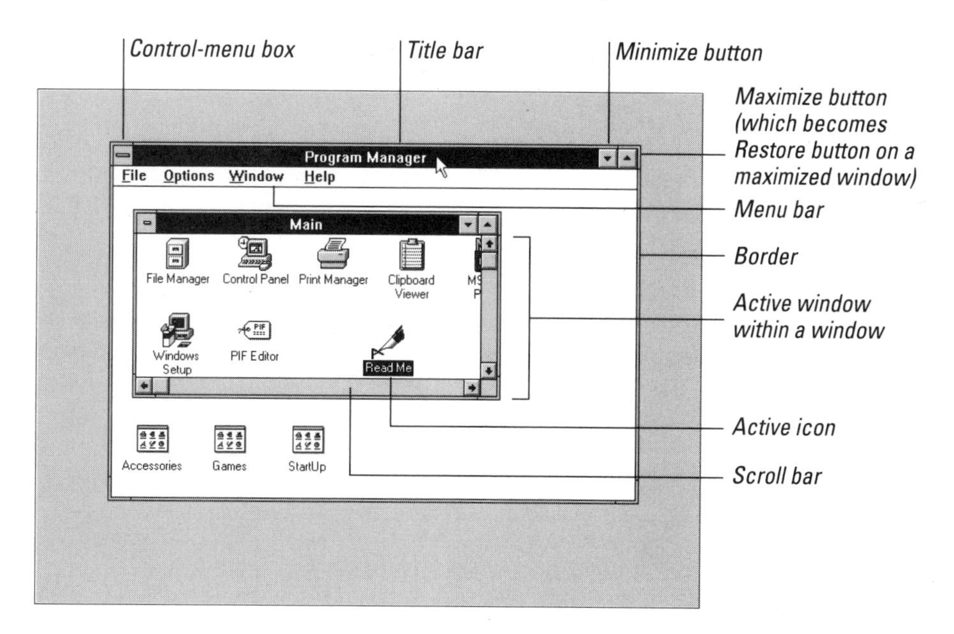

Window element	Function
Title bar	Always appears at the top edge of a window, showing the window's name. Dragging this bar moves the window around the desktop.
Menu bar	Appears just below the title bar. Contains names of available menus. (See Lesson 2.)
Control-menu box	A box in the upper left corner of a window containing a dash-like symbol. Clicking this box displays the Control menu, which includes commands that affect the entire window. Double-clicking this box closes the window. (See Lesson 2 for more about menus.)
Minimize button	A single arrow pointing downward in the upper right corner of a window. Clicking this button shrinks the window to an icon.
Maximize button	A single arrow pointing upward in the upper right corner of a restored window. Clicking this button makes the window fill the entire screen.
Restore button	A double arrow pointing both up and down in the upper right corner of a maximized window (in the same location as the Maximize button). Clicking this button reduces the window to the same size it was before being maximized.
Border	Visible line surrounding all four sides of a restored window. (The border is not visible in a maximized window.) Dragging a side of the border changes the window's size in one dimension. Dragging a corner changes two dimensions at once.
Scroll bar	Moves the display of contents in a window frame either horizontally or vertically without changing the window's size or location. Scroll bars are active only if the window is too small to display all of its contents at one time. (See "Scrolling a Window's Contents" later in this lesson.)

After you have learned how to convert icons to windows and back again, you are ready to select the window or icon that is *active*. Active means that the window or icon is the Program Manager's current focus of attention, and is available to be changed or operated upon in some way.

Only one group window or group icon can be active at a time in the Program Manager window. Only one program-item icon can be active at a time in an open group window. An active window appears in front of other screen objects, and its title bar has a more prominent color. An active icon has a highlighted title (usually a darker background).

Opening and Closing a Group Window

Each group icon within the Program Manager window (such as Games or Accessories) can be opened to become a group window. Any open group window can be reduced to a group icon. You can avoid excessive screen clutter by having no more than two or three group windows open at a time. In the following exercise, you use the mouse to open and close group windows, and to return the Read Me icon to its original place in the Main group window.

Open and close a group window with the mouse

1 Point to the Games group icon.

2 Double-click the left mouse button.

The Games icon expands to a group window. If nothing happens, try again with a slightly faster double-click.

3 In the Main (*not* Games) window, point to the Minimize box in the upper-right corner and click once.

The Main group window shrinks to a group icon at the bottom of the Program Manager window. Your screen looks like this:

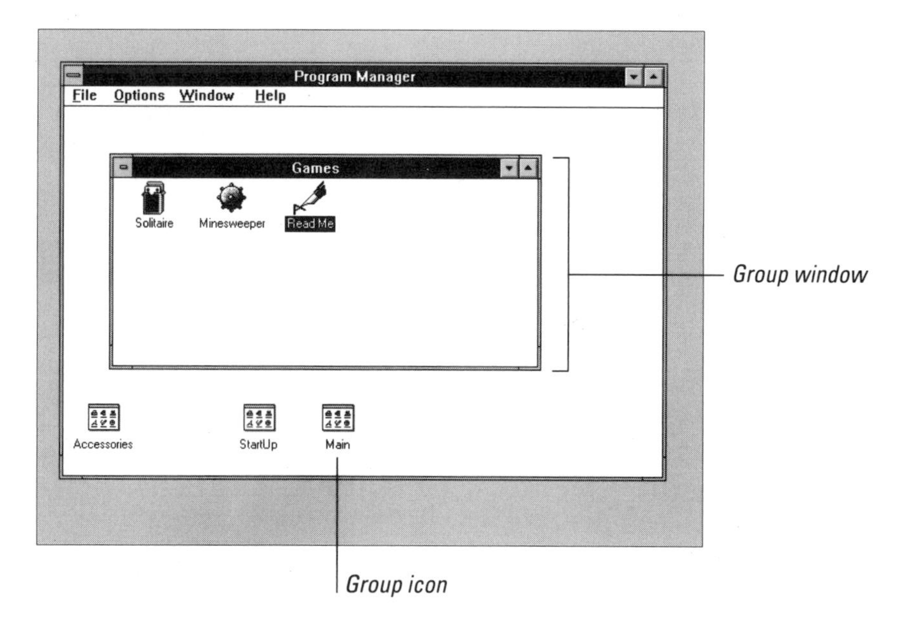

4 Restore the Main group window using the same procedure as in steps 1 and 2.

5 Point to any vacant area of the Games window and click.

If the Main window overlaps part of the Games window, you can still click in any visible part of the Games window. This makes the Games window active and brings it to the foreground. Only one group window can be active at a time.

6 Drag the Read Me icon from the Games window to the Main window, and then drag it back to its original position in the Main window.

7 Click the Minimize button of the Games window.

Your screen should now look the same as it did when you started this exercise.

Minimizing, Maximizing, and Restoring Windows

Each window can appear in one of three ways—a *minimized* form that is represented by a single icon, a *maximized* form that fills the entire available space, or a *restored* form that allows you to move the window around and change its size or shape. You can switch between these forms with the buttons that contain arrows pointing upward or downward, located near the upper-right corner of each window. In the next exercise, you change the Program Manager window to each of these three forms.

Minimize, maximize, and restore the Program Manager window

1 Point to the Minimize button of the Program Manager window (arrow pointing downward in the upper-right corner of the window) and click.

Your screen looks similar to the following:

Program Manager minimized to an icon

2 Point to the Program Manager icon at the bottom of the desktop, and double-click.

This restores the window to its previous condition.

3 Point to the Maximize button of the Program Manager window (the upward-pointing arrow in the upper-right corner of the window), and then click.

The Program Manager window now fills the entire screen. The Maximize button is replaced by a new double-arrow button called the Restore button.

Restore button

4 Point to the Restore button, and then click.

The Program Manager window looks as it did before step 3.

Maximize and restore a window within a window

In the previous exercise, you saw that maximizing an application window, such as Program Manager, makes it fill the entire screen. However, the same principle does not always apply when you have a window within a window—such as a group window within Program Manager, or a document window within a word processor application. In this case, if you restore (not maximize) the application window, maximizing the secondary window makes it fill only the restored application window and not the entire screen. In addition, the title bars of the two windows become merged into one. In this exercise, you maximize and then restore the Main group window.

1 On the Main window, click the Maximize button.

Note that the title bar says "Program Manager - [Main]" to indicate that it is the merger of two windows. The Restore button that appears at the right end of the menu bar belongs to the secondary (Main) window. The Maximize and Minimize buttons at the right end of the title bar belong to the Program Manager window. Your screen now looks similar to the following:

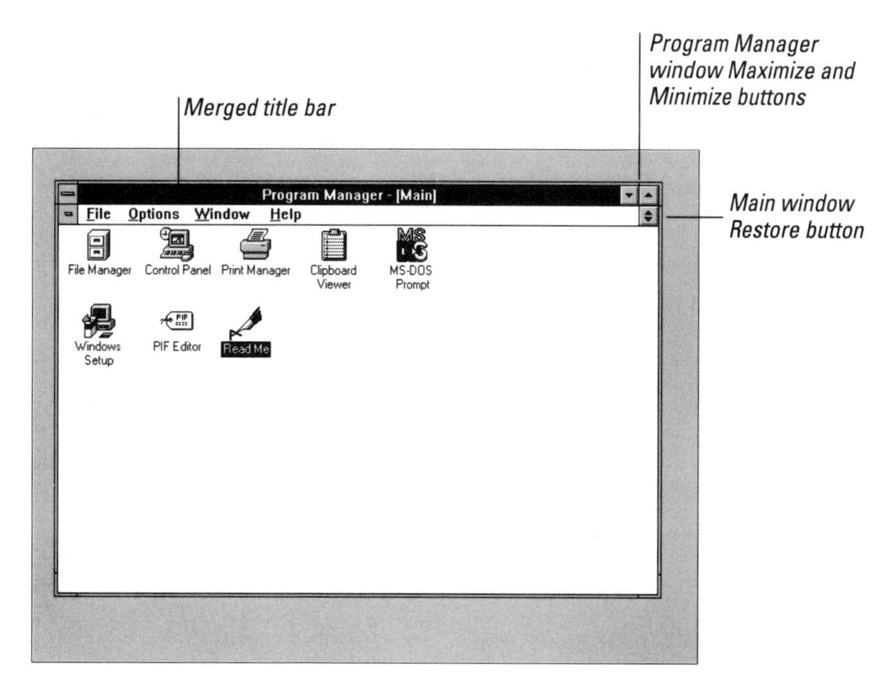

2 Click the Maximize button at the far right end of the title bar.

The combined window is now maximized.

3 Click the Main window's Restore button (at the right end of the menu bar).

The Main window is now restored to its previous size and position.

4 Click the Program Manager's Restore button (at the right end of the Program Manager title bar).

The Program Manager window is also restored.

Controlling a Window's Appearance

Windows are flexible objects. You can change a window's horizontal and vertical size by dragging its sides or corners any time the window is not maximized. You can also move the window around the screen by dragging with the mouse. When a window is not large enough to display everything it contains at the same time (such as all the icons in a group window or additional text in a document window), you can scroll the hidden contents into view with the horizontal or vertical *scroll bars*.

Resizing and Moving a Restored Window

You can change the size or shape of a restored window by dragging its border with the mouse. You can also move a restored window without changing its shape by dragging its title bar. The following table summarizes what actions to take when resizing or moving a restored window.

For this action	Do this with the pointer shape at right
Change a window's width	Place the pointer directly on the window's left or right border and drag it to the side.
Change a window's height	Place the pointer directly on the window's top or bottom border and drag up or down.
Change a window's width and height together	Place the pointer directly on one of the window's four corners and drag in any direction.
Move a window without changing its size or shape	Place the pointer on the window's title bar and drag in any direction.

In the next exercise, you modify the Program Manager window using the actions listed above.

Change the size, shape, and position of a window

1 Place the pointer on the middle of the Program Manager window's left border.

The pointer shape changes to a two-headed arrow pointing to both sides.

2 Drag the border approximately 2 inches to the right.

Be sure to release the mouse button after moving the border.

3 Point to the Program Manager window's lower-left corner.

   The pointer changes to a two-headed diagonal arrow. Be sure you grab the outer border of the Program Manager window, *not* the border of the Main window.

4 Drag the window's lower-left corner approximately 1 inch up and to the right.

5 Point to the words "Program Manager" in the title bar.

6 Drag the window down to the right until it is nearly flush with the lower-right corner of the desktop.

   Your screen now looks similar to the following:

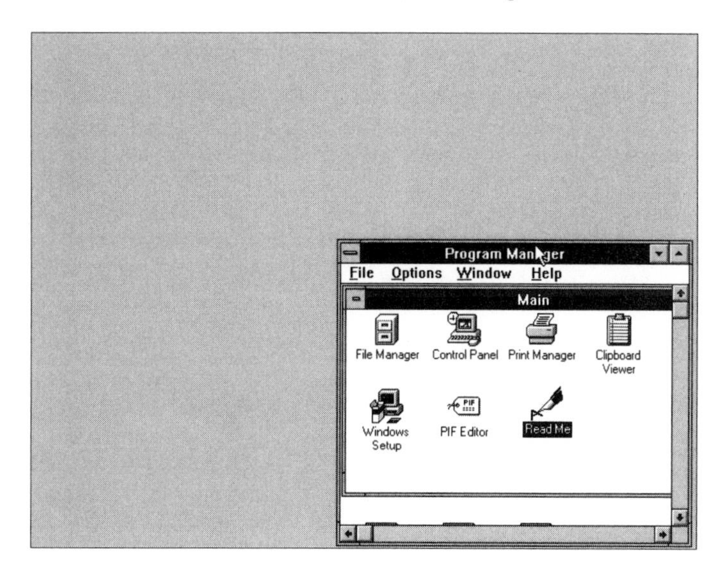

Scrolling a Window's Contents

If a window is large enough to display everything it holds, it is surrounded only by title bars and borders. However, when you decrease a window's size or add more things inside it, only part of the contents might be visible. For example, if you reduce a window in size or add many more icons, not all of the items can be displayed within the window's boundaries at one time. In this case, a set of *scroll bars* might appear on one or two edges of the window.

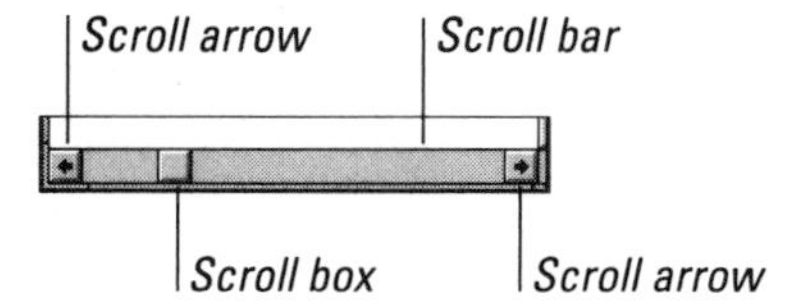

Scroll controls consist of three types of items. A *scroll bar* is a band that appears along a window's right edge for vertical scrolling, and along the bottom edge for horizontal scrolling. A *scroll box* is a small square or rectangle that appears inside a scroll bar. The scroll box's relative location on the scroll bar indicates the position of the window's visible contents relative to its total contents. At the ends of each scroll bar are two *scroll arrow* buttons that you use to move the scroll box.

The following table describes different ways to scroll the contents of a window using scroll controls:

For this scroll operation	Do this
Scroll a window's contents in small steps	Click the scroll arrow button pointing in the direction you wish to scroll. (Each time you click, the window contents move slightly and the scroll box moves toward the scroll arrow.)
Scroll a window's contents in large steps	Click the scroll bar in the area between the scroll box and one of the scroll arrow buttons. (Both the window contents and the scroll box jump in large increments.)
Scroll a window's contents to a specific position	Drag the scroll box to the desired location on the scroll bar.

Scroll bars appear on a window only when necessary to display hidden contents. In the next exercise, you make scroll bars appear on the Program Manager window by reducing the window's size, and then you practice scrolling with the scroll bars.

Scroll the contents of the Program Manager window

1 Drag the lower-right corner of the Program Manager window up and left until the window is about 3 inches square, and then drag the window to the center of the screen.

  Your screen looks similar to the following:

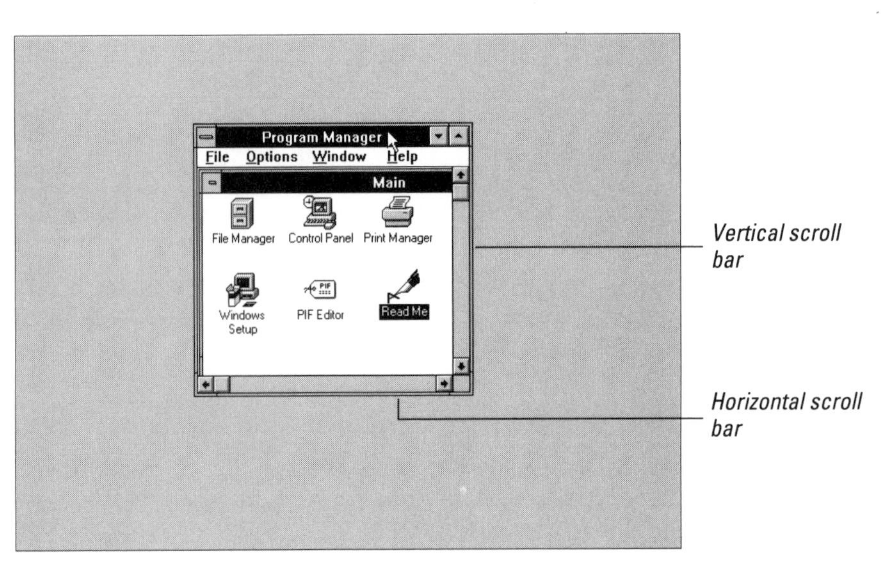

2 On the vertical scroll bar, click the down arrow twice.

3 On the horizontal scroll bar, click the scroll bar area to the right of the scroll box.

4 Drag the horizontal scroll box to the left.

5 Scroll the window's contents using any combination of scroll operations until the Accessories group icon is visible in the window.

Your screen looks similar to the following:

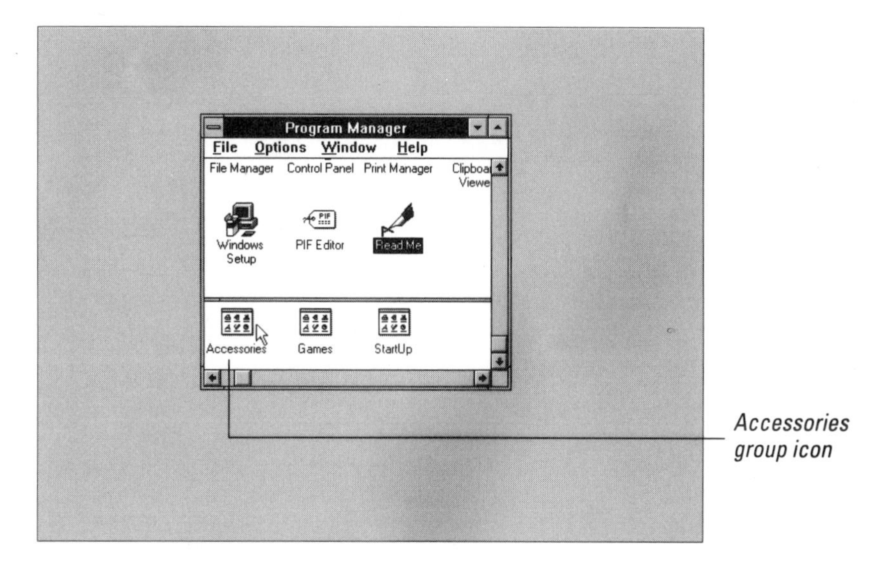

6 Enlarge and center the Program Manager window by dragging its borders, similar to the startup screen.

The window should be large enough so that no scroll bars are visible.

One Step Further

You have learned basic skills involving the mouse, icons, and windows. You used the mouse to open or close group icons, move or resize windows, and scroll the contents of a window. To practice these skills on your own, try the following:

- Minimize, restore, and maximize the Main group window.
- Drag the Read Me and Clipboard Viewer icons so they trade positions in the Main window.
- Move the Main window to the lower right corner of the Program Manager window without changing its size.
- Reduce the Main window's size by dragging the border corner until both the vertical and horizontal scroll bars appear. Then, move all icons into and out of view using the horizontal and vertical scroll bars.

- Put the Main window back to its previous location, size, and shape so that all icons are visible at the same time.

If you want to continue to the next lesson

1. Be sure that the Main group window is open and roughly the same size and location as when you first started Windows.
2. Minimize all other open group windows so they appear as group icons.

If you want to quit Windows for now

1. Press ALT+F4.
2. When the message "This will end your Windows session" appears, press ENTER.

Lesson Summary

To	Do this
Make an icon or window active	Click once on the icon or window.
Move an icon	Drag the icon to the new location.
Move a window	Drag the window's title bar.
Make a window fill the entire screen	Click the window's Maximize button.
Restore a maximized window	Click the window's Restore button.
Change a window's size and shape	Make sure the window is restored, not maximized. Then drag any border or corner to the desired size and shape.
Reduce a window to an icon	Click the window's Minimize button.
Open a window from an icon	Double-click the icon.
Close a window	Double-click the window's Control-menu box.
Scroll a window's contents	Click a scroll bar or scroll arrow, or drag a scroll box.

For more information on	See the *Microsoft Windows User's Guide*
Activating and moving windows and icons	Chapter 1, "Windows Basics"
Arranging windows and icons	Chapter 2, "Application Basics"

For an online lesson about	Do this
Basic mouse operations (Windows Tutorial)	Activate the Program Manager window by clicking on it. Press the following three keys in succession: ALT, H, W. When the windows Tutorial screen appears, press M. Then follow the on-screen directions.
Windows and icons (Windows Tutorial)	Activate the Program Manager window by clicking on it. Press the following three keys in succession: ALT, H, W. When the Windows Tutorial screen appears, press W. Then follow the on-screen directions.

Preview of the Next Lesson

In the next lesson, you expand your basic skills by working with menus, commands, and dialog boxes. These are the primary ways you send instructions to Windows-based programs. You also learn to use commands to place windows and icons into orderly arrangements. Finally, will learn how to use the extensive online Windows Help system.

Menus and Dialog Boxes

Although icons and windows are the major graphical building blocks of Windows, menus and dialog boxes are important tools that contain verbal information. *Menus* are lists of *commands* that can be executed at the click of a mouse. *Dialog boxes* are small, specialized windows that present options and ask you to make a response. The Windows environment also includes a *Help* system that consists of indexed, online (on-screen) documentation, context-sensitive explanations, and interactive tutorials.

In this lesson, you learn how to open menus and choose commands, and then use these skills to place windows and icons in orderly arrangements. You also learn about various types of dialog boxes. Finally, you learn how to explore the wealth of information available through the Windows Help system.

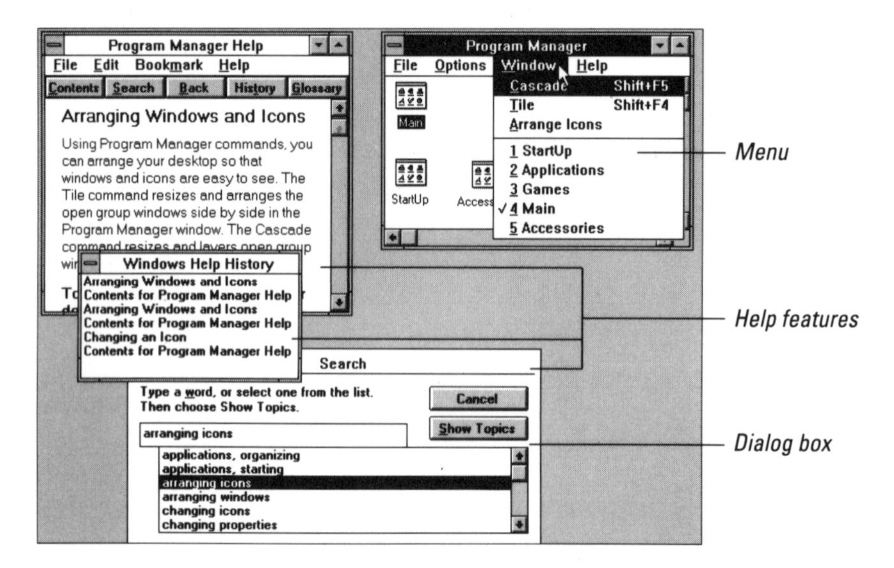

This lesson explains how to do the following:

- Open a menu to examine a list of commands
- Choose a command from a menu
- Arrange windows and icons for an organized display
- Choose from a list of options in a dialog box
- Explore the online Help system, which provides help if you are stuck

Estimated lesson time: 40 minutes

Using Menus and Commands

Choosing a command from a menu is a common way to carry out an operation in Windows-based programs. Each menu has a name describing its overall purpose, and contains a list of related commands.

Immediately below the title bar of most program windows is a horizontal band called the *menu bar,* which contains menu names such as File, Edit, or Help. Clicking any one of these names causes a drop-down menu—a list of commands—to open. After you have opened a menu, you can choose and execute any available command by clicking the command, or close the menu without performing any action.

Every window also has a *Control menu* that you activate from the *Control-menu box* in the upper-left corner of the window. The Control-menu box is the box with a symbol that looks like a dash. The Control menu generally includes commands that allow you to close the window or change its physical appearance.

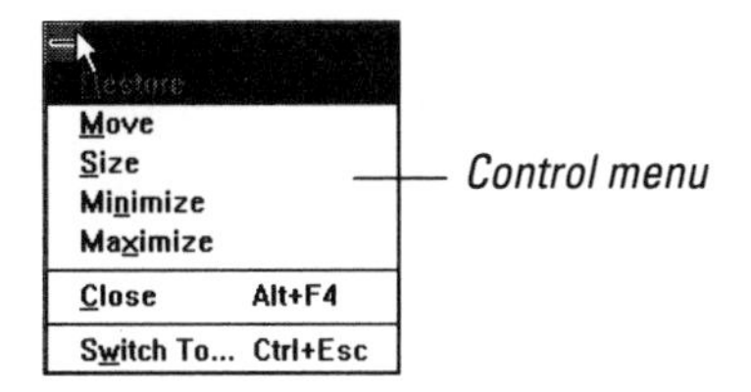

Opening and Closing a Menu

To open a menu, simply click the menu name with the mouse and the menu drops down. You can close the menu in one of several ways—by clicking the menu name again, by opening another menu, or by clicking outside the menu border. The command list also disappears after you choose a command.

Tip As an alternative to using the mouse, you can activate every menu and command in Windows by pressing the ALT key plus the underlined character of the menu name or command (often the first letter). You can close a menu without choosing a command by pressing the ALT key once or the ESC key twice. A few commands can also be executed by using a special key or key combination, listed along the right side of the menu. Using keyboard equivalents is sometimes quicker than using the mouse; with keyboard equivalents, you can keep your hand on the keyboard while you are typing text.

Open, examine, and close menus in the Program Manager window

In this exercise, you practice opening and closing various menus in the Program Manager menu bar. Look at the commands in the menu bar and notice the underlined letter for each one, but do not actually choose any command yet.

1 Point to the name "File" in the menu bar, and click once.

The File menu drops down, as shown here:

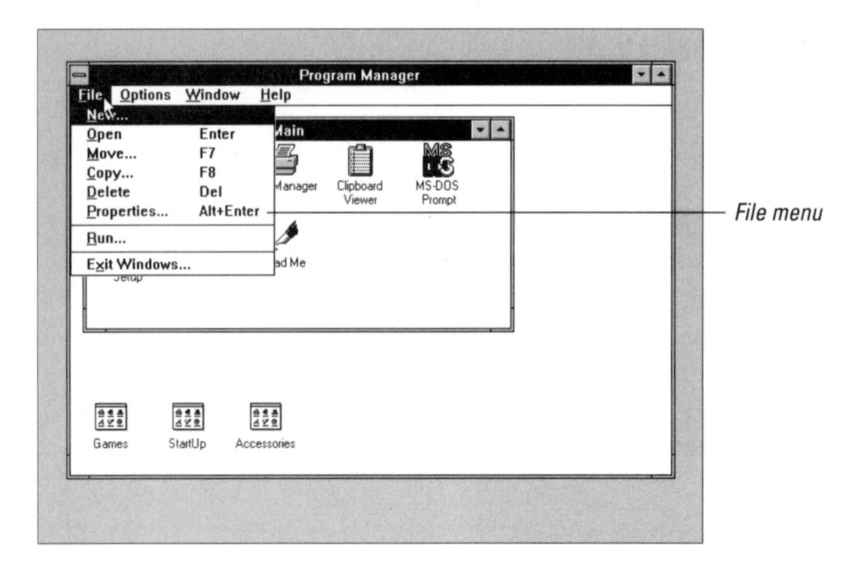

2 Click the Options menu, which is immediately to the right of the File menu.

The File menu closes automatically when the Options menu opens because only one menu at a time can be open.

3 Press ALT.

The menu closes.

4 Click the Window menu.

5 Click anywhere outside the Window menu to close it.

6 Press ALT+H.

This is the keyboard way to open the Help menu. You pressed ALT+H because "H" is underlined in the menu name Help. If you wanted to open the Window menu, you would have pressed ALT+W because "W" is the underlined character in the Window menu name.

7 Close the Help menu by clicking on the Help menu name.

Choosing a Command

After you open a menu, you choose a command with the mouse by pointing to the command and clicking the left mouse button once. You can also choose a command from the keyboard by pressing ALT plus the underlined letter of the command. Either action executes the command immediately. The menu disappears after the command is carried out.

Note Occasionally, you will find that some of the commands on a menu do not respond to the mouse or keyboard. Commands that are unavailable at a given time appear *dimmed*—in a less prominent color (usually gray)—compared with the other commands on the menu. Dimmed commands appear in the list to indicate that they can become available under different circumstances. For example, the Copy command is dimmed unless something on the screen is selected.

The next exercise allows you to practice choosing commands in the Options menu using the techniques explained above. For future exercises, you can use whatever method is most comfortable when you see a step in the form: "From the *X* menu, choose *Y*."

Choose commands from the Options menu

1. In the menu bar, point to the Options menu name, and then click once.

   Notice whether there is a check mark to the left of any of the three commands.

2. Point to the command Save Settings On Exit, and click once.

   This chooses and executes the command, and then closes the menu. You do not immediately see any change from choosing this particular command, but one effect will be apparent in the next step.

3. Point to the Options menu name again, and click once to open the menu.

   With the menu open, you can look at the command to see how it has changed. If there was previously no check mark next to the Save Settings On Exit command, one now appears to indicate that this option is turned on. If the Save Settings On Exit option was previously checked, the check mark is now gone.

4. Click outside the Options menu to close it without choosing a command.

5. Press ALT, then press O, and then press S.

   This keyboard sequence is another way to open the Options menu and choose the Save Settings On Exit command. It returns the Save Settings option to the status it had prior to this exercise. (You will learn more about the effect of the Save Settings On Exit command in Lesson 3.)

Arranging Windows and Icons

In Lesson 1, you learned how to move a window or an icon around the screen, and to change windows. Although this capability allows you to customize your desktop, too much shuffling might result in a disorganized screen. Also, having several windows open can become awkward if they overlap and obscure each other.

Fortunately, the Window menu of the Program Manager includes three commands that help you restore order to the desktop. Two of the commands apply to all open group windows within the Program Manager, and one works on icons in the active window.

Cascading and Tiling Windows

When you have two or more group windows open in the Program Manager, you can arrange them in one of two patterns by using commands in the Window menu. The *Cascade* command makes all open group windows the same size and shape, and places them overlapping each other, except for their title bars. The effect is similar to fanning a deck of cards so that you can see just enough of each one to identify it and, if necessary, select it from the pack.

The *Tile* command divides the Program Manager window into roughly equal areas, and fills the space with open group windows *without* letting them overlap each other. The exact configuration, size, and shape of the rearranged windows depends on how many group windows exist. In the next exercise, you open several group windows and rearrange them with these two commands.

Use commands to cascade and tile multiple group windows

1 Open the Accessories and Games group windows by double-clicking on their respective group icons.

The Main window should remain open.

2 From the Window menu, choose Cascade.

Note that the lowermost window is currently the active one. Your screen looks similar to the following:

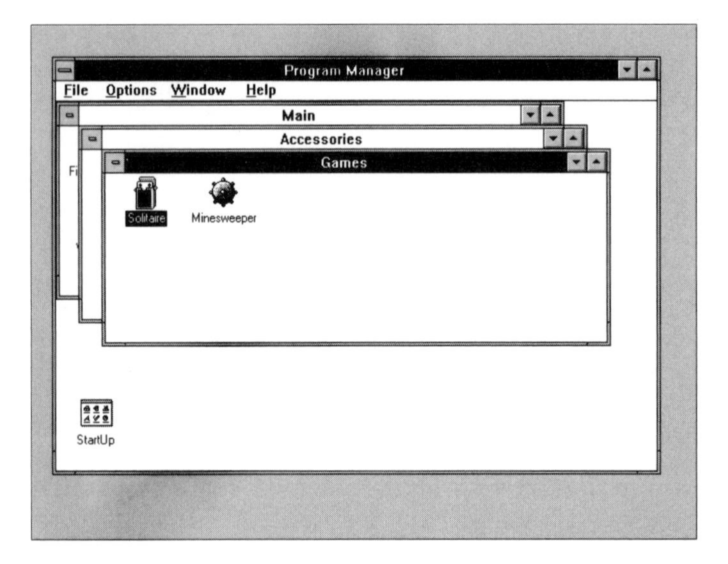

3 Click the Main window title bar.

This window becomes active and moves to the foreground.

4 Click in any visible area of one of the other windows to make it active.

5 From the Window menu, choose Tile.

The windows are rearranged so that none overlap. Scroll bars might appear on some or all windows. Your screen looks similar to this:

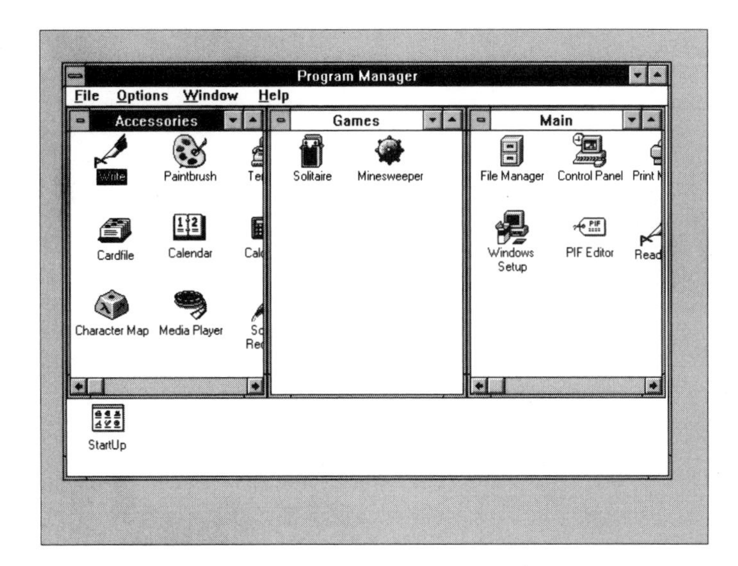

6 Open the Startup window from its group icon.

Any window that you open after you have applied the Tile command is not automatically tiled.

7 From the Window menu, choose Tile.

The open windows are resized to accommodate the new window.

8 Close all group windows *except* Main, and choose the Tile command.

The Main window expands to fill the available space.

Using the Arrange Icons Command

Within an open group window, the Arrange Icons command can serve two purposes. First, after you move icons around with the mouse, Arrange Icons can rearrange them into neat rows and columns. Second, if you change the size or shape of a window, Arrange Icons rearranges the icons to fit the new space most efficiently. If you have more than one group window open, the command applies only to the active window.

You can also apply the Arrange Icons command to the group icons that appear in the Program Manager window. First you must inactivate all open group windows by selecting a group icon. Then you choose the Arrange Icons command to rearrange the entire set of group icons.

In the next exercise, you apply the Arrange Icons command to the icons in the Main window and then to the group icons in the Program Manager window. For the exercise to work successfully, your first step is to be sure that the option called Auto Arrange is not active.

Use a command to arrange icons in a window

1 Open the Options menu. If the Auto Arrange command is checked, then choose Auto Arrange. If the command is not checked, close the menu without choosing a command.

2 With the mouse, drag four program-item icons in the Main window to slightly different positions.

3 From the Window menu, choose Arrange Icons.

   The icons are restored to regular rows and columns.

4 Drag the right border of the Main window approximately 2 inches to the left, and choose the Arrange Icons command.

   The icons are rearranged to fit as well as possible into the new window size, as shown here:

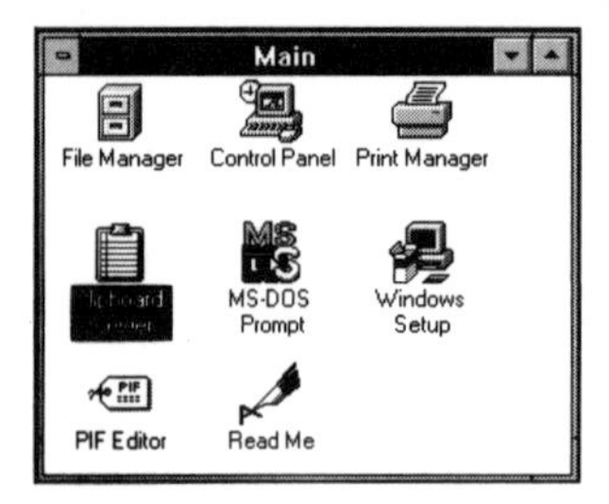

5 Drag the bottom border of the Main window up about 1 inch, and choose Arrange Icons.

   The icons are again rearranged to fit the window.

6 Drag the Accessories and Games group icons to different locations in the Program Manager window.

   The Main window is open but inactive. If you can't find the group icons to move, try looking behind the Main window. The last group icon you moved has its title highlighted, as on the next page:

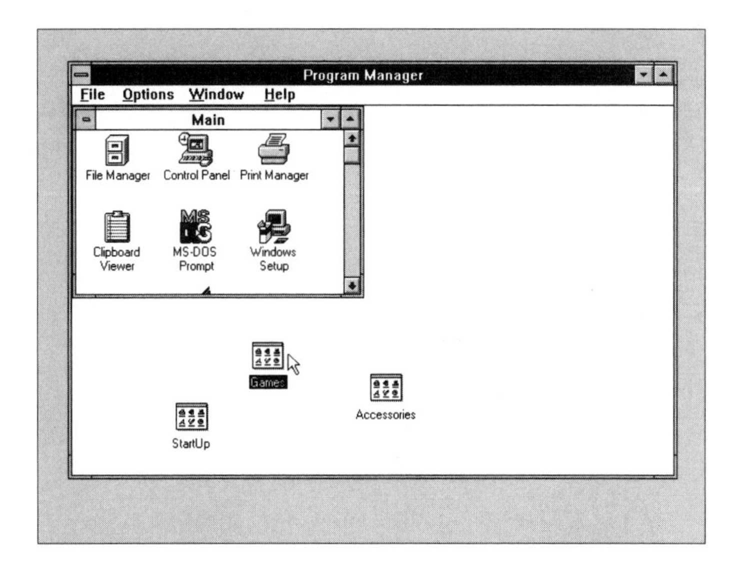

7 From the Window menu, choose Arrange Icons.

All the group icons line up at the bottom of the Program Manager window.

Responding to Dialog Boxes

A dialog box is an information-exchange window that appears at certain times during the operation of a program. Dialog boxes can have many different forms, but they always present pertinent information and require an active response from you before the program can continue. Most often, a dialog box presents a list of options from which you must choose in order to determine how the program will proceed. The following table summarizes the most common forms of these response options.

This type of dialog box option	Works this way
Check box: A small square next to a word or phrase. ☒ Run Minimized	Click in the square to turn the option on or off. When an X appears, the option is selected (active).
Command button: A rectangular button labeled with a command. OK	Click the button to carry out the command. This often closes the dialog box.

<table>
<tr><th>This type of dialog box option</th><th>Works this way</th></tr>
<tr><td>List box: A box containing a list of items. Sometimes has an arrow to make the list drop down.
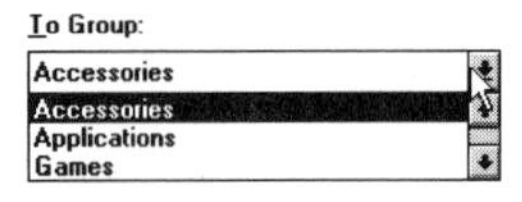
</td><td>Click the desired item to select it. If it is a drop-down list box, click the arrow first to display the option list. Scroll the option list, if necessary.</td></tr>
<tr><td>Option buttons: Round buttons, each representing one in a set of mutually exclusive options.
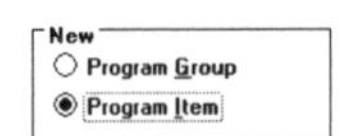
</td><td>Click the button next to the desired option to fill it with a black dot. Only one button in a set can be selected at one time.</td></tr>
<tr><td>Text box: Rectangular box in which you can enter text (letters, numbers, and symbols) from the key-board.
Current Directory: C:\
From:
To:</td><td>First click in the box to display the insertion point (a blinking, vertical bar). Then type the desired text.</td></tr>
<tr><td>Combo box: Combination of text box with list box.
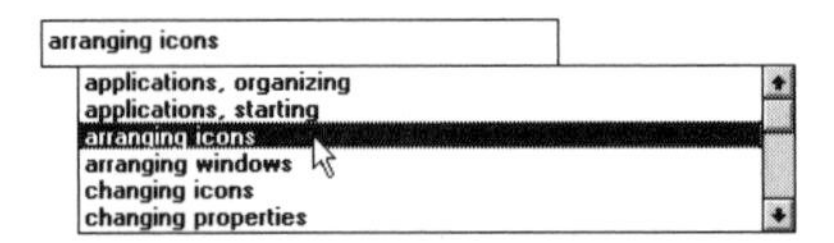
</td><td>Either click the selection from the displayed list, or type the text in the box at the insertion point.</td></tr>
</table>

A dialog box can appear at various times in response to an action you take. You always see a dialog box after choosing a command whose name is followed by an ellipsis (...). A dialog box displayed as a result of choosing a command often includes a command button labeled Cancel. The Cancel button allows you to close the box without changing anything. In the following exercise, you open several dialog boxes from Program Manager commands and close each one with its Cancel button. In later exercises, you will use many dialog boxes to specify options and see them take effect.

Practice with various dialog box options

1 From the File menu, choose New.

Notice that the command "New..." is followed by an ellipsis.

2 Click the empty round button (the one *not* containing a black dot).

When you select one button, the dot in the other one disappears. This demonstrates that only one option button in a set can be selected at a time.

3 Choose Cancel.

This command button closes the dialog box without further action.

4 From the File menu, choose Run.

5 Click the box next to Run Minimized a few times.

This check box makes the option active when the X appears and inactive when it doesn't.

6 Choose Cancel.

7 From the File menu, choose Properties, and then click in the text areas.

You can enter text in these text boxes.

8 Choose Cancel.

9 See that the Main window is active; then from the File menu, choose Copy.

10 Click the down arrow to make the list box drop down, and then select one of the options.

11 Choose Cancel.

Obtaining Online Help

Windows applications include an extensive online Help system that can be accessed either through the Help menu or the keyboard. You can use Help like an electronic user's guide—with the equivalent of a table of contents, an index, and a glossary at your fingertips. Each application has a set of Help screens that present explanations, definitions, and tips about using the program. After you learn how to explore the Help information for one Windows-based application, you'll be able to apply the same skills to other applications.

The following exercises guide you to explore the Help system and use different ways to find information about Program Manager.

Use Help Contents

Each Help screen has a descriptive title at the top, followed by information relevant to the topic. Many screens also display the names of additional topics with a solid underline. When you click an underlined topic, a different Help screen appears with information about the new topic. A Help screen might also contain glossary terms, which are underlined with dots. When you click a glossary term, a small pop-up window appears that contains a definition of the term. In this exercise, you start with the Help Contents screen and then choose a topic and a glossary term to get more information.

1 From the Help menu, choose Contents.

Pressing F1 has the same effect. The Help window opens, as shown below:

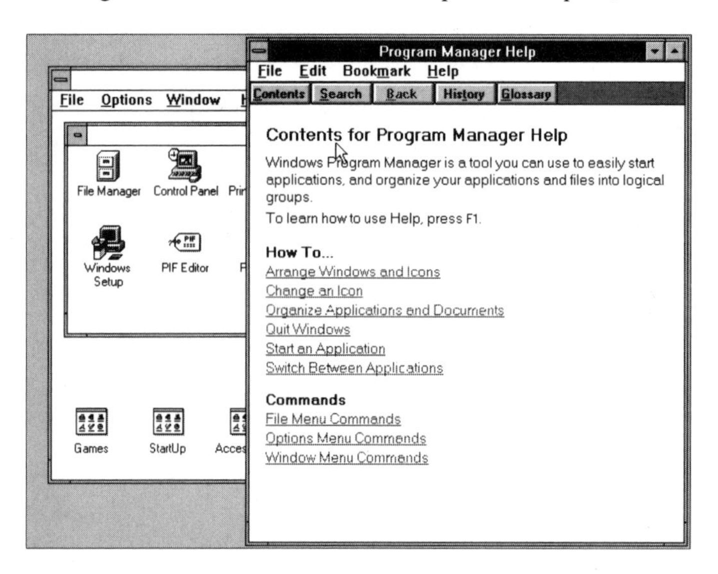

2 Under Commands, click the topic "Window Menu Commands."

Notice that the pointer changes to the shape of a hand when it is on an underlined topic or glossary term.

If necessary, scroll the contents of the window until you see the topic name in the list. After you click the topic, the new screen's contents, titled "Window Menu Commands," appears.

3 Click the term "scroll bar" (with dotted underline) near the top of the screen.

The glossary definition pops up, as shown on the next page.

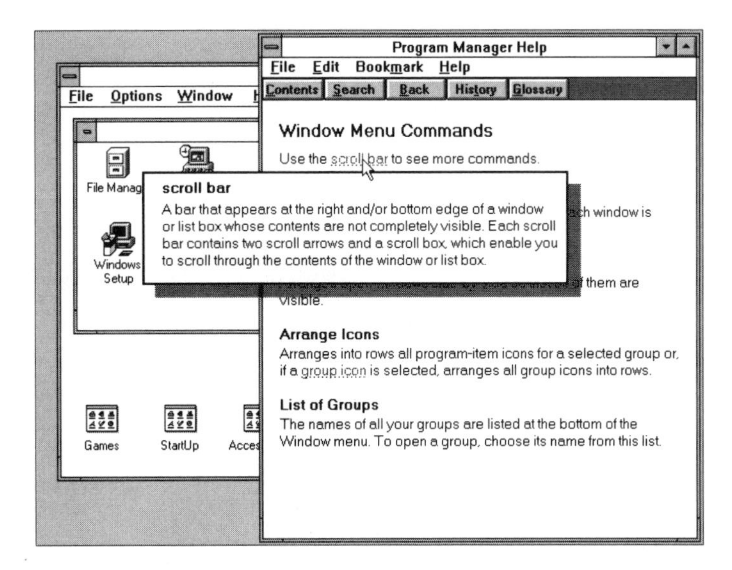

4 Click anywhere else on the desktop to make the definition disappear.

5 Double-click the Control-menu box in the Help window to close the window.

Search the Help topics index

Another way to get Help information in Windows 3.1 is to use the Search function in Help. Choosing the Search For Help On command from the Help menu opens the Search dialog box. It contains a scrollable list box that displays dozens of possible topics in alphabetic order, similar to an electronic index. Selecting a topic from this list leads to the relevant Help screen. You can also type any word or phrase in the adjacent text box above the list to select the most closely related topic. In this exercise, you practice using the search window to find information from the alphabetic list of topics.

1 From the Help Menu, choose Search For Help On.

The Search dialog box appears, as shown below:

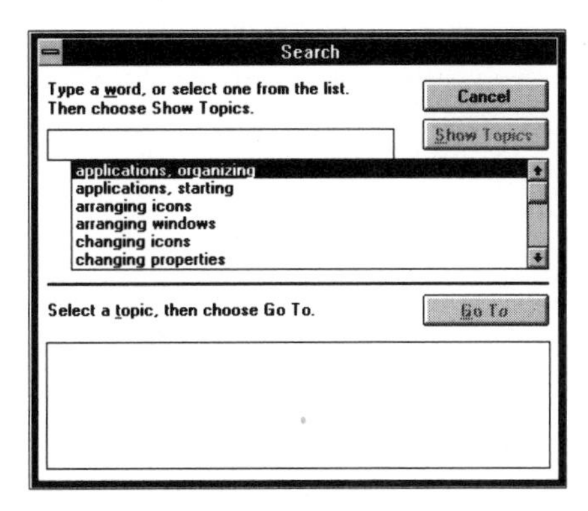

2. In the list box, select "arranging icons."

   You might need to scroll the list to find additional items.

3. Click the Show Topics button.

   In the lower box, one or more relevant topics appear.

4. Click the Go To button.

   The Search window disappears and is replaced by a Help screen about the selected topic, in this case, Arranging Windows and Icons.

5. Close the Help screen.
6. Repeat step 1.
7. Type **moving** in the text box.

   This selects the index item "moving program items." Note how the list box automatically scrolls to the topic that most closely matches what you type.

8. Repeat steps 3, 4, and 5.

Tip Many dialog boxes include a Help command button that opens a Help window with information specific to that dialog box. You can also receive *context-sensitive help* by pressing F1 virtually any time a Windows-based program is running.

Using the Help Window Button Bar

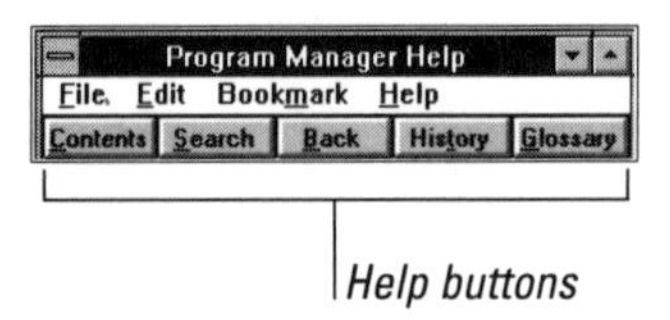

Help buttons

Near the top of the Help window in Windows 3.1 is a row of buttons labeled Contents, Search, Back, History, and Glossary. (Other applications do not necessarily give you the same options in their Help windows.) If you choose the Contents button, you return to the "Contents for Program Manager Help" screen, just as if you had chosen the Contents command from the Help menu. Clicking the Search button opens the same Search dialog box that you saw by choosing the Search For Help On command in the previous exercise.

The Back and History buttons let you return to screens you have viewed previously in the same Help session. Choosing Back displays the previous screen. Initially, the Back button is dimmed because each time you open Help you start from scratch. Choosing History gives you a list of all the topics you have examined during the current Help session in reverse chronological order, allowing you to repeat any one. Choosing Glossary gives you an alphabetic list of all glossary words for the current application. In the next exercises, you use the Back, History, and Glossary buttons to move around and get information in Help.

View previous Help screens with the Back and History buttons

1. From the Help menu, choose Contents.
2. In the button bar, click the Contents button.

   This button returns you to the main Contents list from any Help screen.
3. Under "How To," click the topic "Organize Applications and Documents."

   The previous Help screen is replaced with a new one about the selected topic.
4. Click the topic "Copying a Program Item."

   Again, the previous Help screen is replaced with a new one about the selected topic.
5. In the button bar, click the Back button.

   This returns to the previous Help screen, "Organizing Applications and Documents."
6. Click the topic "Arranging Windows and Icons."
7. Click the History button.

   A box appears listing the topics of all Help screens you have viewed in the current Help session, similar to the following:

   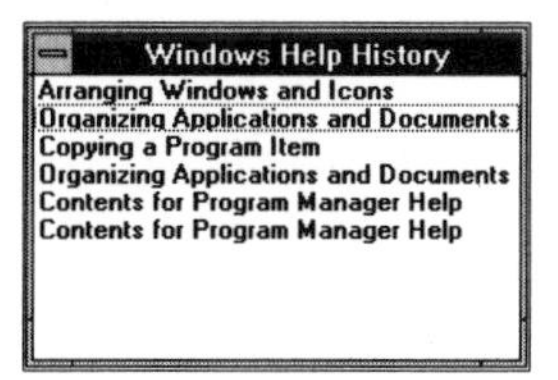

   The most recently viewed topics are at the top of the list. Notice that topics you have viewed more than once (such as "Organizing Applications and Documents") appear repeatedly in the list. "Contents for Program Manager Help" appears twice at the bottom of the list to reflect both steps 1 and 2 of this exercise.
8. In the History box, double-click "Copying a Program Item."

   The selected topic screen is immediately displayed.

View the Glossary list

If you are interested in the definition of a specific term in Windows 3.1, you can view an alphabetic list of all glossary items by clicking the Glossary button on the button bar. Then, from the glossary list, you can click any item to display its definition.

1 Click the Glossary button.

The Glossary window opens, similar to the following:

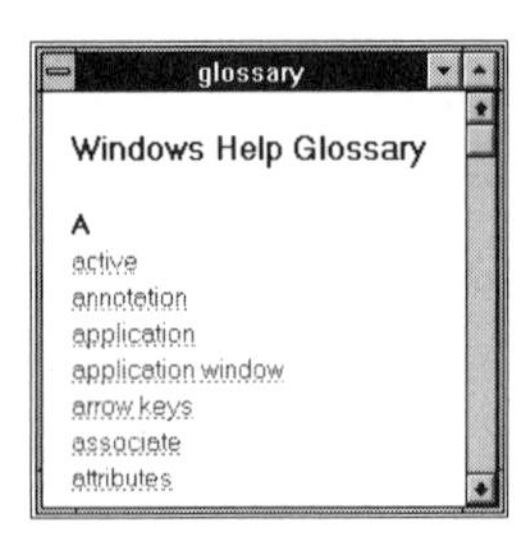

2 Click the term "arrow keys."

A definition box pops up.

3 Click again to close the definition box.

4 Scroll down to the term "group icon," and click. Click again to close the definition box.

5 Scroll through the list and look at the definitions of any other terms that interest you.

6 Double-click the Control-menu box in the Glossary window to close the window.

7 Close the Help window.

One Step Further

- To enhance your experience with dialog boxes, try the following. From the File menu, choose Properties. Identify the response formats that are included in this dialog box. Choose each of the command buttons that are followed by ellipses ("Browse..." and "Change Icon...") to examine additional dialog boxes. Choose the Help button for context-sensitive help about the dialog box. Close each dialog box with its Cancel button.
- Use the Help system to find out information about the following topics and terms: the Open command, program items, and Help buttons.

If you want to continue to the next lesson

- Close all windows except the Program Manager and Main windows.

If you want to quit Windows for now

1 On the Program Manager window, double-click the Control-menu button.

A dialog box appears, saying "This will end your Windows session."

2 Click OK.

Lesson Summary

To	Do this
Open a menu	Click the menu name in the menu bar. *or* Press ALT plus the underlined letter in the menu name.
Close a menu without choosing a command	Click outside the menu area. *or* Press ALT once. *or* Press ESC twice.
Choose a command	Open a menu. Then click the desired command *or* press the underlined letter of the command.
Arrange multiple windows in cascaded form (overlapping)	Choose Cascade from the Window menu.
Arrange multiple windows in tiled form (not overlapping)	Choose Tile from the Window menu.
Arrange program-item icons within a group window	Activate the group window you want to arrange. Then choose Arrange Icons from the Window menu.
Arrange group icons in the Program Manager window	Select any group icon (but do not open it). Then choose Arrange Icons from the Window menu.
Turn a check box item on or off	Click the box. If an X is present, the item is on. If not, the item is off.
Select an option from a list box	If necessary, click the arrow and scroll the list to display the desired option. Then click the option to make it highlighted.
Select from a set of option buttons	Click the round button next to the desired option. (Other options in the set automatically become deselected.)
Search the Help system through its list of topics	Choose Contents from the Help menu, or press F1.
Search for a Help topic through its alphabetic index	Choose Search For Help On from the Help menu. Then select or type a topic name, choose Show Topics, select a topic in the lower box, and choose Go To.
View Help screens that you have previously seen in the same Help session	In the Help window, choose the Back button to see the immediately previous screen; or choose the History button to see a list of all previously viewed screen titles and select the desired one.

To	Do this
View a list of Glossary terms for the current application	In the Help window, choose the Glossary button.

For more information on	See the *Microsoft Windows User's Guide*
Using menus, commands, dialog boxes, and Help	Chapter 1, "Windows Basics"

For an online lesson about	Do this
Using menus and commands	From the Help menu, choose Windows Tutorial. Press W. Choose the Contents button near the lower-right corner of the window. From the list of topics, choose the button next to Using Menus And Commands.
Using dialog boxes	From the Help menu, choose Windows Tutorial. Press W. Choose the Contents button near the lower-right corner of the window. From the list of topics, choose the button next to Using Dialog Boxes.

Preview of the Next Lesson

With the basic skills you've learned, you are ready to learn how to use Windows features to organize your work and start applications. In the next lesson, you will be introduced to the functions of Program Manager, and you will find out how to start and quit application programs using Program Manager as your base of operations.

Part **2**

Application Management

The Program Manager: A Guided Tour

In Lessons 1 and 2, you practiced basic Windows skills by working with icons, windows, menus, and dialog boxes. You saw that each window can be reduced to an icon, that each icon can be opened into a window, and that group icons are different from program-item icons. Yet, you might have wondered, what's the point? Isn't there more to Windows than reading a Help screen, moving an icon, resizing a window, and running tutorials? Well, there certainly is! Starting with this lesson, the book begins to flesh out your understanding of the major Windows functions as well as the specific tasks you can accomplish with its built-in applications.

You can think of Program Manager as the "home base" or "command post" of all work carried out in the Windows environment. Program Manager is usually the first screen element you see when you start Windows and the last one you see before you quit. You use Program Manager for two major purposes: to start a selected application program, and to keep all your available applications organized so you can quickly find any of them. In this lesson you take a closer look at the menus and organizational structure of Program Manager, and start an application from it.

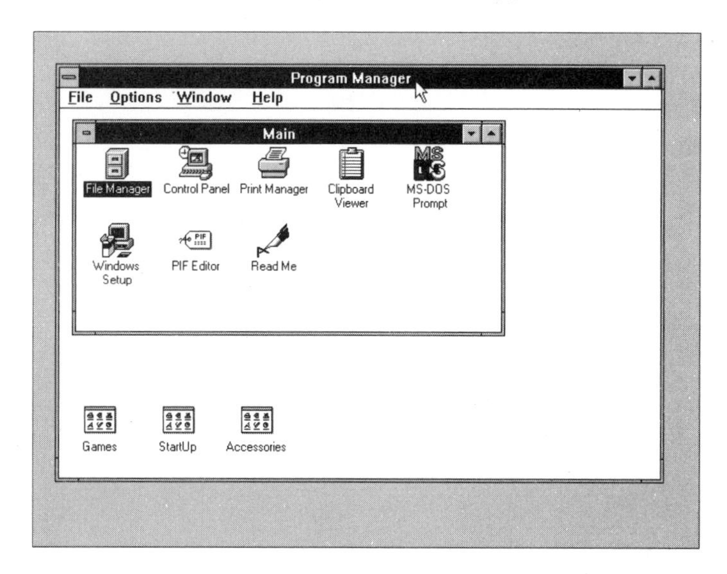

This lesson explains how to do the following:

- Use important commands in the Program Manager menus
- Start and quit application programs from Program Manager

Estimated lesson time: 30 minutes

Exploring Program Manager Menus

In Lesson 2, you used commands under the Window menu to arrange windows, and under the Help menu to explore the Help system. Now let's look at the File and Options menus, and revisit the Window menu.

The File Menu

The File menu is divided into three parts. At the top are six commands that apply to the active program-item or group icon. The Move and Copy commands are available only when a program-item icon is selected. The other four commands (New, Open, Delete, and Properties) can act on either a group icon or a program-item icon. The next command, Run, is used to start any program by typing its filename (up to eight characters plus a three-character extension). The bottom command, Exit Windows, provides an alternate way to quit the Windows program.

You will have a chance to use several of these File menu commands in later exercises. For now, let's look at the Properties command more closely. Choosing Properties opens a dialog box that shows vital information about the active icon. One type of dialog box appears for a group icon, and a slightly different type of box for a program-item icon.

Use the Properties command from the File menu

1 Select the Accessories group icon.

If the Accessories group window is open, reduce it to an icon by clicking the Minimize button.

2 From the File menu, choose Properties.

The Program Group Properties dialog box appears, similar to this:

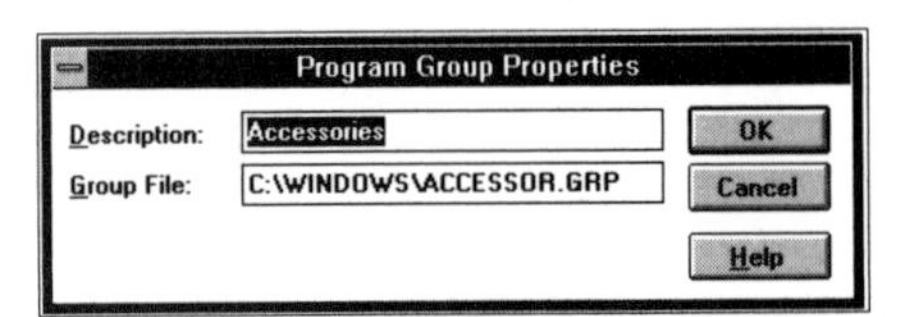

The Description text box shows the name that appears as the title for both the Accessories group icon and group window. The Group File text box names the specific file that contains information about the group.

3 Choose Cancel.

4 In the Main window, select the Clipboard Viewer icon.

5 From the File menu, choose Properties.

This time a different dialog box appears, one that applies to a program-item icon.

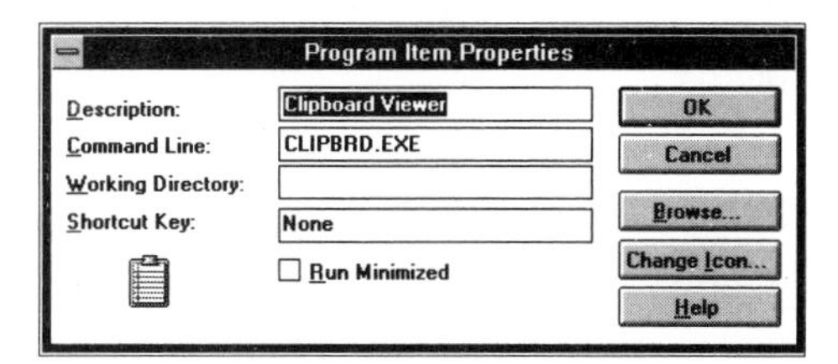

The Description box contains the title that appears under the icon. The Command Line text box contains the name of the program file associated with the icon. Other items on this dialog box are optional, and you include information in them depending on how you wish to run the application itself.

6 Choose Cancel.

The Options Menu

As you saw in Lesson 2, choosing a command from the Options menu either removes or places a check mark next to the command. The following table summarizes the effect of each command in the Options menu.

Command	Effect when checked
Auto Arrange	Icons in group windows automatically align themselves in straight rows and columns after being manually moved.
Minimize on Use	The Program Manager window shrinks to an icon whenever you start an application. This is useful for reducing desktop clutter when running multiple programs.
Save Settings on Exit	If you open, close, or move any group window or icon in Program Manager before quitting Windows, these changes remain in effect the next time you start Windows. Do not activate this command if you prefer to see the same startup screen each time.

Activate the Auto Arrange command from the Options menu

This exercise lets you see the effect of turning on and off the Auto Arrange option.

1 In the Main window, drag the Control Panel icon about a half-inch to the right.

The icon stays wherever you put it. (If it jumps back, carry out step 2 and then repeat the exercise from step 1.)

2 From the Options menu, choose Auto Arrange.

3 Drag the Control Panel icon about a half-inch again.

Notice how the icon jumps back to line up with all the other icons in straight rows and columns.

4 From the Options menu, choose Auto Arrange.

Now the command is deactivated.

The Window Menu

In Lesson 2, you used the first three commands in the Window menu (Cascade, Tile, and Arrange Icons) to rearrange windows and icons. In this lesson, you look at the lower part of the menu, which lists all available group names.

When you choose a group name from the Window menu, that group window becomes active. If the chosen group had been previously reduced to a group icon, it is opened to a window. If you maximize one group window, then any window you activate later using the Window menu is also maximized. The following exercise involves activating group windows from the Window menu.

Activate a group window from the Window menu

1 From the Window menu, choose Accessories.

The Accessories group window opens and is the active window.

2 From the Window menu, choose Games.

The Games window also opens, and moves to the front of the other group windows. Games is now the active window.

3 Maximize the Games window.

If the Maximize button of the Games window is not visible within the Program Manager window, either enlarge Program Manager or move the Games window until you can see the button.

If you are not sure how to restore a window, refer to the section "Minimizing, Maximizing, and Restoring Windows" in Lesson 1.

4 From the Window menu, choose Main.

When one group window is maximized, each group window that you subsequently activate from the Window menu also appears maximized.

5 Restore the Main window.

Your screen should now look similar to the one on the next page.

The relative size and position of each window might vary, depending on how you have previously manipulated them.

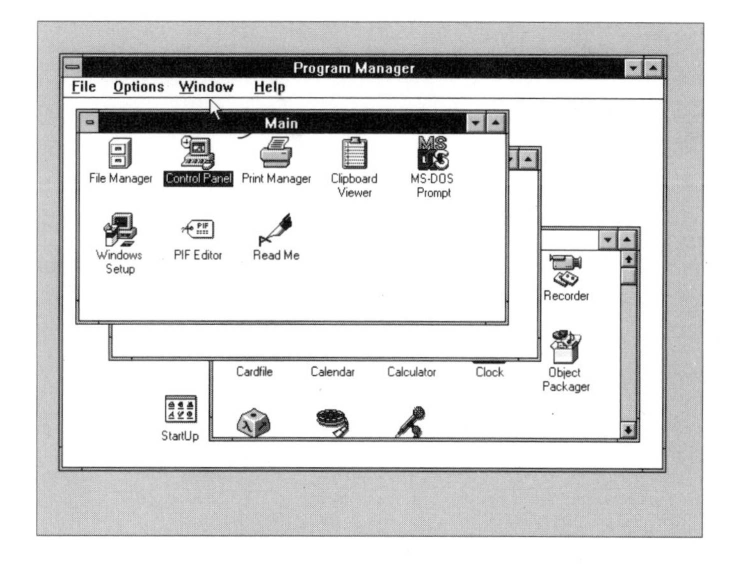

6 Minimize all group windows except Main.

You might want to rearrange or cascade the windows to make their Minimize buttons accessible.

Note Minimizing a group window (with either the Minimize command or the Minimize button) has the same effect as closing the group window from its Control menu. In both cases, the window is reduced to an icon on the screen.

Starting and Quitting Application Programs

Starting an application from an icon is straightforward. First, you open the group window containing the application. Next, you select the program-item icon for the application. Finally, you either choose the Open command from the File menu of Program Manager, or double-click the icon.

Quitting an application in Windows can usually be accomplished in any of three ways. One is to choose Close from the Control menu. Another is to choose Exit from the File menu. The quickest method is to double-click the application's Control-menu box.

Note Quitting an application is *not* the same as minimizing an application window. When you *minimize* an application window, the program is technically still running in the computer's memory, and an icon representing the application appears at the bottom of your screen. When you *quit, close,* or *exit* an application, however, it is removed from memory and *no* icon remains at the bottom of the screen. This distinction is important when you run two or more applications.

In the next two exercises, you use two types of methods to open, minimize, and quit an application called Cardfile in the Accessories group. First you use menu commands, and then you use mouse shortcut techniques. These general procedures apply to any Windows-based application that is installed on your system.

Open, minimize, and close the Cardfile application using menu commands

1 Open the Accessories group window.

2 Point to the icon labeled Cardfile and click once to select it.

If necessary, scroll the window's contents until you see the Cardfile icon.

3 From the File menu, choose Open.

The Cardfile application window opens, similar to the following:

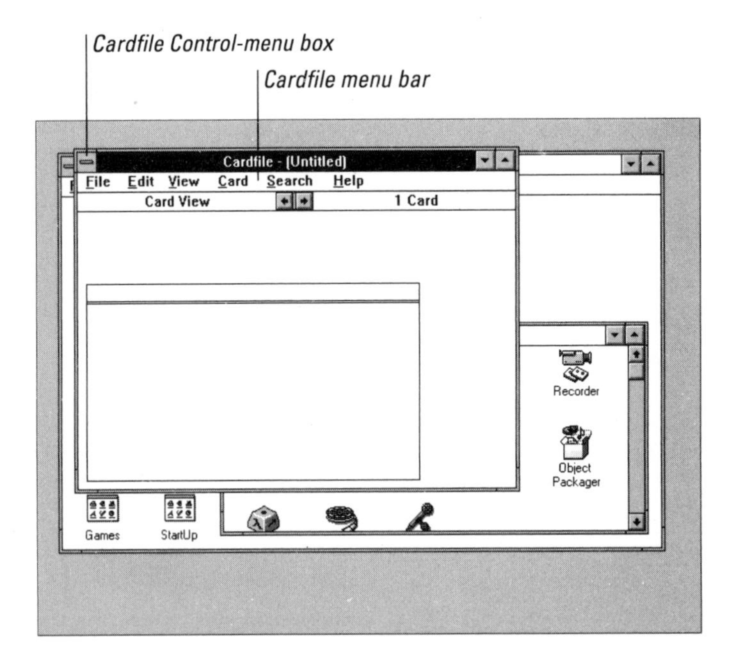

4 From the Control menu on the Cardfile window, choose Minimize.

The application window is reduced to an icon at the bottom of the screen, as shown in the following illustration. Remember that the Cardfile application is still running in the computer's memory.

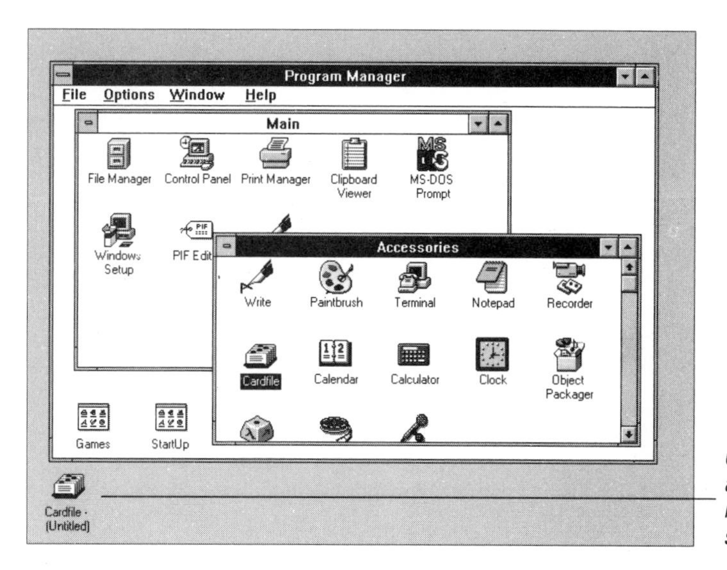

Cardfile application minimized but still running

5 Click the minimized Cardfile icon once.

This makes the Control menu pop up.

6 Choose Restore.

7 From the File menu on the Cardfile window, choose Exit.

An alternate method would be to choose Close from the Cardfile Control menu. Either way, you quit the application.

Open, minimize, and close the Cardfile application using mouse shortcuts

In this exercise you accomplish exactly the same results as in the previous exercise, but without choosing menu commands.

1 Activate the Accessories group window, if necessary.

2 Double-click the Cardfile icon.

This starts the application and opens the Cardfile window. If nothing happens, perhaps you didn't click fast enough. Try it again.

3 Click the Minimize button on the Cardfile window.

The Cardfile icon appears at the bottom of the screen, indicating that Cardfile is still running.

4 Double-click the minimized Cardfile icon.

The Cardfile window is now restored.

Note In step 4 above, you must double-click the Cardfile icon that is minimized at the bottom of the screen, *not* the program-item Cardfile icon in the Accessories window. If you accidentally double-click the program-item icon, then two sessions of the Cardfile application would be running at the same time. With more than one Cardfile running, you must quit each session individually.

5 Double-click the Control-menu box on the Cardfile window.

This closes the Cardfile window and quits the application.

6 Close the Accessories group window.

You can use any of these menu and mouse techniques interchangeably, depending on whichever makes you more comfortable.

One Step Further

- From the Options menu, activate Minimize On Use, which minimizes the Program Manager window when you start any application. Locate the Write application icon under Accessories and start the program.
- Minimize Write, and then restore both the Write and Program Manager windows. Finally, quit Write and deactivate the Minimize On Use option.

If you want to continue to the next lesson

- Be sure that the Main group window is open and that all other groups appear as group icons.

If you want to quit Windows for now

1 Double-click the Control-menu box in the Program Manager window.

2 When the message "This will end your Windows session" appears, click OK or press ENTER.

Lesson Summary

To	Do this
Examine information about a group or program-item icon	Select the icon, and then choose Properties from the File menu.
Activate a Program Manager option	Open the Options menu. If the desired option has no check mark, choose that option. Otherwise, close the menu.
Deactivate a Program Manager option	Open the Options menu. If the desired option has a check mark, choose that option. Otherwise, close the menu.

To	Do this
Activate a group window that appears as a group icon	Double-click the group icon. *or* Choose the group name from the Window menu.
Start an application	Double-click the program-item icon. *or* Select the program-item icon and then choose Open from the File menu in Program Manager. *or* Select the program-item icon and then press ENTER.
Minimize an application window without quitting	Click the Minimize button on the application window. *or* Choose Minimize from the Control menu of the window.
Quit an application	Double-click the application's Control-menu box. *or* Choose Close from the application's Control menu. *or* Choose Exit from the application's File menu. *or* Press ALT+F4.

For more information on	See the *Microsoft Windows User's Guide*
Choosing commands and starting applications from Program Manager	Chapter 3, "Program Manager"

Preview of the Next Lesson

In the next lesson, you learn how to customize the visible elements of Program Manager to meet your needs. These skills include moving and copying program items between groups, creating new groups and program items, and modifying icon names.

Managing Program Groups and Items

You can easily customize the initial organization of groups and items in Program Manager to fit your individual software mix and work needs. For example, suppose you own five different word-processing programs and would like to keep their application icons together in one group called Word Processors. Or, suppose you manage three unrelated projects, and would like to create a separate group of program-item icons for the documents and programs of each project. In this lesson, you learn how to customize the contents of your Program Manager window by moving and copying program items, renaming icons, and creating new groups and program items.

By the end of this lesson, you will have learned the skills needed to reorganize program items and groups in Program Manager, as shown in the following example:

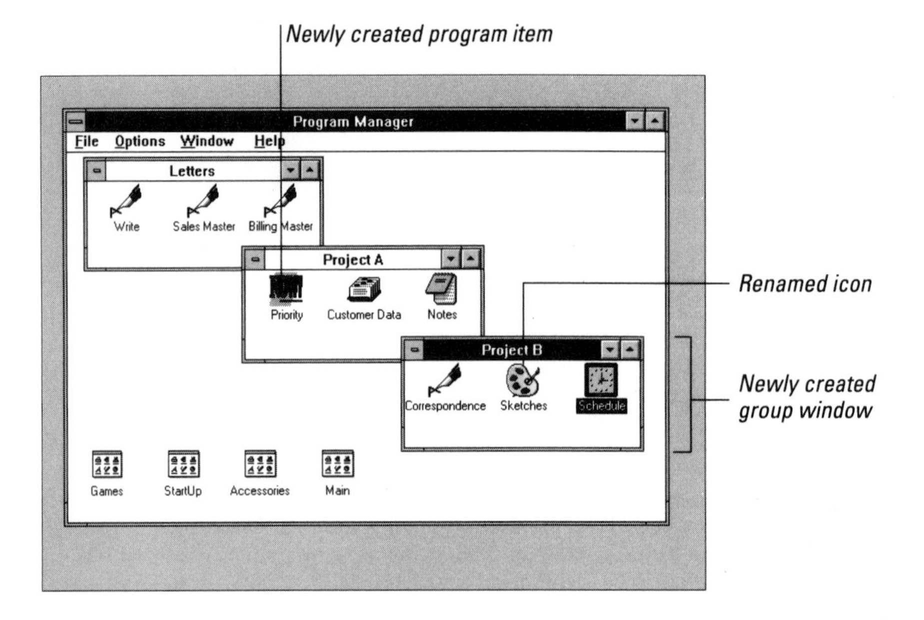

This lesson explains how to do the following:

- Organize program items by moving and copying them between groups
- Create and delete program items and groups to fit your work needs
- Alter item names and change icons

Estimated lesson time: 40 minutes

Moving and Copying Program Items

The designers of Windows 3.1 created a generic set of program groups that appear in Program Manager after you install Windows. They grouped program items together in a way that they thought would be a good starting point for most people. However, the built-in applications do not all have to stay in a group called Accessories, and entertainment programs do not have to be so obviously grouped under Games. (If you use Windows at work, this group name might not help you convince your boss that you play Solitaire only to develop mouse skills and reduce stress.) Because you probably plan to have a long-term relationship with Windows, it's not too early to consider how to organize the icons according to your personal needs and preferences.

As you saw in Lesson 1, to *move* a program-item icon between groups, you simply drag it from one group window to another. If you prefer, you can also move an item by selecting the icon and choosing the Move command from the File menu. You can also *copy* an existing program item easily by dragging the icon while holding down the CTRL key. It can be very convenient to have multiple copies of the same frequently used program item available in several groups.

Tip You can also move or copy a program item without using the mouse. Choose the Move or Copy command from the File menu, and then indicate the destination group in the dialog box. The exercises in this lesson, however, show you the more direct mouse technique.

The StartUp Group

A new feature of Windows 3.1 is a special group within Program Manager called *StartUp,* whose name represents its function rather than merely a description of its contents. Program Manager automatically activates any program item that appears in the StartUp group whenever you start Windows. If you want certain accessories or applications to be running as soon as Windows begins, then you should place their icons in the StartUp group.

In the next exercises, you move the Cardfile accessory and copy the Clock accessory into the StartUp group, and then restart Windows to observe the effect. Finally, you remove these applications from the StartUp group.

Move and copy program items into the StartUp group

1 Open both the Accessories window and the StartUp window, and adjust them so they do not overlap.

  You do not have to open the destination group window (StartUp) to place icons in it, but doing so makes it easier to watch the transfer of icons.

2 Drag the Cardfile icon from the Accessories window to the StartUp group icon.

  Because you moved, rather than copied, the Cardfile icon, it is no longer in its original group window.

3 Hold down CTRL and drag the Clock icon from Accessories to StartUp.

   Because you have copied the Clock icon, it appears in both group windows.

4 Open the Options menu, and be sure that Save Settings On Exit is not checked.

5 Quit Windows.

6 Restart Windows.

   Both Clock and Cardfile start after Windows is loaded. Your screen looks similar to the following:

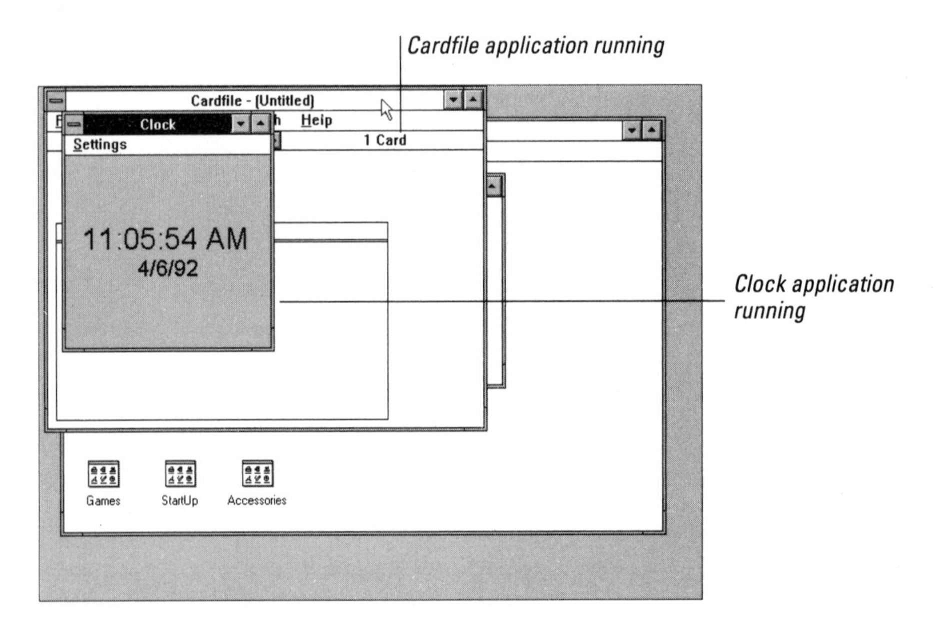

Remove program items from the StartUp group

1 Open both the StartUp and Accessories group windows, and move them as necessary so they don't overlap.

2 Drag the Cardfile icon from StartUp to Accessories.

3 In the StartUp window, select the Clock icon.

4 From the File menu, choose Delete; or press the DELETE key.

   Because the Clock icon in StartUp is a duplicate, another copy is still in Accessories. Therefore, you do not have to move it back, as you did for Cardfile in step 2.

5 At the confirmation message dialog box, choose Yes.

6 Quit and restart Windows.

Setting Up Groups and Program Items

So that you can gain complete control over the organization of Program Manager, you will learn to create, rename and delete both group and program-item icons in addition to copying and moving them. After you have these skills, you can set up the exact number and types of groups that fit your needs, and then move, copy, or create the appropriate program-item icons to fill the groups.

There are two types of program items. The first type simply starts an application. The second type opens a specific document at the same time that it starts an application. For example, suppose you have a Microsoft Excel spreadsheet that you use for a particular project. You can create a group for that project, and then add a program item that starts Microsoft Excel and opens the spreadsheet file at the same time.

In this section, you create one new group and two new program-item icons using the New command from the File menu. The first program item starts an application, and the second opens a specific document associated with an application.

Create a new group

In this exercise, you create a new group called "My Letters."

1 From the File menu, choose New.

The following dialog box appears:

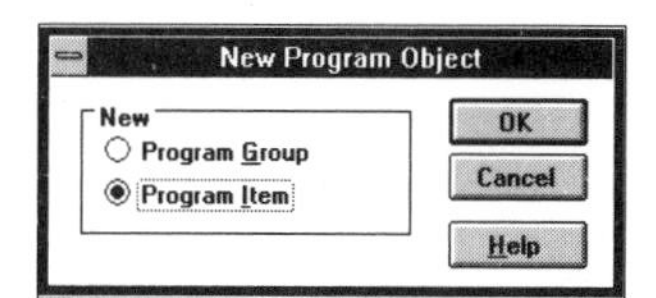

2 Select Program Group, and then choose OK.

You see the Program Group Properties dialog box.

3 In the Description text box, type **My Letters**

The dialog box now looks similar to the following:

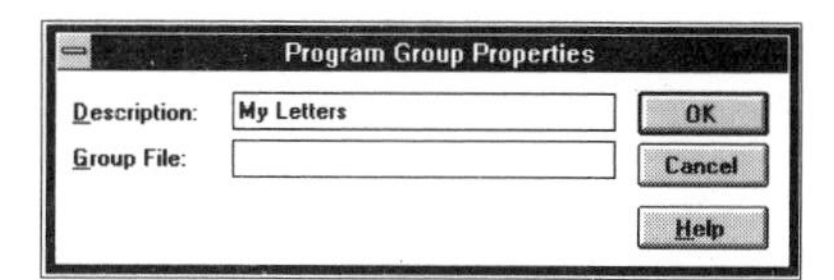

4 Choose OK.

Program Manager automatically creates a new group file name, so you can leave the second text box blank. The new group window appears on your screen, as shown on the next page.

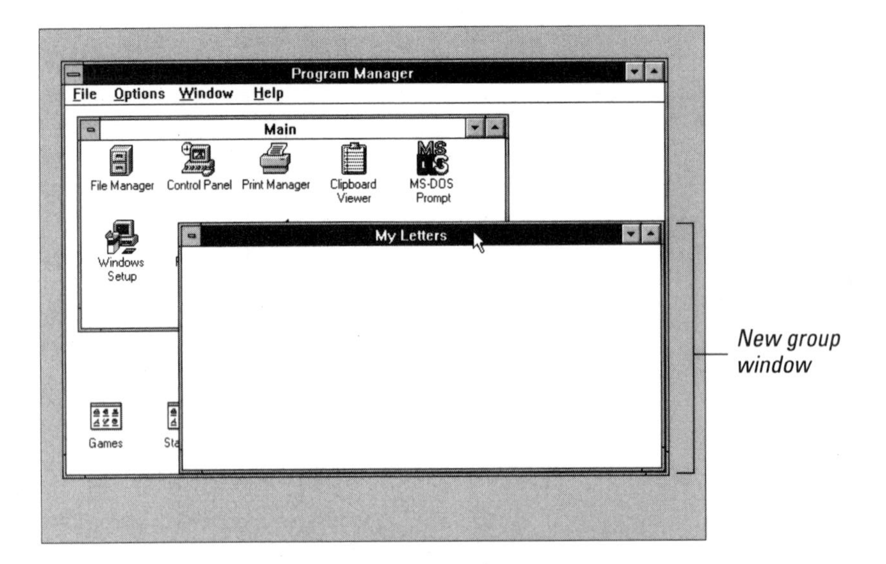

Create a new program-item icon for an application

In this exercise, you set up an icon in the My Letters window that starts the Write application. The description of the new program item is "My Write." You must enter the specific name of the Write program file.

1. Click the My Letters window to make sure it is active.
2. From the File menu, choose New.
3. In the dialog box, see that Program Item is selected, and click OK.

   Your screen displays the Program Item Properties dialog box.
4. In the Description text box, type **My Write**, and then press TAB.

   Pressing TAB selects the next text box or control area in a dialog box. You can also click with the mouse to select any text or control area.
5. In the Command Line box, type **WRITE.EXE**

   This is the name of the Write program file.

Note In some cases you must include a drive letter and directory name in the Command Line box. You will learn about drives and directories in Lesson 5.

---

6. Click OK.

   The other text boxes are optional, and so can be left blank in this example. When the dialog box closes, the My Write icon appears in the new group window.

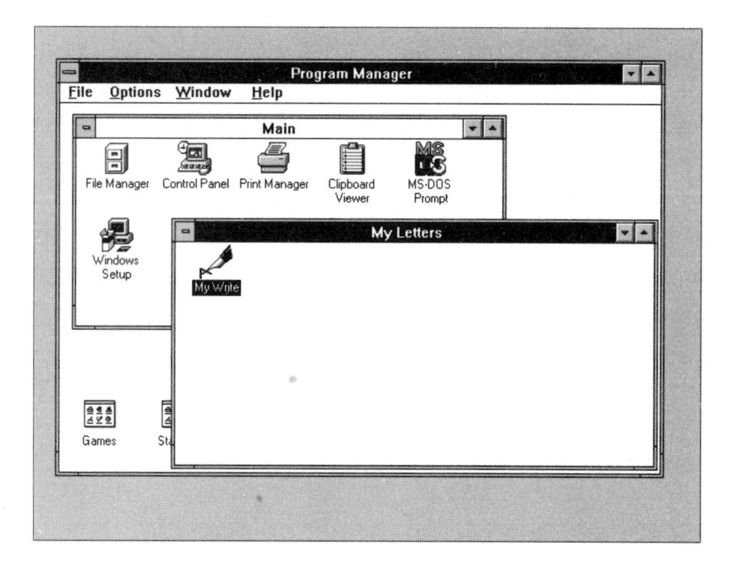

7 Double-click the My Write icon to start the Write application.

8 Double-click the Control-menu box in the upper-left corner of the Write window to quit the Write application.

Create a new program-item icon for a document with an application

As mentioned above, you can create a program item that opens a specific document as well as the application that was used to create the document. The process is similar to setting up an application-only icon, except that the document file name is added to the command line. In this exercise, you create a program item that opens the document PRINTERS.WRI in Write. PRINTERS.WRI is a supplementary document about using printers that comes with Windows. The program-item icon you create in this exercise allows you to open this document directly whenever you want to view it.

1 Click the My Letters window to be sure it is active.

2 From the File menu, choose New.

3 In the dialog box, see that Program Item is selected, and click OK.

   The Program Item Properties dialog box appears.

4 In the Description box, type **PrinterInfo**, and then press TAB.

5 In the Command Line box, type **WRITE.EXE PRINTERS.WRI**

   Be sure to leave a space between the program name (WRITE.EXE) and the filename (PRINTERS.WRI).

6 Click OK.

7 Click the new PrinterInfo icon.

Your screen looks like the following:

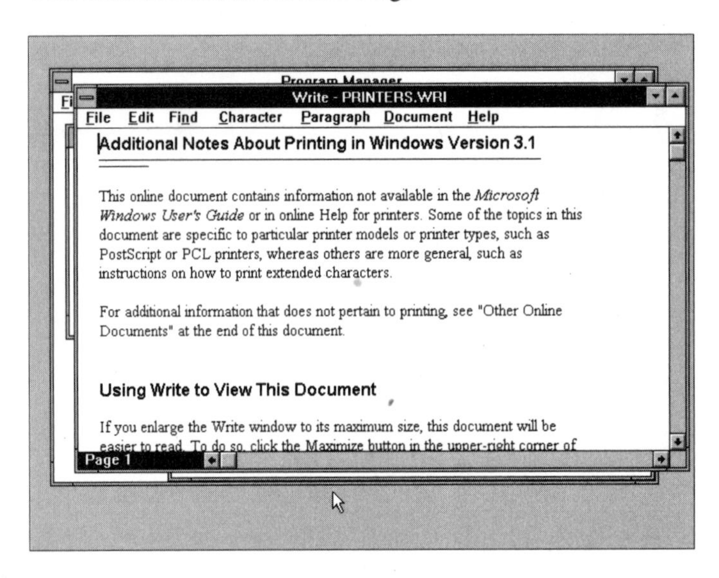

8 Double-click the Control-menu box to quit the Write application.

Modifying Groups and Program Items

Suppose you have a partner who objects to the exclusive-sounding names you have applied to the new group and application icon, and would like the icon names to suggest that they belong to more than one person. Also, you prefer to have a variety of icons within each group window to help distinguish between application and document items. Fortunately, you can easily alter the name of a group or program item, and change the icon itself, through the Properties command in the File menu.

Rename a group and a program-item icon

In this exercise, you change the group name "My Letters" to "Our Letters," and the application program item "My Write" to "Our Write."

1 Minimize the My Letters group window.

2 Select the My Letters group icon.

You can tell that an icon is selected when its name is highlighted.

3 From the File menu, choose Properties.

The Program Group Properties dialog box appears.

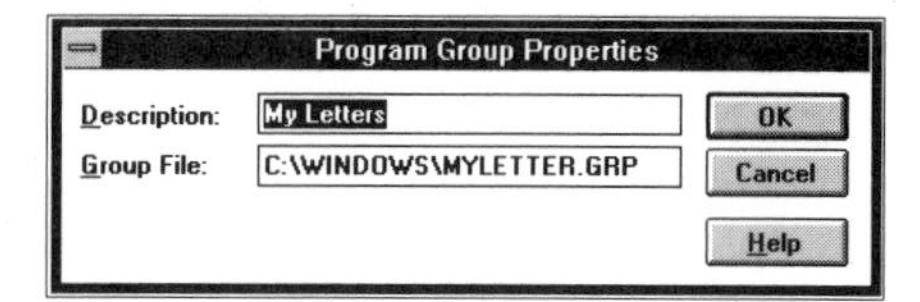

Program Manager created a new file that holds information about the group. The name of this file is now listed in the Group File box.

4 With "My Letters" highlighted, press DELETE.

5 Type **Our Letters** and press ENTER.

6 Open the Our Letters group and select the My Write icon.

7 From the File menu, choose Properties.

8 Replace the description with **Our Write**, and press ENTER.

The name of the My Write icon changes to Our Write.

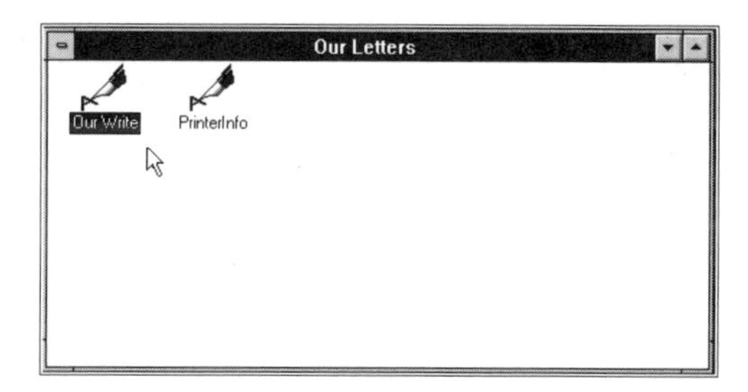

Change the icon for a program item

The icon displayed for both program items in this group is associated with the Write application program. Suppose you would like to display a different icon for the document items (such as PrinterInfo) than for the generic application icon. Program Manager provides several sample icons that you can use for any program item. In this exercise, you change the PrinterInfo icon to an image of a typewriter.

1 Select the PrinterInfo icon.

2 From the File menu, choose Properties.

3 Choose the Change Icon button.

A dialog box appears, similar to this:

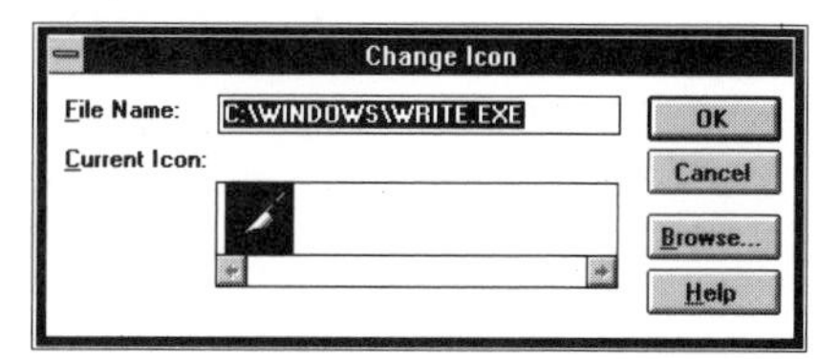

4 In the File Name text box, delete the existing name and type **PROGMAN.EXE**, and then press ENTER.

PROGMAN.EXE is the master file for Program Manager, and contains a variety of alternative icons. The Change Icon dialog box now looks similar to this:

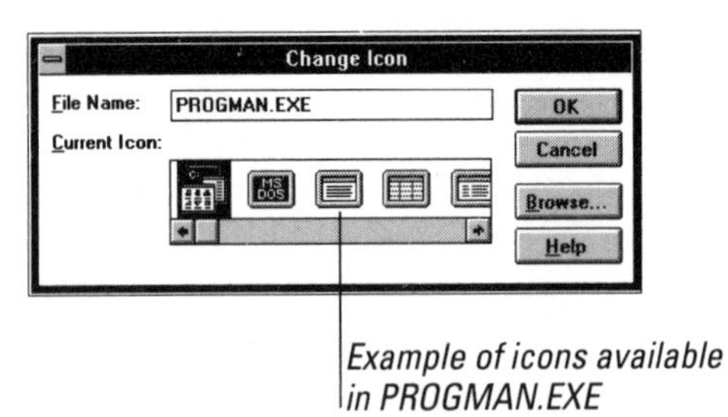

5 Click the right arrow of the scroll bar repeatedly to view all the available icons.

6 Scroll to the icon that looks like a typewriter, and select the icon with the mouse.

7 Click OK, and then click OK again.

The typewriter icon now appears as the PrinterInfo item, similar to the following:

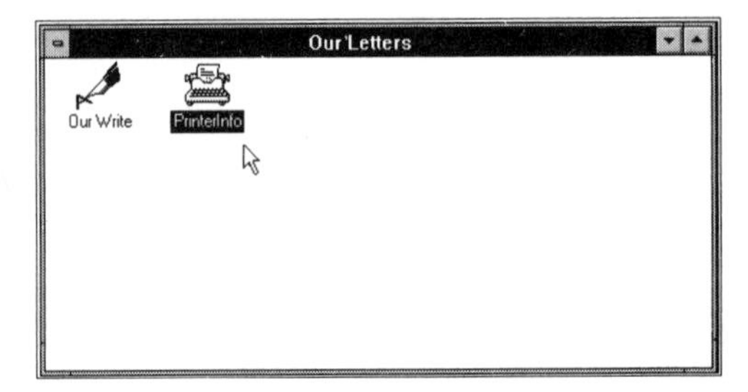

Tip Additional icons are provided in a file called MORICONS.DLL. To examine these icons, go through the exercise above, but in step 4 type the name of this file.

Delete a program group from Program Manager

Earlier, you deleted a program item from the StartUp window with either the DELETE key or the Delete command from the File menu. The same procedure applies to deleting an entire group. Do not delete a group too hastily, because deleting a group also removes all the program items in that group. If you accidentally delete a group that you want to keep, it can be difficult to reconstruct. In this exercise, you delete the Our Letters group and both of its items in a single operation.

1 Reduce the Our Letters group to an icon.

2 Select the Our Letters group icon by clicking once.

Be sure you have selected the correct icon.

3 From the File menu, choose Delete.

4 At the confirmation dialog box, choose Yes.

If you prefer to keep the new group, choose No at this point.

One Step Further

- Create a new group called "More Games." Copy Solitaire from the existing Games group into More Games. Copy Calculator from the Accessories group into More Games.
- You might want to give the new group a more respectable appearance in case your supervisor walks by. Change its name to "Weekend Work." In the group, change the name of the Solitaire program-item to "Overtime," and change its icon to the picture of Mona Lisa.
- Finally, erase all traces of your attempted subterfuge. From the Weekend Work group window, delete Calculator. Then close the group window and delete the group icon.

If you want to continue to the next lesson

- Be sure that the Main group window is open and that other groups are icons.

If you want to quit Windows for now

1 Double-click the Control-menu box in the Program Manager window.

2 When the message "This will end your Windows session" appears, click OK or press ENTER.

Lesson Summary

To	Do this
Move a program item from one window to another	Open the window that contains the item you want, and select the icon. Then drag the icon to the other group window or group icon; *or* choose Move from the File menu and specify the destination group in the dialog box.
Copy a program item from one window to another	Open the window that contains the desired item, and select the icon. Then hold down CTRL and drag the icon to the other group window or group icon; *or* choose Copy from the File menu and specify the destination group in the dialog box.
Make an application start automatically whenever you start Windows	Move or copy the program item(s) into the StartUp group.

To	Do this
Create a new group	Choose New from the File menu, and select Program Group in the first dialog box. Type a descriptive name next to Description in the second dialog box.
Create a new program item for an application	Activate the group window in which you want to create the new item. Choose New from the File menu, and select Program Item. Type a descriptive name next to Description and the application program's filename next to Command Line.
Create a new program item for a document with an associated application	Go through the steps to create a new program item for an application. After the program file in the Command Line text box, type a space and then the document's filename.
Modify the name of an icon	Select the icon and choose Properties from the File menu. Modify the Description as desired.
Change the icon displayed for a program item	Select the icon and choose Properties from the File menu. Choose the Change Icon button. Type the name of a file that contains one or more icons (such as PROGMAN.EXE) and choose OK. Select an icon from those displayed.
Delete a group or program item	Select the item or group icon to be removed. Choose Delete from the File menu, or press DELETE. Choose Yes at the confirmation dialog box.

For more information on	See the *Microsoft Windows User's Guide*
How to manage program groups, items, and icons	Chapter 3, "Program Manager"

Preview of the Next Lesson

In the next lesson, you are introduced to File Manager—an application in Windows that helps you keep track of all the program and data files stored on your floppy and hard disks. Those familiar with MS-DOS might appreciate how the menu-driven graphical environment makes it much easier to visualize your overall file organization, and to search for specific files or file groups. If you have used the File Manager in Windows 3.0, you'll also notice how it has been improved in version 3.1.

Part 3 File Management

The File Manager: A Guided Tour

One advantage of working with computers is that creating and using many electronic files is easy. Unfortunately, the large number of files is also one of the problems. Major application programs stored on your disk, as well as document files you create, can amount to hundreds of files that would be hard to manage without excellent tools.

The Microsoft Disk Operating System (MS-DOS) lets you organize your files into groups and subgroups called "directories." The Windows 3.1 File Manager brings to life the file structure of your disks with a graphical representation that is logical, flexible, and quick to respond. By the end of this lesson, you will be able to control and interpret the display of files and directories similar to the following:

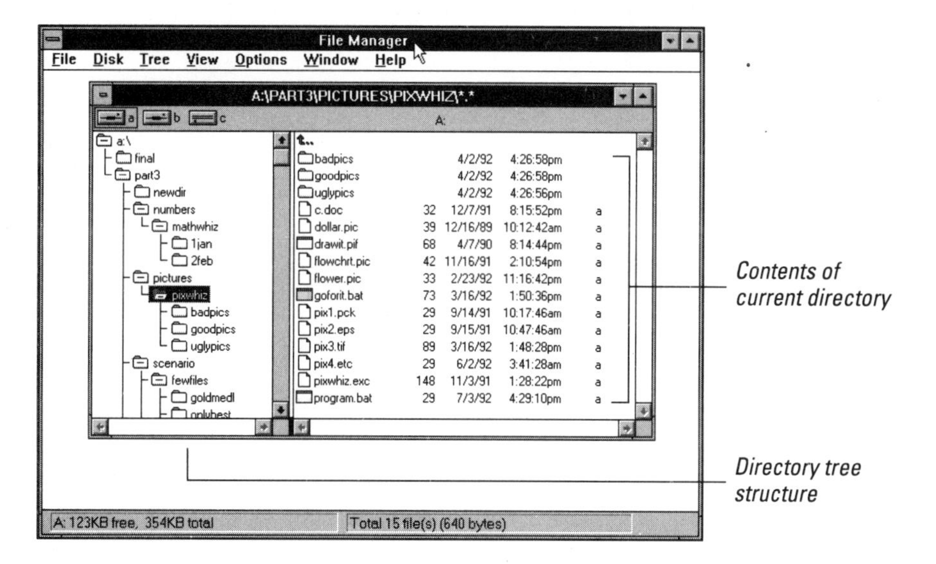

This lesson explains how to do the following:

- Start File Manager
- Display the contents of selected drives and directories in a directory window
- Modify the directory tree level to display desired branches
- View and interpret essential details about files and icon types
- View file lists sorted by name, type, size, or date
- Use the Search function to find a file

Estimated lesson time: 40 minutes

Starting File Manager

As far as Program Manager is concerned, File Manager is just another application like Write or Cardfile. You can usually find the File Manager icon, which looks like a tiny file cabinet, in the Main group window. As with any program item, this icon can be moved or copied to other groups, or placed in the Startup group if you want it to run whenever you start Windows. Starting File Manager is the same as starting any application from Program Manager, as you learn in the next exercise.

Start File Manager from its icon in the Main group window

1 If necessary, open the Main group window.

2 Double-click the File Manager icon.

The initial File Manager screen looks something like the following. Not all of the specific details you see on your own computer screen necessarily match this picture because different computers have different file structures. However, the major window elements should be comparable.

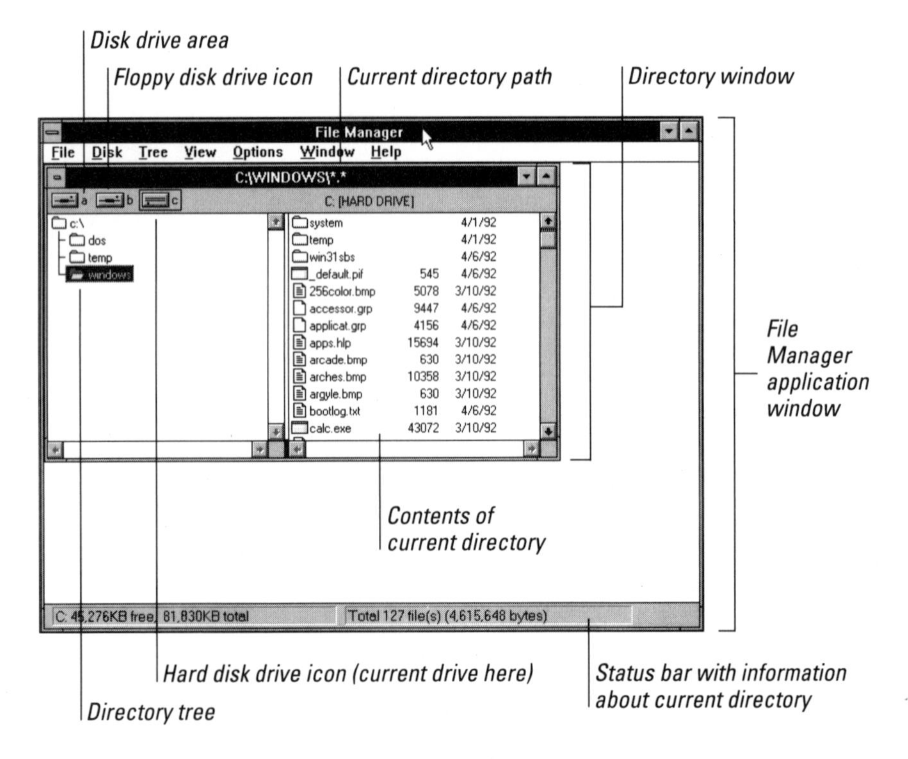

3 Locate each labeled element in this picture and note its definition in the list of terms that follows.

Directory window A window within the File Manager application window. It can display both the directory tree of a specified disk and the contents of the current directory.

Disk drive area A horizontal band just below the title bar of a directory window that shows the available disk drives in your system. Each drive is represented by a letter and by an icon that indicates its type (floppy, hard, network, and so on).

Current drive The disk drive whose information is currently displayed in a directory window. In the disk drive area, the current drive is surrounded by a rectangle.

Directory A named organizational unit within a disk. A directory can contain individual files and/or other directories.

Subdirectory A directory contained in another directory.

Directory tree A visual representation of the directory structure on a disk, usually found on the left side of a directory window.

Current directory The directory that is selected within a directory tree. Only one directory can be current at a time in a directory window. The current directory path is shown in the title bar of the directory window, and its contents are displayed on the right side of the window.

Directory path The name of a directory preceded by the names of all other directories to which it belongs, as well as the disk drive letter.

File A named unit of electronic information. There are two types of files commonly found in your system. A *program file* contains instructions that control the computer as it performs an application or system task. A *data file* consists of information you create with an application, such as a word processor document.

Status bar A band of information along the bottom edge of an application window. In File Manager, the status bar gives data about the capacity of the current disk and the size of files in the current directory.

Exploring the Structure of Drives and Directories

By looking through the directory window, you can see both the directory structure of a disk and the specific files contained in each directory. Using the mouse, you can scroll either side of the directory window, as necessary, to show all available information. You can also quickly change both the current drive and the current directory within a drive. Finally, you can control how many levels of a tree structure are displayed.

Scrolling a Directory Window

If a directory tree and contents list are too long to display all items within a directory window at one time, you can scroll them with their respective scroll bars. As you can see, a directory window is divided into two sides, each with its own set of vertical and horizontal scroll bars.

When you open File Manager, the current directory shown in the directory window is probably the one that contains your Windows program and system files—C:\WINDOWS. (Your Windows directory might have a different name, depending on what was assigned during the software installation process. The exact directory showing at this point is not important.) This directory has more files than can be shown in the window at one time. In the next exercise, you scroll the directory window vertically to display its contents.

Scroll the directory window

1 If no vertical scroll bars are active, drag the bottom border of the directory window up to reduce the window's height.

Your screen now looks similar to the following:

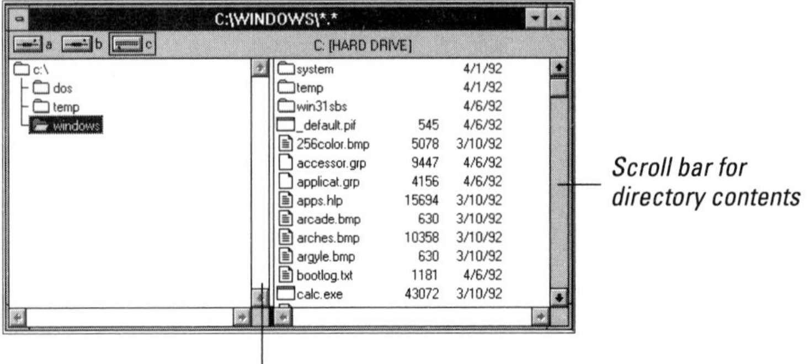

Scroll bar for directory tree (currently inactive)

2 If you see an active vertical scroll bar in the middle of the directory window, scroll it up and down.

This is how you examine the entire directory tree of the current drive if its length exceeds the window's space.

3 If you see an active vertical scroll bar at the right edge of the window, scroll it up and down.

This allows you to view all the files and subdirectories contained in the current directory.

Selecting Drives and Directories

If you want to change the current drive, click the icon with the drive letter you want in the area below the title bar. The directory tree structure of the new drive appears in the left part of the directory window. (Of course, you must first have a disk in a floppy drive to read its files.) If you want to change the current directory, click the desired directory icon in the directory tree. The contents of the new directory appear on the right side of the window.

Every disk contains a primary directory called the *root directory*. (Just like every tree in nature must have a root.) The root directory on any disk is named with a single character, the backslash (\). If you have just a few files to store on a disk, you might as well put them in the root directory. However, if you have many files, then it's better to group them in separate directories.

In the next exercises, you change the current drive from your hard disk to your floppy disk drive, and examine the directory structure of the practice disk that accompanies this book.

Important *Do not double-click any individual file in the contents list as you go through Lessons 5 and 6.* Double-clicking a program file usually starts the program. Double-clicking a data file can also start the program with which its name is associated (for example, files whose names end with ".WRI" are associated with the Write application). To conserve disk space, however, the files used in these lessons are not working program or data files. Therefore, if you accidentally click one of these files, you might get an unexpected result. If you see an error message, acknowledge it and follow any directions in the dialog box to recover. If you inadvertently start an application program, close it. Then continue with the lesson.

Change the current drive and directory

1 Be sure that your practice disk is securely locked in your disk drive.

2 In the drive area of the directory window, click the drive icon next to A. (If your practice disk is in drive B, choose the B icon instead.)

The directory window looks similar to the following:

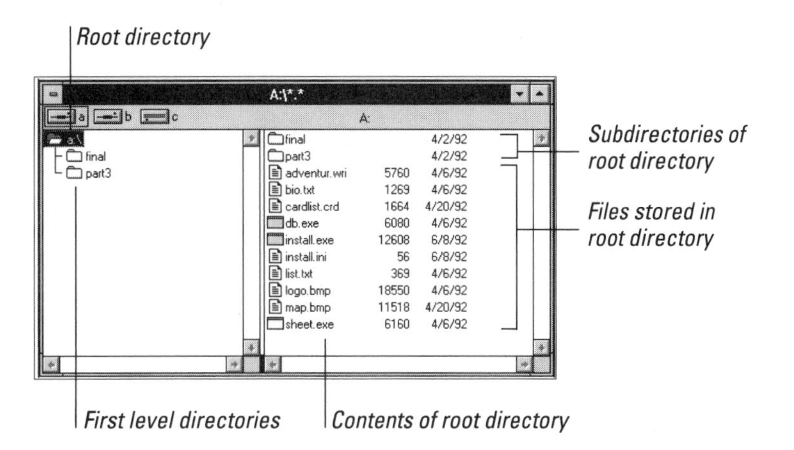

In the directory tree on the left, the highlighted line is "A:\" (or "B:\" if you are using drive B), which represents the root directory.

Note Uppercase and lowercase letters are used interchangeably for drive letters, directories, and filenames.

For the display of directories and filenames, you can easily switch between uppercase and lowercase letters. Choose Font from the Options menu; and in the dialog box, select or clear the Lowercase check box.

3 In the directory tree on the left, click PART3.

The directory icon, which looks like a file folder, changes to look like an open folder when selected.

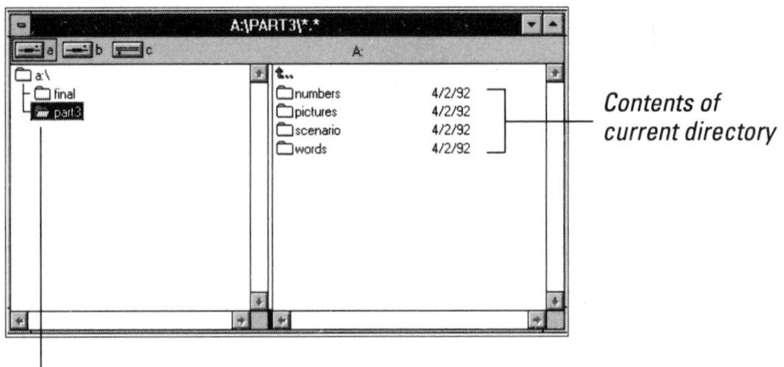

Notice that the contents list on the right is automatically updated to show what is contained in the current directory, PART3.

4 Click each of the other directories in the directory tree and observe the contents of each one. Be sure to select the root directory before going to the next section.

Both individual files and subdirectories of the current directory are shown in the contents list.

Moving Through Levels of a Directory Tree Structure

Why is the file structure of a disk called a "directory tree"? Imagine how a tree develops. A single branch grows from the root. Individual leaves and other branches grow from the branch. Every leaf is ultimately connected to the tree's trunk and root through a line of one or more connected branches. If you compare a file to a leaf and a directory to a single branch, then each file is connected to the root directory through a *path* of connected directories.

Another analogy that can help you understand the structure of a disk is the "parent-child" relationship between directories. For example, if a directory called ALLDOCS contains a directory called NEWONES, then ALLDOCS is the *parent* of NEWONES, and NEWONES is the *child* of ALLDOCS. A child can have only one parent directory, but a parent can have many children (subdirectories). The root directory is the parent of all first-level directories in a disk. A first-level directory, such as PART3, is a child of the root directory, and can be the parent of one or more subdirectories. A *branch* consists of any directory plus all of its subdirectories at all lower levels.

The directory tree on the left side of the directory window can show one or more levels of a disk's directory structure. Usually, when you first view a disk, the directory tree shows at least the root directory and all first level directories. If a directory contains one or more subdirectories (or "child" directories) that are not currently shown in the tree, it is considered to be an *expandable branch.* Expandable and expanded branches can be marked if you activate the Indicate Expandable Branches command from the Tree menu, as shown in the next exercise.

Note The following discussion of expanding and collapsing branches applies only to how the directory tree is displayed in a directory window at a given time. The actual directory structure on the physical disk is not affected.

Mark expandable branches in the directory tree

1 Open the Tree menu.

2 If there is *no* check mark next to the Indicate Expandable Branches command, choose this command. If it *has* a check mark, close the menu.

Your directory window now looks like the following:

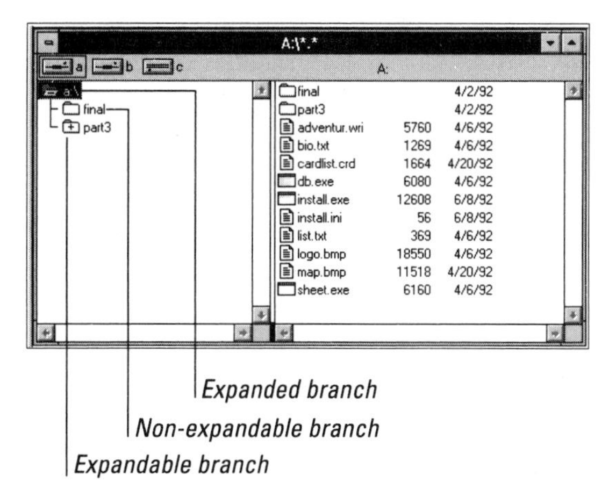

A directory icon marked with a plus sign (+) is an expandable branch because it contains at least one subdirectory that is not currently shown in the directory tree. A directory icon that is marked with a minus sign (-) is expanded, and its subdirectories are displayed in the directory tree. Any directory that is not marked contains no further subdirectories. Using either Tree menu commands, the mouse, or the keyboard, you can expand and collapse branches to display any number of directory levels. In the next exercises, you use these controls to expand and collapse branches of the practice disk's directory tree.

Expand and collapse a branch by one level

The PART3 directory is marked as an expandable branch. You first expand it by one level and then collapse it using Tree menu commands. Then you do the same operation with the mouse.

1 In the directory tree, select PART3.

2 From the Tree menu, choose Expand One Level.

   A keyboard equivalent is to press the plus (+) key. Notice that the expanded directory icon is marked with a minus (-) sign. Your directory window now looks like the following:

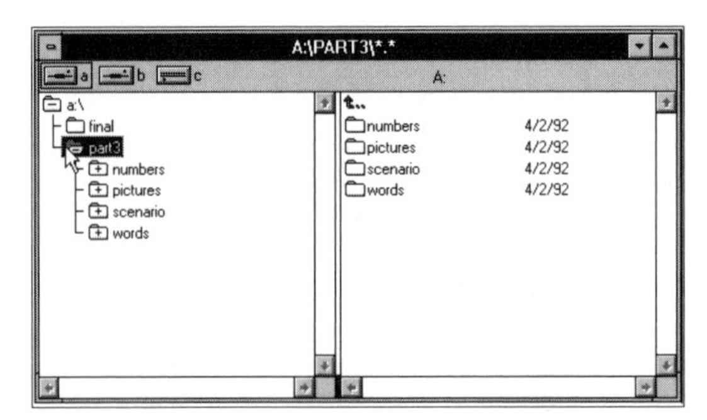

3 From the Tree menu, choose Collapse Branch.

   The PART3 subdirectories disappear from the directory tree, and the directory icon is marked with a plus sign again.

4 In the directory tree, double-click the PART3 directory.

   You can point to either the directory icon or its name. This mouse action expands the directory by one level, having the same effect as step 2 above.

5 Double-click the PART3 directory again.

   This collapses the branch, as in step 3 above.

Expand and collapse an entire branch

If a directory has more than one level of subdirectories, you can display all levels by choosing the Expand Branch command. When you collapse a branch showing multiple levels of subdirectories, all levels below the selected directory are hidden. In this exercise you expand and collapse the entire PART3 branch.

1 Select the PART3 directory.

2 From the Tree menu, choose Expand Branch.

   All levels of subdirectories below PART3 are now shown, similar to the one on the next page.

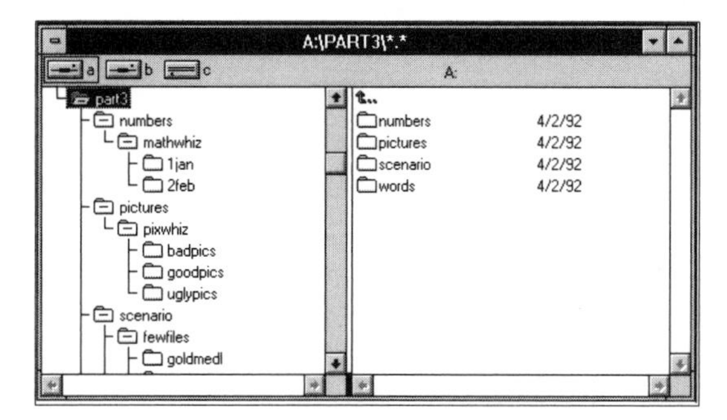

3 From the Tree menu, choose Collapse Branch, or double-click the PART3 directory.

The entire branch below PART3 is collapsed.

Expand and collapse an entire directory tree

There are two ways to expand an entire tree in a single step. One is to select the root directory and expand its branch. (The branch of a root directory is the same as the full tree). Another is to choose the Expand All command, regardless of which directory is currently selected. To collapse an entire tree in one step, select the root directory and collapse it. In this exercise you expand and collapse the directory tree of your practice disk.

1 Select the root directory at the very top of the directory tree.

2 From the Tree menu, choose Expand Branch.

Because the root directory is current, expanding its branch is the same as expanding the entire tree. Your directory window now looks similar to the following:

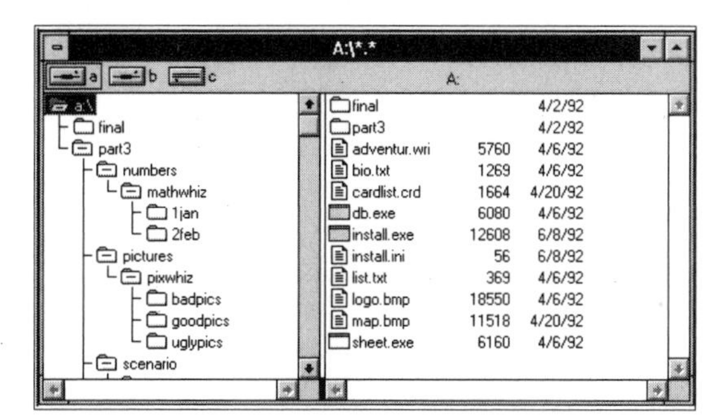

3 Double-click the root directory.

The tree is fully collapsed.

4 Double-click the root directory again.

The first-level subdirectories are displayed.

5 Select any of the first-level directories.

6 From the Tree menu, choose Expand All.

The full tree is displayed again. Because you made a lower-level directory current in step 5, this demonstrates that the Expand All command expands the entire tree regardless of which directory is current.

Displaying File Information

Now that you have explored the left part of the directory window, which displays the directory tree structure, we can turn to the other side, which shows the contents of a directory. As you have seen previously, when you select any directory in the directory tree, its contents are listed in the right side of the window. The relative size of the contents side can be adjusted by moving a vertical split bar. The amount and type of information listed for each file can be modified with dialog boxes. The order and type of files displayed can also be customized to suit your needs.

Adjust the width of the contents list

A vertical split bar separates the left and right sides of a directory window. In this exercise, you move the split bar so that the contents list side is as large as possible without overlapping the directory tree.

1 In the directory window, point to the vertical bar that separates the left side from the right side.

When your pointer is on the bar, it appears as a black, two-headed arrow pointing left and right, like this:

2 With the pointer on the split bar, drag the split bar left until it almost touches the names of the directory tree.

Your directory window looks similar to this:

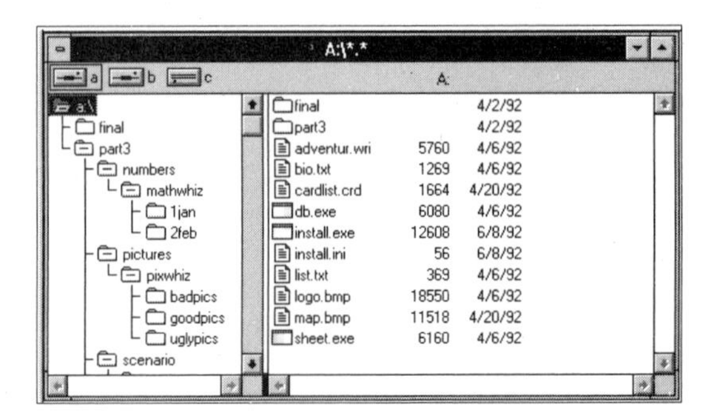

Tip If you accidentally lose the split window by moving the split bar all the way to an edge, or by choosing Tree Only or Directory Only from the View menu, you can get it back in one of the following ways: Choose Tree and Directory from the View menu; choose Split from the View menu and click once; or drag the split bar from the extreme left edge of the directory window.

Viewing File Details

Filenames

Every file has a *filename*. Under the rules of MS-DOS, each filename consists of a string of one to eight characters, plus an optional one-to-three-character extension preceded by a period. Letters, numbers, and certain punctuation marks (but no spaces) are allowed. There is no distinction between uppercase and lowercase letters.

Each filename within a directory must be unique—that is, two files with identical names *and* extensions cannot exist in the same directory. However, identically named files can exist in different directories. The same rules of form and uniqueness apply to directory names. By convention, however, directory names usually do not include extensions.

Other File Details

Four additional pieces of information are available for each file in the contents list: the file's *size* measured in bytes, the *last modification date*, the *last modification time*, and file *attributes*. Attributes tell you, for example, whether a file can be modified, or whether it is a special system file.

Using the View menu, you can select whether any or all of these file details are displayed in the list of directory contents. In the next exercise, you specify which details are shown.

Modify the file details displayed in the directory window

1 In the directory tree, select the WORDS directory.

2 From the View menu, choose Name.

   One of the Tree commands—Name, All File Details, or Partial File Details—is checked to indicate which is currently in effect. With Name active, only the file and directory names are shown in the contents list.

3 From the View menu, choose All File Details.

The directory window looks similar to the following:

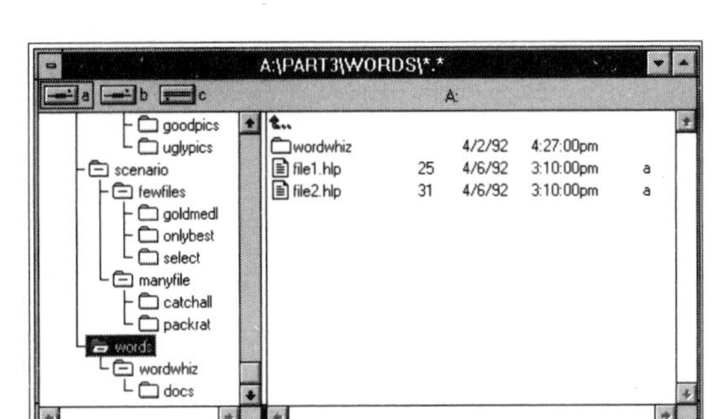

You can see each file's name, size, date and time last modified, and any attributes.

4 From the View menu, choose Partial Details.

The following dialog box appears:

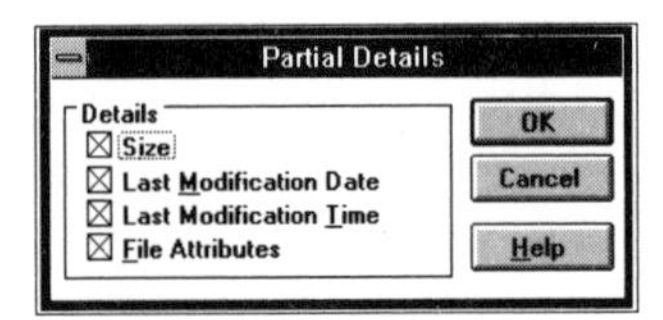

5 Click the check boxes so that Size is checked but the other three boxes are not checked.

6 Choose OK.

Now only the name and size of each file are listed.

7 Choose Partial Details again, and check the box for Last Modification Date, and then click OK.

Name, size, and date are displayed for each file.

Viewing Sorted and Selected File Lists

If a directory contains a large number of files, you might want to list them in a certain order. The four "Sort by" commands in the View menu let you modify the order in which files are listed. These commands rearrange the listed files on the basis of specified file details. The "By File Type" command allows you to select which types of contents to display. These commands are summarized in the following table.

This View menu command	Has this effect on the contents list
Sort by Name	Directories are listed in alphabetic order by name, followed by files listed in alphabetic order by name.
Sort by Type	Directories are listed in alphabetic order. Then files are listed in alphabetic order by extension. Files with identical extensions are grouped together and alphabetized by name.
Sort by Size	Directories are listed in alphabetic order. Then files are listed in order by size, from largest to smallest.
Sort by Date	Directories are listed in order by creation date, most recent first. Then files are listed in order by last modification date, most recent first.
By File type	A dialog box with check boxes appears. You can choose to display or hide any of the following categories: *Directories*, *Programs* (files with the extensions EXE, COM, BAT, or PIF), *Documents* (files associated with particular applications), or *Other Files*.

View a contents list sorted by file details

In this exercise, you select a directory containing several subdirectories and files, and then view the effects of sorting based on different types of file details.

1 From the fully expanded directory tree of your practice disk, select the directory PIXWHIZ.

2 From the View menu, choose Sort by Type.

Your directory window looks similar to the following. The files are listed in alphabetic order by their extensions. Notice that each item in the contents list has an icon that indicates what type of item it is.

In the contents list, of a directory, subdirectories are listed before files.

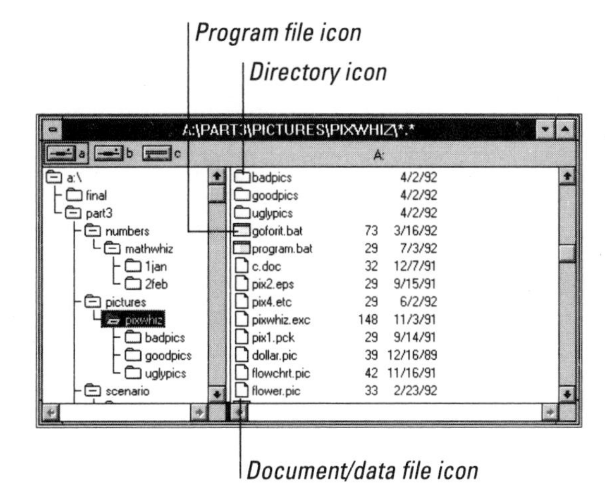

3 From the View menu, choose Sort by Size.

The files are now ordered according to their size.

4 From the View menu, choose Sort by Date.

Both directories and files are sorted by date, with the most recent on top.

5 From the View menu, choose Sort by Name.

The files are now listed in alphabetic order according to filename. This is the standard way that contents lists are initially displayed.

View a contents list by selected categories

When you choose the By File Type command from the View menu, a dialog box appears that allows you to display or hide different types of items in the contents list. In this exercise, you see the effects of deselecting Directories and Programs in this dialog box.

1 From the View menu, choose By File Type.

2 In the dialog box, remove the X from both Directories and Programs.

The dialog box now looks like the following:

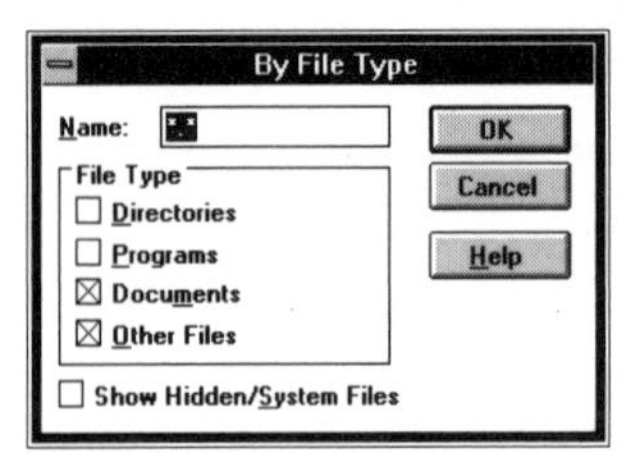

3 Choose OK.

The contents list no longer displays directories or program files (those files with the extensions EXE, COM, BAT, or PIF.

4 In the directory tree, select other directories to examine their contents lists.

The selection of displayed file types applies to any directory in this directory window.

5 From the View menu, choose By File Type.

6 Restore the Xs in the Directories and Programs check boxes, and choose OK.

The contents list is restored to its previous status.

Searching for a File by Name

Suppose you think a certain file is stored on a disk but you are not sure of its directory. You can use the Search command to examine all the directories in a specified branch and report the file's path if it is located. To search an entire disk, start from the root directory. In the next exercise, you search for a file named B.TXT on the practice disk.

Search for a specified file on a disk

1 In the directory tree, select the root directory of the practice disk.

2 From the File menu, choose Search.

The dialog box below appears:

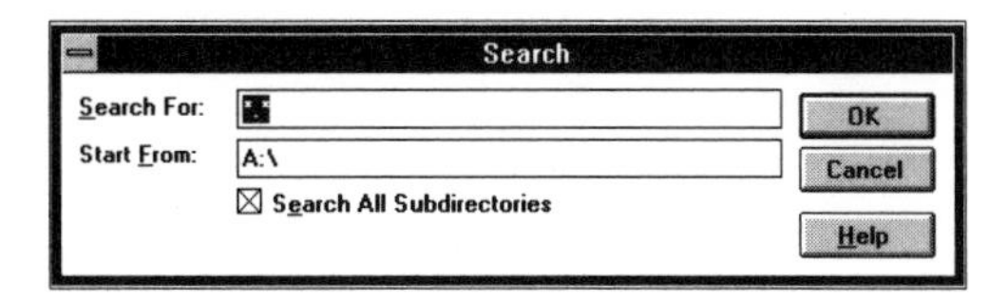

3 In the "Search For" line, type **B.TXT**

4 Be sure there is an X in the Search All Subdirectories check box.

This assures that the search covers the entire branch, including all subdirectories under the specified directory. If not checked, the search occurs only in the specified directory.

5 Choose OK.

After a few moments, the Search Results window appears, similar to the following:

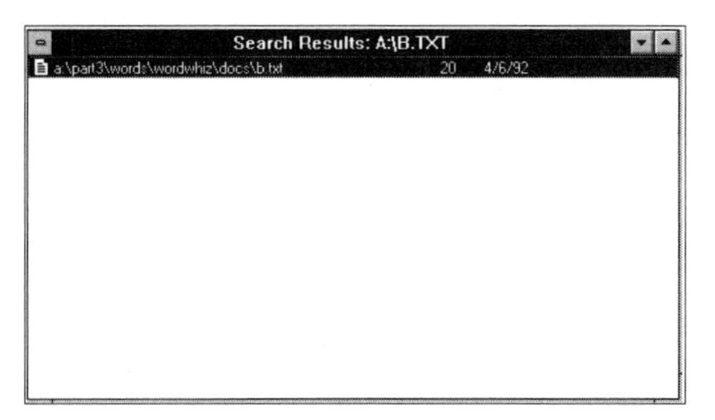

The result of the search shows the full path of the file. You can move or resize the Search Results window to reveal more of the directory window.

6 In the directory tree, select the directory containing B.TXT (as indicated in the Search Results window) to display the file in the contents list.

7 Close the Search Results window.

Tip If you want to search for a file but are not sure of the exact filename, you can use the asterisk (*) as a *wildcard* character to represent the part(s) of the name you don't know. For example, suppose all you know is that the file starts with L and ends with the extension DOC. In the Search For line, enter L*.DOC. The Search Results window lists every filename that has the specified initial character and extension.

One Step Further

- ▶ Switch to your hard disk, and select a first level directory that has a long list of files, including one or more subdirectories. The \WINDOWS directory would be a good choice.
- ▶ Expand the branch by one level. Then expand the branch to all lower levels. Next, expand the full tree. Finally, collapse the tree so that only first level directories are shown in the directory tree.
- ▶ For the contents list, change the view to show name only, all file details, and partial details. Sort the list by size. Then change the display to show only program files, and then restore it to show all files.
- ▶ Search for a file in your Windows directory branch called WIN.INI.

If you want to continue to the next lesson

1 Exit File Manager.

2 In Program Manager, make sure that the Main group window is open and that all other groups appear as group icons.

If you want to quit Windows for now

1 Exit or minimize File Manager.

2 Double-click the Control-menu box in the Program Manager window.

3 When the message "This will end your Windows session" appears, click OK or press ENTER.

Lesson Summary

To	Do this
Start File Manager	Double-click the File Manager icon, initially found in the Main group window.
Change the current drive in a directory window	In the directory window, click the icon of the desired drive located in the area below the title bar.
Change the current directory in a directory window	In the directory tree, click the desired directory. If the directory name is not showing, expand the branch containing the directory.

To	Do this
Expand a directory tree branch by one level	Select the directory whose branch you want to expand. From the Tree menu, choose Expand One Level, *or* double-click the selected directory.
Expand a directory tree branch to all lower levels	Select the directory whose branch you want to expand. From the Tree menu, choose Expand Branch.
Completely expand an entire directory tree in one operation	From the Tree menu, choose Expand All. *or* Select the root directory; then, from the Tree menu, choose Expand Branch.
Collapse a branch	Select the directory whose branch you want to collapse. Then either double-click that directory, *or* choose Collapse Branch from the Tree menu.
Search for a specific file in a branch	Select the directory whose branch contains the file. Then, from the File menu, choose Search. In the Search For text box, type the desired file name, using wildcard characters (*) if necessary. With Search All Subdirectories checked, click OK.

For more information on	See the *Microsoft Windows User's Guide*
Controlling a directory window's display in File Manager	Chapter 4, "File Manager"

Preview of the Next Lesson

In this lesson, you have learned how to use File Manager as a tool to navigate around directories and display files. In the next lesson, you find out how to use File Manager for the basic disk management functions of formatting and copying. You also discover ways to reorganize the directory structure of a disk by renaming, copying, and moving files and by creating new directories.

Managing Disks, Directories, and Files

As you saw in Lesson 5, File Manager is a versatile window through which you can view a disk's overall directory structure and lists of files in any directory. But there is more to file management than simply climbing around a directory tree. How do you copy a file, change a file's name, or add a new directory to a directory tree?

To fully control how your files are organized on a disk, you must be able to move and copy files between directories, rename files, and create new directories. Formatting and copying floppy disks are necessary skills for storing backup files and transferring data to other computers. In this lesson, you use File Manager to perform file and disk management operations. The following illustration shows how you can set up two directory windows to transfer files between disks with the mouse.

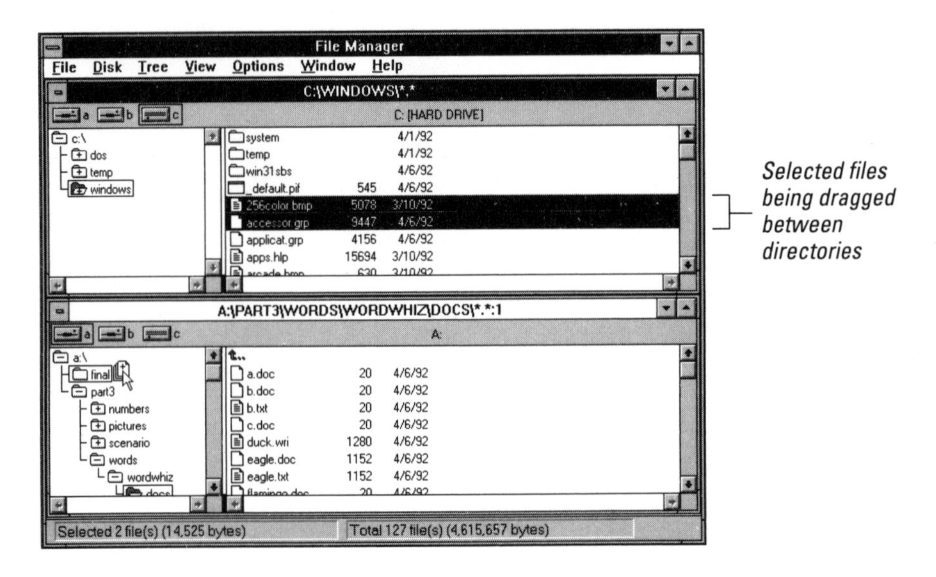

This lesson explains how to do the following:

- Format a floppy disk to prepare it for use
- Copy a disk's contents to another disk for data transfer and storage
- Rename a file without altering its contents
- Create directories for better file organization
- Copy and move files between directories and disks

Estimated lesson time: 45 minutes

Formatting and Copying Disks

Before a new floppy disk can be used to store data, it must be prepared with magnetic markers that act like electronic road signs for your disk drive. This process, called *formatting*, is performed at least once in the life of any active disk. (If you format a disk for the second time, the data stored previously on that disk is usually destroyed.) The Format Disk command in the Disk menu is an easy way to carry out this task. You can also use the Copy Disk command to copy the contents of an entire floppy disk to another one. If the second disk is brand new, the disk copy process also formats it.

Distinguishing Disk Types

When you format a disk, you need to know three important pieces of information: (1) the size of the floppy disk you want to format (5.25-inch or 3.5-inch); (2) the letter of the drive that holds the floppy disk (usually A or B); and (3) the storage capacity of the disk. The size of a disk is fairly obvious, but in addition to their sizes, 3.5-inch disks have a hard, permanent outer covering while 5.25-inch disks are bendable. You should know the letter associated with each floppy disk drive as a basic aspect of your system installation. The trickiest part of formatting is knowing the correct disk capacity.

In commercial disk packaging, high-capacity disks are generally called "high-density" or HD disks, and low-capacity disks are called "double-density" or DD disks.

Both 5.25 and 3.5-inch disks are made in two capacities—*low* (also called *double-density*) and *high* (or *high-density*). A high-density disk can hold two to four times as much information as a low-density disk. The main physical difference between low- and high-density disks is the nature of the metallic coating on the disk's magnetic surfaces. Visible differences between a low- and a high-density disk of the same size are very subtle and easy to overlook.

Important *It is essential that you know the capacity of a disk before you format it.* The electronic formatting process for low-density disks is different from that for high-density disks. If you format a disk for the wrong storage capacity, it will not work properly and might lose data that is later stored on it.

The best way to tell a disk's storage capacity is to look at its original package for the terms "double density" (DD) or "high density" (HD). If you have a disk that is separated from its box, then look for the physical identifiers listed in the chart below:

Type of Disk	Data Storage Capacity	Physical Identifiers
5.25-inch low-density (also called double-density)	360 kilobytes (360 KB)	Ring around center hole (hub) on at least one side of disk.
5.25-inch high-density	1.2 megabytes (1.2 MB) or 1,200 KB	Lack of a hub ring.
3.5-inch low-density (also called double-density)	720 KB	A little square hole in only one corner.

Type of Disk	Data Storage Capacity	Physical Identifiers
3.5-inch high-density	1.44 MB or 1,440 KB	A little square hole in each of two corners. Cover is often imprinted with an "HD" symbol.

Using the Format Disk Command

After you place a fresh disk in your drive and are sure you know whether it is low- or high-density, you are ready to use the Format Disk command from the Disk menu. The Format Disk dialog box has list boxes in which you specify both the drive letter and the disk's format capacity. It also presents the following options:

Label At the time of formatting, you can electronically *label* a disk with an 11-character name for identification purposes. Later, you can add or change the label through the Disk menu.

Make System Disk A *system disk* includes special files from which you can start your computer without using the hard drive. Unless you have a special need for a system disk, leave this option turned off because system files reduce the room available for your own data.

Quick Format If you are reformatting a disk that has previously been formatted, you can save a few minutes by turning on the *Quick Format* option. However, quick formatting does not check the entire disk surface for defects, as normal formatting does. You cannot quick format a fresh disk that has never been formatted.

In the next exercise, you format a disk and label it MYDISK.

Format a floppy disk

A high-capacity drive can format either high- or low-density disks. A low-capacity drive can format only low-density disks.

1 Start File Manager if it is not already running.

2 Place a new floppy disk (or a used one whose data you can discard) in your floppy disk drive, and be sure you know both its size and whether it is a low-density or a high-density disk.

   If you have more than one floppy disk drive, be sure you know the letter of the one you are using (A or B).

3 From the Disk menu, choose Format Disk.

   The following dialog box appears:

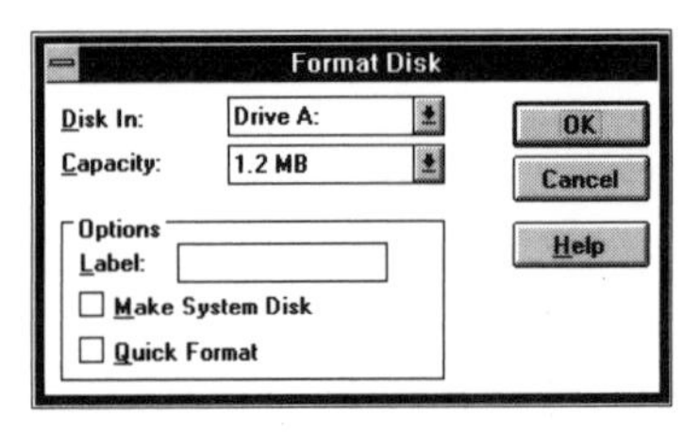

4. In the "Disk In" list box, click the arrow and choose the appropriate drive letter.
5. In the "Capacity" list box, click the arrow and choose the storage capacity that corresponds to the disk.

   Refer to the table above, if necessary, to determine the correct capacity.
6. Click in the Label text box, and type **My Disk**
7. Choose OK, and then choose Yes in the confirmation box.

   A Formatting Disk dialog box appears (shown below) that tells how far along the formatting process is at any moment. When it reaches 100% the job is done.

8. On the Format Complete dialog box that eventually appears, be sure that the disk capacity displayed is what you expected, and then choose No.

   If you choose Yes, you can continue formatting additional disks of the same capacity on the same drive.

Using the Copy Disk Command

You might want to duplicate a disk to make a backup or to share data with someone else. In File Manager, the Copy Disk command does the job. You need a *source disk* that contains some files, and a *destination disk* of the same size and capacity (density). The destination disk can be either formatted or unformatted. If the destination disk contains any files, they are destroyed in the process of copying. The following exercise takes you through copying the practice disk using one disk drive.

Copy a floppy disk

1. Hold your practice disk (source disk) in one hand, and hold a fresh disk of identical size and density (destination disk) in the other hand. (The fresh disk can be the one you formatted in the previous exercise.)

   For this exercise, it is a good idea to write-protect the source disk by sliding the little plastic window in the corner of a 3.5-inch disk so you can see through it, or placing an adhesive tab on the square notch of a 5.25-inch disk.
2. From the Disk menu, choose Copy Disk.

   If you have more than one floppy drive, a dialog box appears, similar to the one on the following page.

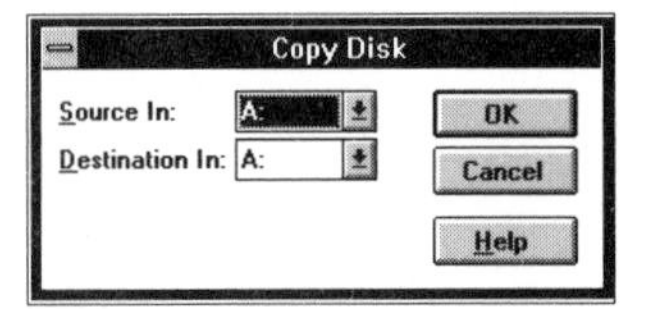

3 If this dialog box appears, select the appropriate drive letters and click OK. Otherwise, continue to the next step.

   Unless your computer has two floppy drives of identical size and capacity, set both the source and destination drive letters to the same one that matches the floppy disk you are copying.

4 Respond positively to the confirmation dialog box.

   A message box appears that says "Insert source disk."

5 Insert the source (practice) disk in the drive and click OK.

   A dialog box appears showing the progress of the copy operation.

6 When you see a box saying "Insert destination disk," do so, and then click OK.

   You might be asked to insert the source disk and destination disk one or several more times. The entire process takes a few minutes. Follow the directions on screen until the job is done.

7 Leave the *copy* of the practice disk in your disk drive for the rest of this lesson.

Renaming a File

There are several possible reasons for renaming a file. Maybe you accidentally hit a wrong key when you first created the filename. Or perhaps you want to preserve the file as an archive copy with a different name while generating a new file with the original name.

The Rename command in the File menu presents a dialog box that shows you the current name of a selected file and lets you type a new name. The new name must correspond to the file naming rules described in Lesson 5 (up to eight characters plus a three character extension, no spaces, unique within the same directory). In the next exercise, you search for the file RENAME.ME on the practice disk, and then give it a new name.

Rename a file after locating its directory

1 Click the icon for drive A (or drive B, if that drive holds the copy of your practice disk).

2 In the directory tree, select the root directory.

3 Search the entire disk for the file named RENAME.ME.

   If you are not sure how to search for a file, review the section on Searching in Lesson 5.

4 In the directory tree, select the directory that contains RENAME.ME. Then close the Search Results window.

You might have to expand a branch to reveal the directory.

5 In the contents list, select the file RENAME.ME.

Be careful to *click only once* when you select a file. If you accidentally double-click, refer to the note labeled "Important" in the early part of Lesson 5.

6 From the File menu, choose Rename.

The following dialog box appears:

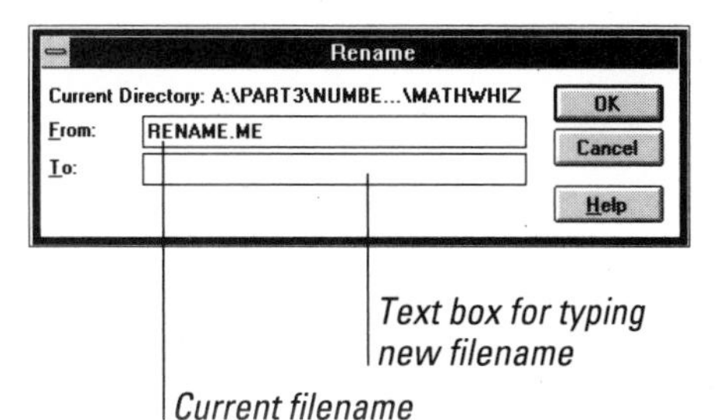

7 In the To box, type **NAMEIS.NEW**, and then press ENTER or click OK.

In the contents list, the old filename is replaced by the new one, as shown here:

Even though the filename has changed, the data within the file remains exactly the same.

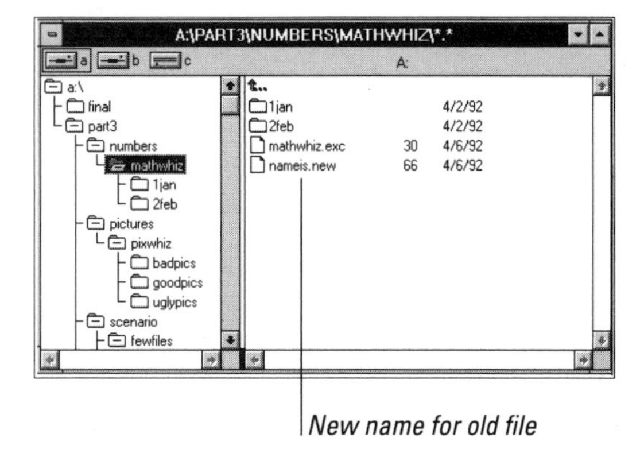

Tip File Manager provides a quick way to start an application and open a document by double-clicking on the document's data file in the contents list. The file must be *associated* with an application that is installed in Windows. Each associated data file in the contents list appears with a shaded document-file icon. A non-associated file has a hollow icon. You can use the Associate command from the File menu to create a new association between an application and document files that have a specified filename extension.

Creating a New Directory

You can create and name a new directory anywhere on a directory tree. First, you select any existing directory at any level. Using the Create Directory command from the File menu, you create a new directory that is a subdirectory (child) of the selected directory. The name of the new directory must be different from any other subdirectory or file contained in the selected directory. A newly created directory is always empty. In the next exercise, you create a directory called NEWDIR under the existing PART3 directory.

Create a new directory

1 Select the directory called PART3.

2 From the File menu, choose Create Directory.

The following dialog box appears:

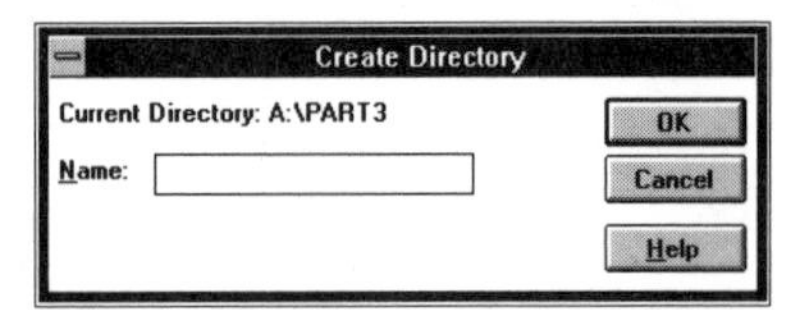

3 In the Name box, type **NEWDIR**, then press ENTER, or click OK.

The new directory appears on the directory tree as a subdirectory of PART3, as shown here:

Newly created directory

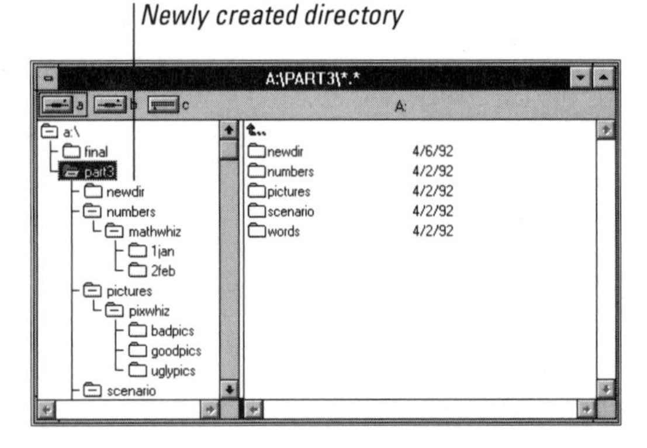

4 Repeat steps 2 and 3.

When you type the same directory name, you get a message saying “Directory already exists” because a directory cannot contain two files or subdirectories with the same name.

5 Click OK.

6 In the directory tree, select NEWDIR.

As you can see, the contents list of a new directory is empty.

Moving and Copying Files and Directories

Suppose you create a new directory and would like to place some files into it from an old directory. You can transfer a file from one directory to another in either of two ways—moving or copying. If you *move* a file, it disappears from the old directory when you put it in a new one. If you *copy* a file, it remains in the old directory while an exact duplicate appears in the new directory. (Remember that you can have two files with the same filename *only* if they reside in different directories.)

With File Manager, transferring a file from one place to another within a disk can be done in a single mouse action. With a directory window open, you move or copy a file between directories by dragging the file from the contents list to the desired directory in the directory tree.

Transferring a file from a directory on one disk to a directory on another disk is slightly more complicated because you work with two directory windows at the same time. Otherwise, the mouse actions are the same.

File Manager also makes it easy to transfer more than one file in a single operation. You can select multiple files from a directory, or select an entire directory or branch, and move or copy them in the same way as individual files.

Transferring a File Between Directories

You carry out the following general steps to move or copy a file in a directory window. First, select the file's current directory in the directory tree at left. Second, make sure the destination directory is visible in the tree (expand a branch if necessary). Third, select the file you need in the contents list at right. Fourth, drag the file from the contents list to the destination directory in the tree, while holding down either the SHIFT key (to move the file) or the CTRL key (to copy the file). Fifth, respond positively to the confirmation dialog box that appears. File Manager does the rest.

In the next exercises, you move a file called MOVE.ME from the WORDWHIZ directory of the practice disk to the NEWDIR directory. Then you copy a file called COPY.ME between the same directories.

Move a file between directories

1 Collapse all branches under PART3 except WORD, and then select WORDWHIZ as the current directory.

2 Be sure the destination directory (NEWDIR) is visible in the directory tree.

You might have to scroll the contents list to view the destination directory.

3 In the contents list, select the file MOVE.ME.

4 Hold down SHIFT and drag MOVE.ME to the NEWDIR directory in the tree.

After you drop the file at its destination, a confirmation dialog box appears, similar to the following:

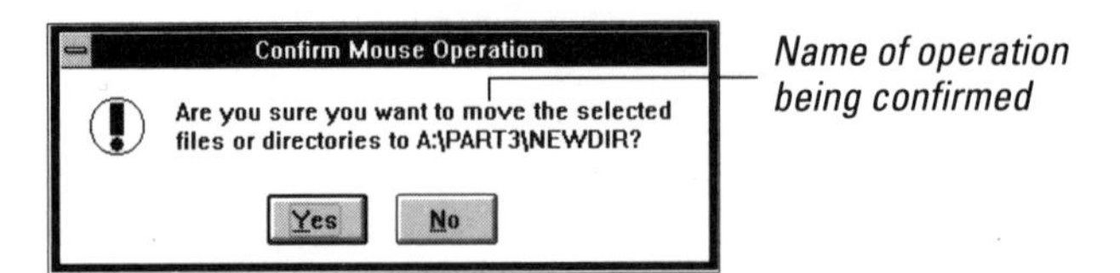

Name of operation being confirmed

5 Click Yes.

The selected file disappears from the contents list of WORDWHIZ.

6 In the directory tree, select NEWDIR.

The file MOVE.ME is now contained in the new directory.

Tip When you move a file between directories *in the same disk*, holding down the SHIFT key while dragging is optional. In other words, if you drag the file without holding down any key, the effect is the same. However, we recommend that you develop the habit of holding down SHIFT when moving a file with the mouse because it is necessary to do so when you move a file to a different drive, as shown later in this lesson.

Copy a file between directories

The mouse action for copying a file is nearly identical to that for moving, except that you hold down the CTRL key while dragging.

1 In the directory tree, select WORDWHIZ as the current directory.

2 Be sure the destination directory (NEWDIR) is visible in the directory tree.

3 In the contents list, select the file COPY.ME.

4 Hold down CTRL and drag COPY.ME to the NEWDIR directory in the tree.

Notice that while you drag a file to *copy* it, the file icon attached to the pointer contains a small plus sign (+). After you drop the file at its destination, a confirmation dialog box similar to the following appears.

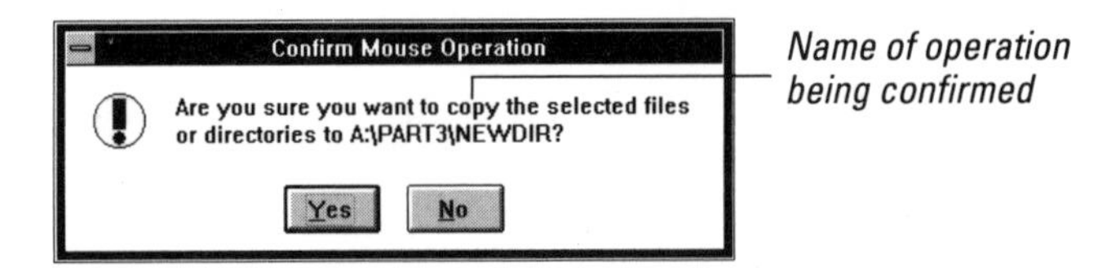

Name of operation being confirmed

Notice that this confirmation box says "copy" rather than "move." Always examine this confirmation box to be sure the program carries out the exact operation you want.

5 Click Yes.

The selected file still appears in the contents list of WORDWHIZ.

6 In the directory tree, select NEWDIR.

A duplicate of COPY.ME is in the new directory.

Transferring a File Between Two Drives

You can move or copy a file between two directories on different disks using similar procedures as outlined above. However, in order to see the original directory contents and the destination directory tree at the same time, you must open a second directory window. In the next exercise, you set up two directory windows in tiled layout, with one window showing your hard disk and the other your floppy disk.

To open a second directory window, you double-click one of the drive icons in the drive area. The second window might completely overlap the first one, so it is not immediately apparent that you have two directory windows open. Clicking the Window menu is a quick way to check how many directory windows are actually open, because the bottom part of the menu lists all open directory windows. You can tile the directory windows to view them both at the same time.

Set up two directory windows in tiled format

1 In the drive area, double-click the icon for your primary hard disk drive (usually drive C).

2 Open the Window menu.

The bottom section of the menu should list two drive/directory paths, similar to the following:

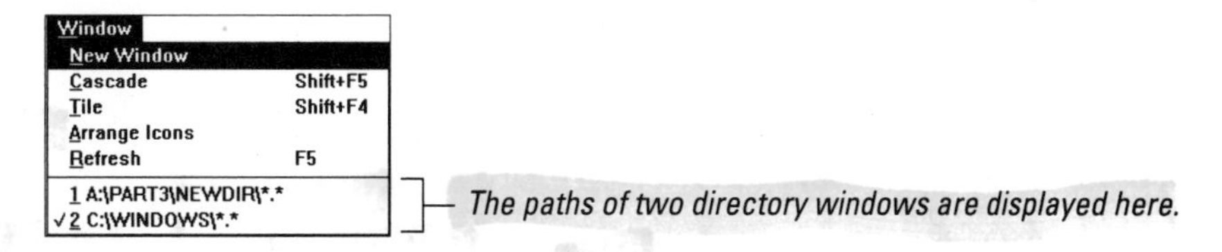

If only one window is listed, repeat step 1. If three windows are listed, close one and then continue to step 3.

3 From the Window menu, choose Tile.

Your screen now looks similar to the one on the following page.

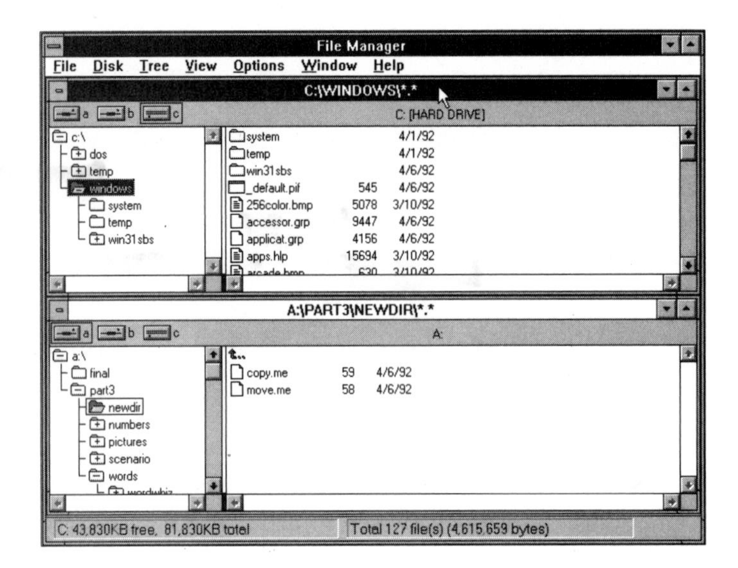

4 Be sure that one directory window is set for the floppy disk drive with your practice disk (usually drive A), and the other is set for your primary hard disk drive (usually drive C).

Move and copy a file between two drives

In this exercise, you set up a temporary directory on your hard disk called SBSTEMP. Then you move a file called CROSS.DRV from the NUMBERS directory on your practice floppy disk to the new temporary directory on your hard disk. Finally, you copy the same file back to its original directory on the floppy disk. (The steps refer to drives A and C, but if you are using different drives, please substitute accordingly.)

1 In the directory window for drive C, select the root directory.

2 Create a new directory under C:\ called SBSTEMP.

   If you are not sure how to create a new directory, refer to the section "Creating a New Directory" earlier in this lesson.

3 In the directory window for drive A, select the directory NUMBERS.

4 In the contents list, select the file CROSS.DRV.

5 Holding down SHIFT, drag CROSS.DRV to the SBSTEMP directory in the drive C directory tree, and click Yes at the confirmation box.

   You might have to scroll the contents list to see the SBSTEMP directory before selecting CROSS.DRV. This move operation is illustrated in the picture on the following page.

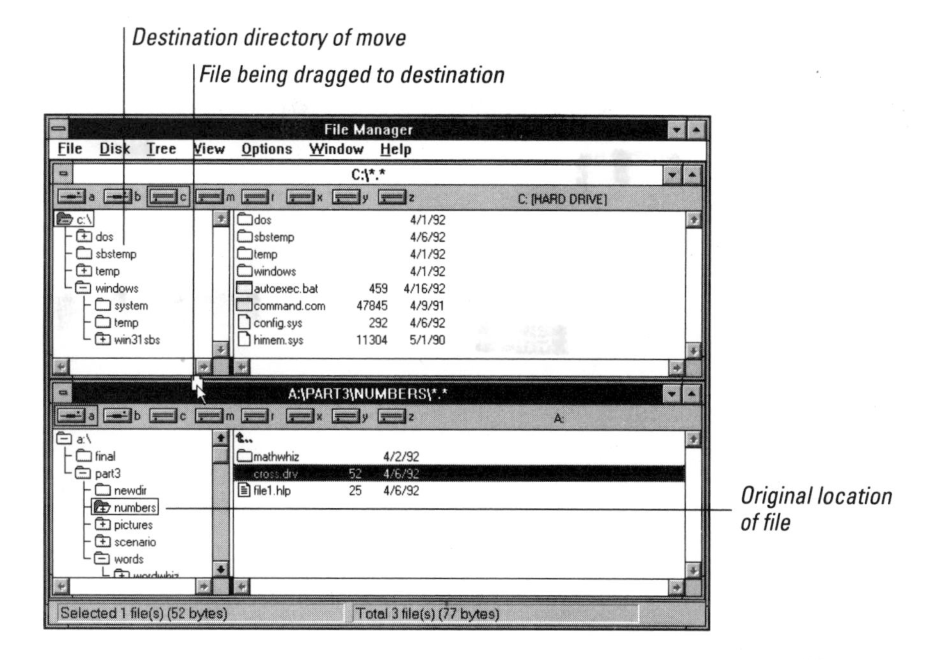

Having been moved from drive A to drive C, the file is listed in the C:\SBSTEMP contents but is gone from the NUMBERS directory under drive A.

6 Holding down CTRL, drag the file CROSS.DRV from the contents list in the drive C window to the NUMBERS directory in the drive A tree, and click Yes at the confirmation box.

This copies the file from drive C to A, so that duplicate files exist in both drives.

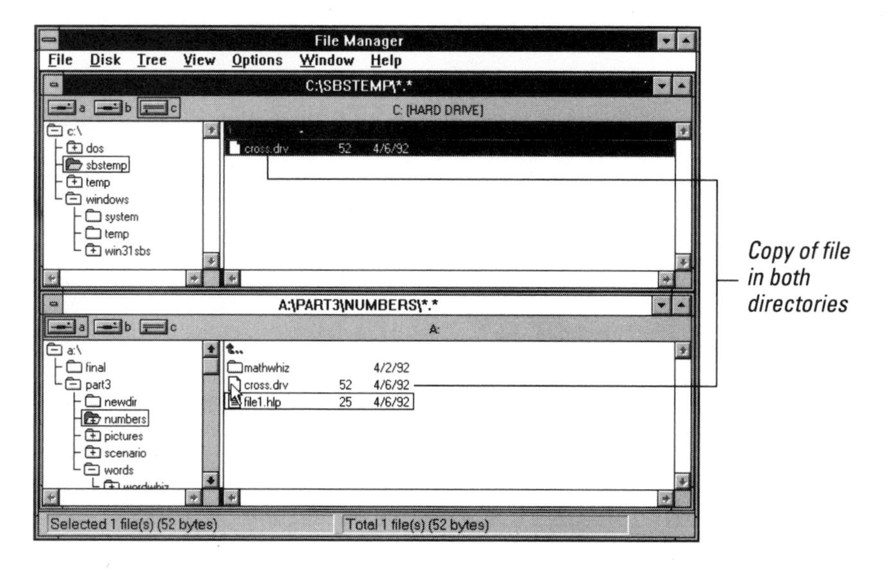

7 Close the drive C directory window, and maximize the remaining directory window.

Tip When you copy a file between directories *in different disks*, holding down the CTRL key while dragging is optional. In other words, if you drag a file to a different disk without pressing any key, File Manager copies rather than moves it. (Remember that SHIFT is optional for *moving* a file within the *same* disk.) However, we recommend that you develop the habit of always holding CTRL when copying a file or SHIFT when moving a file with the mouse in order to avoid confusion. As a mnemonic device to know which is which, remember that "CTRL" and "copy" both start with C, and that the words "SHIFT" and "move" have similar meanings.

Transferring Multiple Files

In the previous exercises, you copied and moved one file at a time between directories. Often you must transfer a large number of files from a directory at the same time, or transfer an entire directory or branch to a different place on a tree. For example, suppose you had accumulated 100 letter documents in the same directory over several months, and now decide to split them by date into three-month groups. You would create new subdirectories for each time period, and then move the files. With this many documents, performing the transfers file-by-file could be tedious and time-consuming.

To streamline this task, File Manager allows you to move or copy a group of files in a single operation. First you select the desired files in the contents list. Then you drag any selected files to the destination directory in the directory tree. All currently selected files are automatically transferred as a group.

There are three different ways to select multiple files in a contents list. If you want to select a group of files that are all adjacent in the list, select the first one with the mouse, hold down SHIFT, and then select the last one. If you want to select files that are *not* adjacent in the list, hold down CTRL while you click each desired file. If you want to select files that have parts of their names in common, choose the Select Files command from the File menu and specify the common parts in the text box. In the following exercises, you practice these techniques of selecting multiple files, and then move a group of files to the NEWDIR directory.

Select a group of files with the Select Files command

1 Expand the entire directory tree of the practice disk, and select the directory DOCS (under WORDS\WORDWHIZ\).

2 In the View menu, be sure that both All File Details and Sort By Name are active (checked).

Your directory window looks similar to the following:

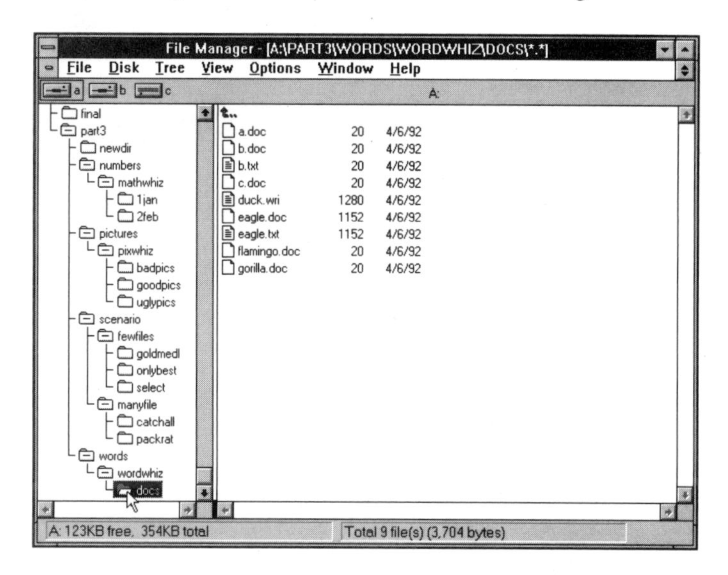

3 From the File menu, choose Select Files.

The following dialog box appears:

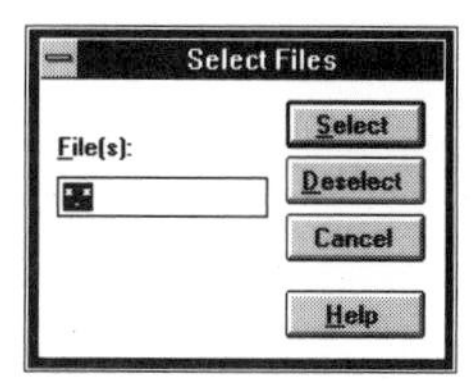

4 Type ***.DOC** in the text box.

As mentioned at the end of Lesson 5, the asterisk (*) is a wildcard character. In this case, it represents any character or group of characters in a filename.

5 Click the Select button, and then click Close.

All files with the extension DOC are selected, as shown on the following page.

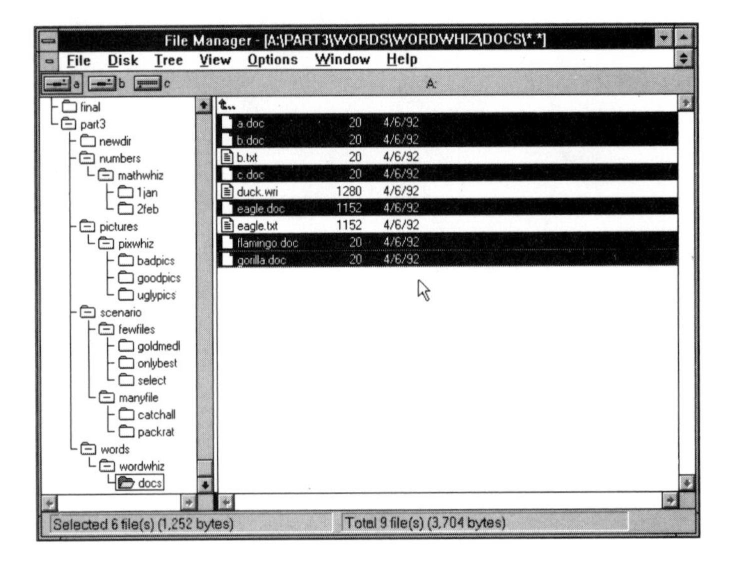

Select and move a group of files with the mouse

In this exercise, you first select a continuous group of files. Then you select a non-adjacent group of files and move this group to the NEWDIR directory.

1. In the contents list, click the second listed file.

   Any other file that had been selected is now deselected. Only the file you clicked is highlighted. (Ignore the very first line that shows an up arrow and two dots. Double-clicking this line is a way of moving up one level in the directory tree.)

2. Hold down SHIFT and click the fourth file listed.

   By using SHIFT, you select all files from the second to the fourth.

3. Hold down CTRL and click the third file (previously selected).

   By using CTRL and clicking on a selected file, you deselect the file.

4. Hold down CTRL and click the sixth file (not previously selected).

   The sixth file is selected, while all other selected files remain highlighted. Your directory window now looks like the one on the following page.

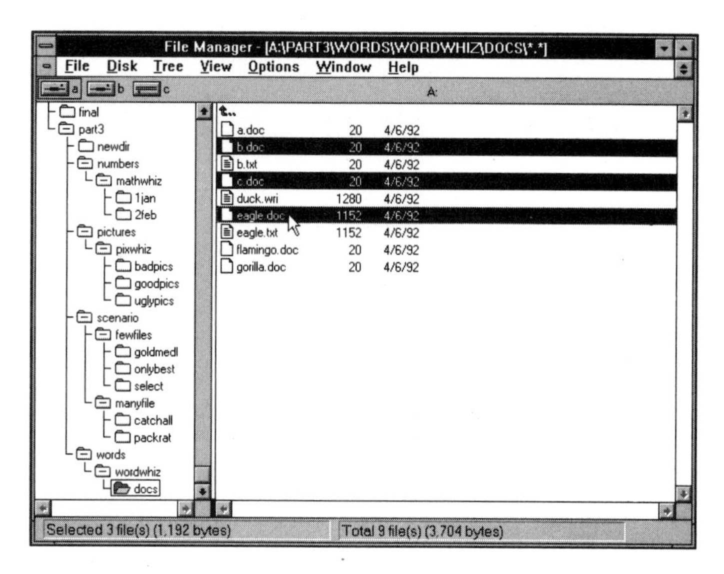

5 Drag any of the selected files to the NEWDIR directory, and respond positively to the confirmation box to complete the move.

Dragging one file of a selected group takes the whole group of files with it. The selected files disappear from the DOCS contents list.

6 In the directory tree, select NEWDIR.

The files you moved are contained in the new directory, as shown here:

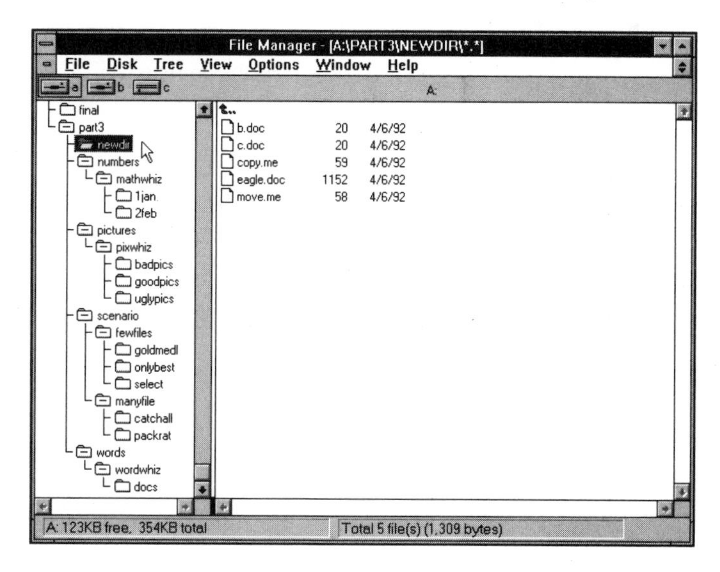

Tip You can use a shortcut to transfer a directory with all of its contents to another location. Simply select the source directory icon and drag it to the destination directory in a tree on either the same or a different disk. While dragging, press SHIFT to move the directory or press CTRL to copy it. This transfers the entire branch, including all of the directory's files and subdirectories.

One Step Further

- Search for the file 1.DOC on your practice disk, and change its name to ONE.DOC.
- Under the root directory of your practice disk, create a new directory called CURRENT. Then copy all the files under PIXWHIZ that have PIC and TIF extensions to the CURRENT directory.
- Format a floppy disk, and copy the practice disk (or any disk containing files) to it. Be sure you have two disks of identical size and capacity.

If you want to continue to the next lesson

1. Exit File Manager.
2. In Program Manager, be sure that the Main group window is open and that all other groups appear as group icons.

If you want to quit Windows for now

1. Exit or minimize File Manager.
2. Double-click the Control-menu box in the Program Manager window.
3. When the message "This will end your Windows session" appears, click OK or press ENTER.

Lesson Summary

To	Do this
Format a floppy disk	Determine the size and capacity of the disk, and insert it into the drive. Then choose Format Disk from the Disk menu and follow the messages that appear on screen.
Copy a floppy disk	Obtain a destination disk that is the same size and capacity as your source disk. Choose Copy Disk from the Disk menu and follow the messages that appear on screen.

To	Do this
Rename a file	Select the file in the contents list. Choose Rename from the File menu. Type the new name of the file in the text box.
Create a directory	Select the parent of the new directory in the directory tree. Choose Create Directory from the File menu. Type the new directory name in the text box.
Move a file to another directory	Select the file in the contents list. Hold down SHIFT and drag the file to its new directory.
Copy a file to another directory	Select the file in the contents list. Hold down CTRL and drag the file to its new directory.
Transfer a file to another disk drive	Open two directory windows and tile them. Select the file and move or copy it as described above.
Select multiple files in a contents list by name similarity	Choose Select Files from the File menu. In the text box, type the common characters of the filenames and use asterisks (*) to represent the different elements.
Select multiple adjacent files in a contents list	Select the first file. Hold SHIFT and select the last file. All files in between are automatically selected.
Select multiple files that are not necessarily adjacent	Hold CTRL and click each of the files to select.
Move or copy multiple files in a single operation	Select the desired files in the contents list. Then drag any of the selected files to the destination while pressing SHIFT or CTRL.

For more information on	See the *Microsoft Windows User's Guide*
Using File Manager to manage files, disks, and directories	Chapter 4, "File Manager"

Preview of the Next Lesson

Windows 3.1 includes a number of small, useful applications called Accessories, which can help speed your work in several ways. In Lesson 7, you learn how to use Calculator, Clock, and Calendar in your everyday activities. You also work with Character Map, which extends the range of available keyboard characters, and with Recorder, which allows you to automate repetitive operations in Windows.

Part

4 Accessories for Windows

Using Accessories for Windows

Windows includes several useful applications to help you to manage various tasks. These applications, called *accessories*, were installed into the Accessories group when you installed Windows.

In this lesson you use several of these accessories to perform some daily tasks. You use Calculator to solve a simple problem. You run Clock to display the system time and date, and you use Calendar to set and review your appointment schedule. You also use Recorder to perform repetitive tasks quickly.

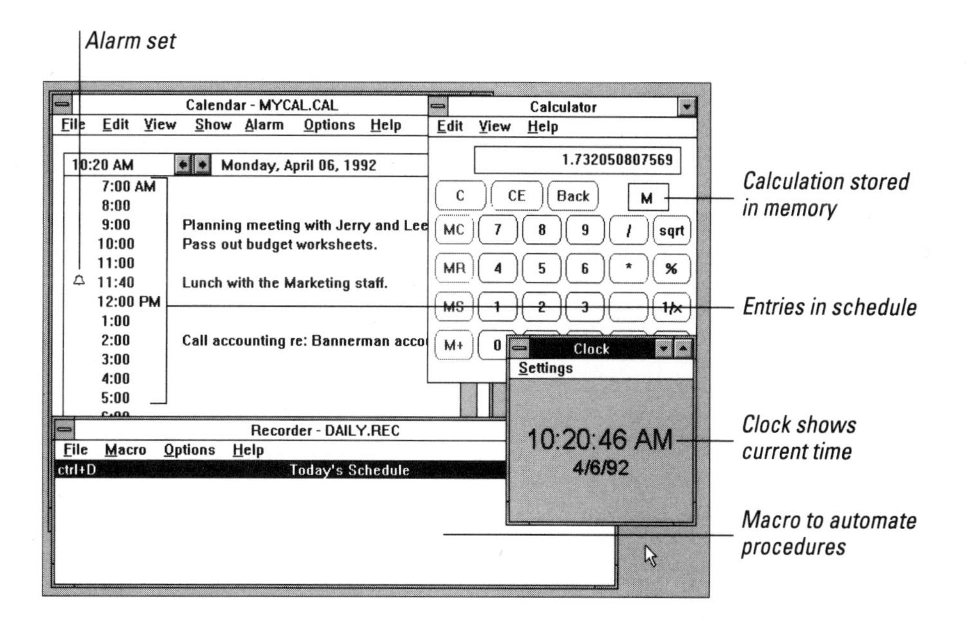

This lesson explains how to do the following:

- Use Calculator
- Use Clock
- Use Calendar
- Use Recorder

Estimated lesson time: 40 minutes

Using Calculator

You use Calculator to solve mathematical problems. Using Calculator will save you time and help you to avoid the nuisance of tracking down your pocket or desk calculator to find quick answers to simple problems.

Start Calculator

1 Double-click the Accessories group icon in the Program Manager window.

2 Find the Calculator icon in the Accessories group in the Program Manager window.

Calculator icon

3 Double-click the Calculator icon.

Calculator appears on the desktop.

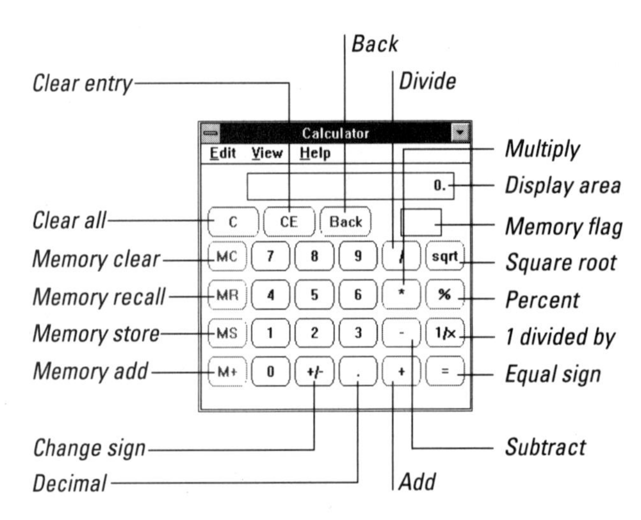

Views of the Calculator

Calculator has two views of its layout. You can display a standard calculator as well as a scientific calculator. You use the standard calculator to solve simple problems. You can store the results in memory. You use the scientific calculator to do scientific and statistical calculations. Refer to Chapter 12 in the *Microsoft Windows User's Guide* for more information about using the scientific calculator.

Solve a simple problem

In this exercise, you add 159 and 164 together. Then you divide the result by 17.You can either click on each numeral on the keypad shown on the screen, or use the keyboard to enter each numeral. You use the other keys on the Calculator keypad to manipulate these values.

1 Click **159** +

You can also use the keys on your keyboard to enter this information. Make sure NUMLOCK is off.

2 Click **164** /

3 Click **17** =

The answer, 19, appears in the display area.

4 Click **C**

The display area is cleared.

Using Calculator's Memory

Calculator has an internal memory to store intermediate values during a longer calculation. You access this memory with four keys on Calculator's keypad.

Add the value into memory

In this exercise you store 323.25 into memory. Then, you add 122.38 to the value already in Calculator's memory. Finally, you review the contents of Calculator's memory without clearing it.

1 Click **323.25**

2 Click **MS**

This button, Memory Store, stores the value in Calculator's memory. Notice the M that appears in the memory flag box.

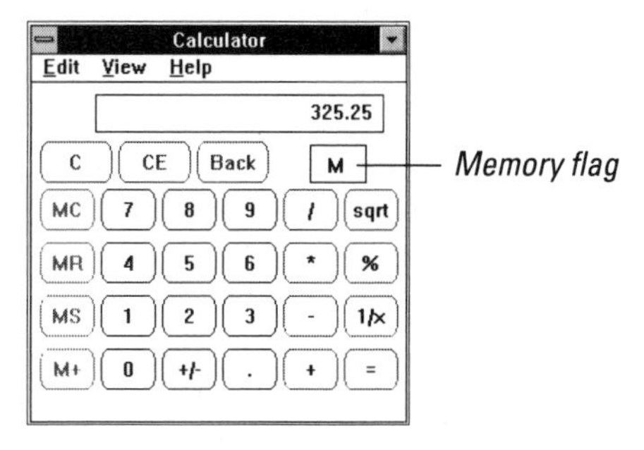

3 Click **122.38**

4 Click **M+**

This button, Memory Add, adds the value to the amount already in Calculator's memory.

5 Click **MR**

This button, Memory Recall, recalls and displays the amount, 445.63, currently in memory.

Subtract a value from memory

In this next exercise you will subtract 59.30 from the value in memory. Because you cannot directly subtract a value from Calculator's memory, you must change the *sign* of the value you will use. The sign of the value shows whether it is positive or negative. Calculator assumes the value is positive.

You use the +/- key to change the sign of a value. When you have changed the sign of the value, you use the M+ key to add it into Calculator's memory. (Adding a negative value is the same as subtracting a positive value.)

1 Click **59.30**

2 Click +/-

   This changes the sign of the value to negative.

3 Click **M+**

   This subtracts the value from Calculator's memory.

4 Click **MR**

   This recalls and displays 386.33, the value currently in Calculator's memory.

Perform an intermediate calculation

You can perform separate calculations with Calculator and add these results to the value in Calculator's memory.

Note Click C to clear the display area before starting a new calculation.

---

1 Click **C**

   This clears the display area.

2 Click **256.32** *

3 Click **75** %

   The result, 192.24, appears in the edit line.

4 Click **M+**

   The result is added to the value (386.33) already in Calculator's memory.

5 Click **MR**

   The value in Calculator's memory, 578.57, is displayed.

Use the contents of Calculator's memory

In this exercise you add the contents of Calculator's memory to 179.89.

1 Click **C**

2 Click **179.89** +

3 Click **MR**

This recalls the value, 578.57, from memory

4 Click =

The result, 758.46, is displayed in the edit box.

Clear the memory

When you have finished with the values stored in memory, you can erase memory.

▶ Click **MC**

This clears the value from memory.

Close the application

When you have finished working with Calculator, you can close it. Closing Calculator removes it from the desktop.

▶ Double-click the Control-menu box in Calculator's window.

Calculator closes.

Using Clock

You use Clock to view the current date and time. You can change the size and appearance of the Clock's display, and also prevent Clock from being covered by other windows.

Start Clock

1 Find the Clock icon in the Accessories group.

2 Double-click the Clock icon.

Clock icon

For information on how to change the date and time, see Lesson 12, "Using the Control Panel."

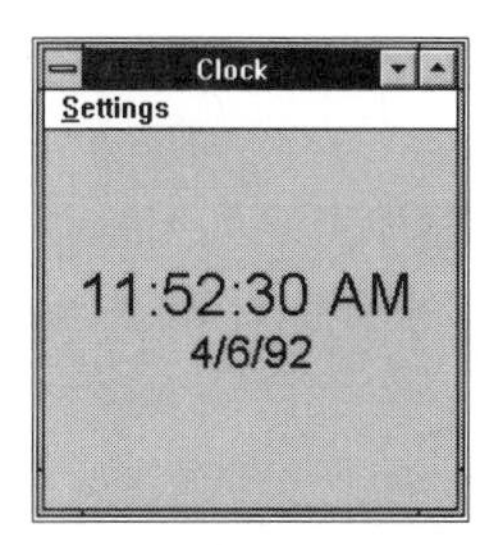

Changing the Clock Display

The Clock face is displayed in one of two formats: *digital* and *analog*. The digital view shows a clock with digits only. The analog view shows a clock with sweep hands. You change the view with commands from the Settings menu. You also use the Settings menu to prevent other windows from covering Clock.

Change the display settings

1 From the Settings menu, choose Analog.

   You see a round clock face.

2 From the Settings menu, choose Digital.

   Clock changes from showing an analog clock to a digital clock, and displays the time using numerals.

3 From the Settings menu, choose No Title.

   This removes the title bar from the Clock display.

4 Double-click the Clock.

   The title bar reappears.

Keep Clock on top of all windows

1 Choose Always On Top from the Control menu.

   This setting forces Clock to be displayed on top of all other windows.

2 From the Settings menu, choose Analog.

   This changes the display to show a clock face with hour and minute hands.

3 Click the Minimize icon in the Clock window.

   Clock shrinks to an icon.

4 Click the Maximize icon in the Program Manager window.

   Notice that the Clock icon remains on top of the Program Manager window.

5 Click the Restore icon in the Program Manager window.

   The size of the Program Manager's window is restored.

Close the application

When you no longer need to view the current time and date, you can close Clock. Closing Clock removes it from the desktop.

1 Click the Clock icon on the desktop.

   The Control menu appears.

2 Click Close.

   Clock closes.

Using Calendar

Calendar combines a monthly and daily scheduling book into one application. By keeping your appointments in Calendar, you maintain easy access to your schedule. Using Calculator also helps to keep your appointments up-to-date. And the built-in alarm feature reminds you of important tasks or meetings.

Start Calendar

1 Find the Calendar icon in the Accessories group.

2 Double-click the Calendar icon.

Calendar icon

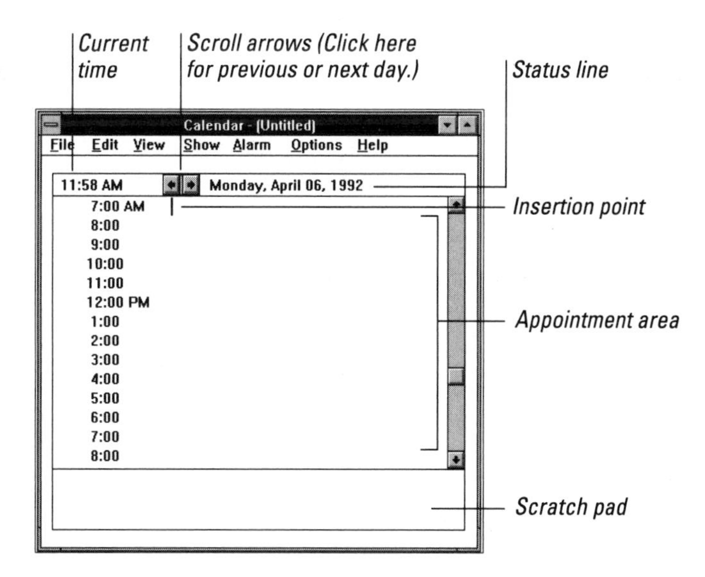

Scheduling an Appointment

You schedule an appointment in two steps. First you choose the date of the appointment. You can choose any day from January 1, 1980 to December 31, 2099. After you choose the appointment day, you click the appropriate time interval to place the insertion point, and then type a short description of your appointment.

Calendar has a list of time default intervals, each an hour apart. If your appointment time does not appear on the list, you can insert a special time. You mark special events with a symbol. You can set an alarm to sound before the event is to occur.

Add an appointment

In this exercise you set several appointments using the time intervals set by Calendar. You also use the scratch pad to jot down a reminder for the day.

1 Click next to 9:00 A.M. to set the insertion point.

  Your appointment is for today, so you do not need to go to another day. However, you may need to use the scroll arrows to find this time interval.

2 Type **Planning meeting with Jerry and Lee.**

3 Click 10:00 A.M. and type **Pass out budget worksheets.**

4 Click in the scratch pad area.

  The scratch pad area is in the bottom of the Calendar window.

5 Type **Don't forget to collect budgets!**

  Use this scratch pad area to write general notes or reminders for each day.

Add a special time

You insert a special time into your schedule for appointments that don't fit in the default time intervals.

1 From the Options menu, choose Special Time.

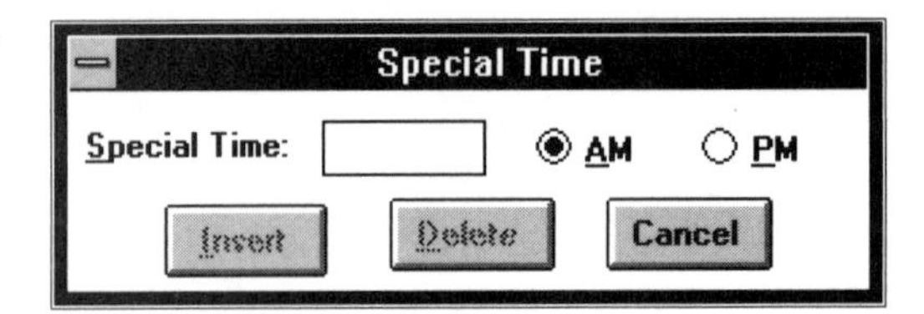

2 Type **11:40** and click the AM button.

  This inserts a space for an appointment between the default time intervals.

3 Click Insert.

  The insertion point blinks in the new 11:40 A.M. time interval.

4 Type **Lunch with the Marketing staff.**

Add an appointment on a different day

You move to a different day when you want to schedule an appointment on a day before or after the selected date.

1 Click the right scroll arrow in the status line.

  You use the scroll arrows to move through your schedule one day at a time.

2 Click 10:00 A.M.

3 Type **Review marketing allocations.**

4 From the Show menu, choose Date.

This is an alternate way to select a date. Use this method to select a specified date.

5 Type a date three days from the current date.

Be sure to use the slash "/" key to separate the day, month, and year so that your entry matches the format "mm/dd/yy".

6 Click OK.

7 Click 9:00 A.M.

8 Type **Collect final budgets.**

9 From the Show menu, choose Today.

This is the shortcut to select today's schedule.

Set an alarm

You can set an alarm for any appointment. This alarm sounds a bell and displays a message reminding you of your appointment. You can choose to have the alarm alert you at the time of the appointment, or you can choose to be alerted up to 10 minutes before the appointment. This early alarm feature is useful when you need extra time to meet your appointment.

1 Click the 11:40 A.M. meeting.

You can click on the appointment text, or click on the appointment time.

2 From the Alarm menu, choose Set.

A bell symbol appears to the left of this time. Clock sounds the speaker when it is 11:40 A.M. To clear the alarm, choose Set again from the Alarm menu.

3 From the Alarm menu, choose Controls.

4 Type **10** in the box.

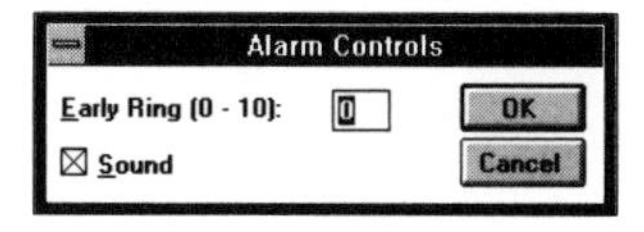

5 Click OK.

Your computer speaker will beep at 11:30 A.M. (10 minutes before the 11:40 A.M. meeting). An alert message will also appear to remind you of your appointment.

Change views from daily to monthly

You change the view of Calendar from the daily view when you want to see the current month. You use the same menu to return to see the day's activities.

1 From the View menu, choose Month.

The current month appears.

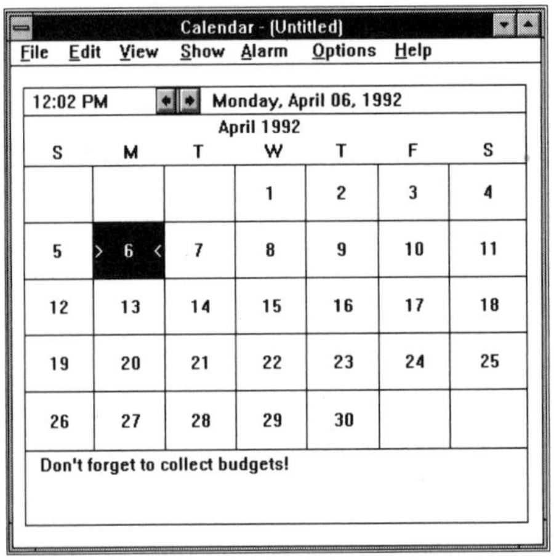

Calendar - [Untitled]

File Edit View Show Alarm Options Help

12:02 PM Monday, April 06, 1992

April 1992

S	M	T	W	T	F	S
			1	2	3	4
5	> 6 <	7	8	9	10	11
12	13	14	15	16	17	18
19	20	21	22	23	24	25
26	27	28	29	30		

Don't forget to collect budgets!

2 From the View menu, choose Day.

The current day's schedule reappears.

Mark a special event

You mark a day to highlight a special event. Calendar has five different symbols. You can set these symbols to mark the day while in either the daily or monthly view. However, they *appear* only in the monthly view.

Tip To use this feature effectively, you should use the same symbol for similar events. That way, you can quickly determine the event type based on the symbol you see in the monthly view.

1 From the View menu, choose Month.

You cannot see the mark for the special event unless you are in the monthly view.

2 From the Options menu, choose Mark.

3 Click the Symbol 1 box.

4 Click OK.

Today's date shows a box around it.

Saving and Retrieving a Calendar File

You save each schedule you create in Calendar with a descriptive name. You can keep separate schedules for different tasks by saving each one with its own name.

In the following exercise you will save your schedule to the WIN31SBS subdirectory. This subdirectory was created when you installed the practice files in the Getting Ready section of this book.

Save the Calendar file

1 From the File menu, choose Save.

2 Type **MYCAL** in the File Name box.

  This gives a name to your schedule. You can retrieve this schedule later, and it will contain all the appointments you have just entered.

3 Scroll down in the Directories box and double-click the WIN31SBS folder icon.

  Double-clicking sets the default directory to the WIN31SBS subdirectory.

4 Click OK.

  This saves your schedule on your hard drive. Calendar adds the CAL extension when you save the file.

5 From the File menu, choose New.

  The current schedule is removed from the computer's memory, but it is saved on your hard drive.

Retrieve a Calendar file

1 From the File menu, choose Open.

  Because you reset the default directory in the previous exercise, you do not need to set it again to see the files in the WIN31SBS subdirectory.

2 In the File Name box, double-click MYCAL.CAL.

  The Calendar file with your appointments appears.

Printing a Calendar File

If you have connected and installed a printer, you can print your Calendar file. Calendar prints to the default (current) printer. Usually, Calendar prints only the current day's appointments, but you can select any range of days.

Print a Calendar file

1 From the File menu, choose Print.

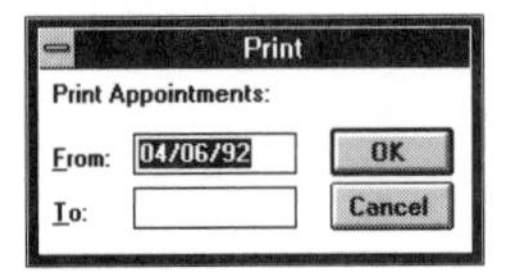

2 Click OK.

Calendar print all the appointments.

3 From the File menu choose Print.

4 Type a date three days from today in the From box.

Make sure you separate the day, month, and year with a "/" (slash).

5 Type the same date in the To box.

This selects the appointments that you have scheduled three days from today.

6 Click OK.

The daily appointments you scheduled in the previous exercises begin to print. If there are any days with notations in the scratch pad, these notes print between that day's appointments and the next day's appointments.

Add a new appointment

1 Click the 2:00 P.M. time interval.

2 Type **Call accounting re: Bannerman account.**

You have added a new appointment.

Print the new appointment

1 From the File menu, choose Print.

2 Click OK.

Calendar prints today's schedule including the new appointment.

Closing Calendar

When you have finished working with Calendar, you can close it. This removes it from the desktop. If you have made changes to your schedule, Calendar asks you if you want to save your file before closing.

Close Calendar

1 From the File menu, choose Exit.

Calendar displays a message box asking you if you wish to save the modified Calendar file before you quit.

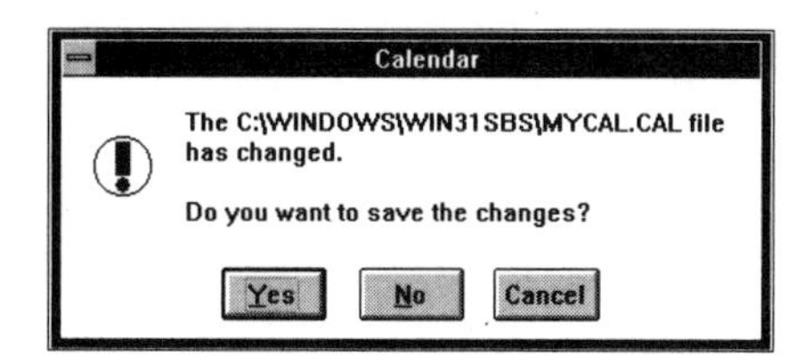

2 Click Yes.

After Calendar saves the file MYCAL.CAL, it closes.

Using Recorder

You will find that you repeat many actions (keystrokes and mouse actions) during your work with Windows. You use Recorder to record these actions as a *macro*, and later play them back to save yourself time. A macro is simply a recorded list of keystrokes and mouse actions that perform an action.

To create a macro, you start Recorder and begin recording. Recorder remembers all your keystrokes and mouse actions and stores them as a macro. You can assign each macro a name or a shortcut key, or both. You use the macro name to run the macro from Recorder. The name you choose can be any combination of uppercase or lowercase letters up to 40 characters long. You use the shortcut key to run the macro without switching to Recorder.

Start Recorder

1 Find the Recorder icon in the Accessories group.
2 Double-click the Recorder icon.

Recorder appears on the desktop.

Recorder icon

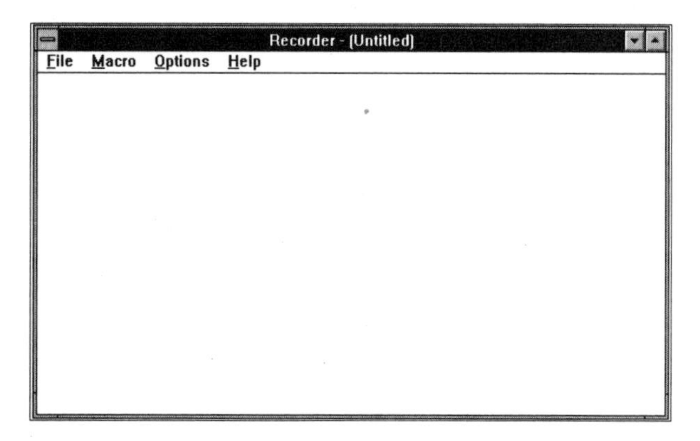

Creating a Macro

You create a macro using Recorder. Before you begin recording your macro, however, you should have the correct application or accessory as the active window on the desktop. When you activate the Recorder window and start recording the macro, Recorder "remembers" the last window you had active and automatically switches to that window.

Start Calendar

In this exercise you start Calendar and arrange the windows on the desktop.

1 Move the Recorder window down and to the right so you can see the Program Manager window.

2 Click in the Program Manager window to make it the active window.

3 Double-click the Calendar icon in the Accessories group.

   Calendar appears on the desktop.

4 Move the Calendar window to the upper left.

5 Choose Open from the File menu.

6 Double-click the WIN31SBS folder in the Directories box.

7 Double-click MYCAL.CAL.

   The file opens.

Switch to Recorder

In this next exercise you record a macro to open a schedule in Calendar and print your daily schedule. Before you begin recording your macro, however, be sure the window you last had as the active window is the Calendar window.

1 Click the Program Manager window to make it the active window.

2 Click the Minimize icon in the Program Manager window.

   Program Manager shrinks to an icon.

3 Click the Calendar window to make it the active window.

4 Click the Recorder window to make it the active window.

   You are ready to record your macro.

Start recording the macro

1 From the Macro menu in the Recorder window, choose Record.

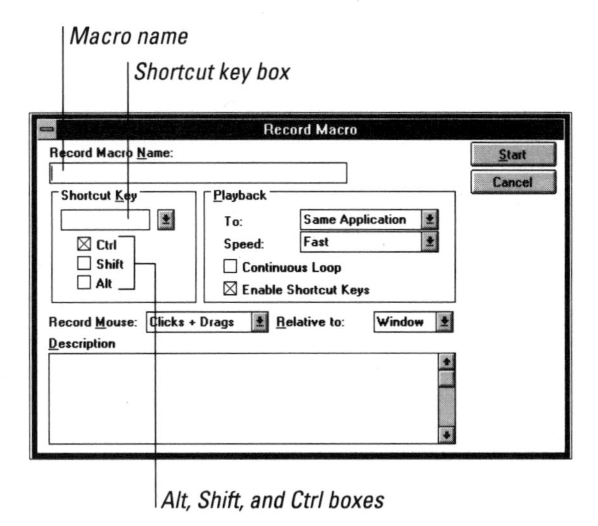

2 Type **Daily Schedule** in the Record Macro Name box.

Your macro name can be up to 40 characters long, using uppercase or lowercase characters.

Tip The Recorder transcribes *every* action, whether you use the keyboard or mouse. Don't use the mouse unless you need to. You cannot always ensure that the mouse will click the correct point on the screen when you run the macro.

---

3 Click in the Shortcut Key box and type **d**

You can also use uppercase or lowercase characters in the Shortcut Key box.

4 Be sure only the Ctrl box is checked.

If the Alt and Shift key boxes are checked, click in each to remove the check mark.

5 Click Start.

The Calendar window comes to the foreground, and the Recorder application shrinks to a flashing icon.

6 Choose Print from the File Menu.

7 Click OK.

The daily appointments print.

8 Press CTRL+BREAK.

The macro recording is suspended, and a dialog box appears.

9 Click Save Macro and click OK.

Run a macro

You run a macro by highlighting its name in the Recorder window box and choosing the Run command.

1 Click the Calendar window to make it the active window.

Note Because this Daily Schedule macro is designed to run with Calendar, you must have this application as the active window before switching to Recorder to run the macro.

---

2 Double-click the Recorder icon to restore it and to make it the active window.

3 Highlight the Daily Schedule macro.

4 From the Macro menu in the Recorder window, choose Run.

The highlighted macro Daily Schedule runs. Calendar prints the schedule. Recorder is minimized.

Modify a macro

In this exercise, you change the name of the macro Daily Schedule by changing the properties of the macro.

1 Double-click the Recorder icon to restore it and to make it the active window.

2 From the Macro menu in the Recorder window, choose Properties.

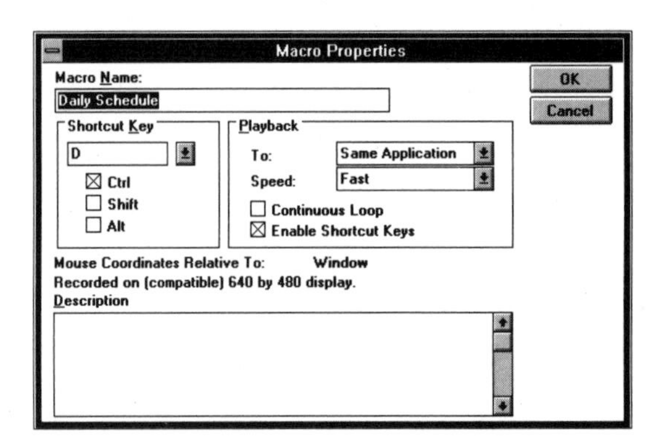

3 In the Macro Name box, type **Today's Schedule**

This is the new name for the macro.

4 Click OK.

This changes the name of the macro from "Daily Schedule" to "Today's Schedule." You can also change the shortcut key assigned to the macro by changing its properties.

Saving and Retrieving a Macro

You should save your macros for later use in a Recorder macro file. Each macro file can contain a single macro, or a variety of macros. You can store macros for one application or for several applications in the same file. However, you can easily find the right macro for an application if you keep each application's macros in separate files.

Save the macro

1 From the File menu in the Recorder window, choose Save.

2 In the File Name box, type **DAILY**

3 Double-click the WIN31SBS folder icon.

Double-clicking sets the default directory to the WIN31SBS subdirectory.

4 Click OK.

Recorder adds the REC extension when you save the file.

Retrieve the macro

1 From the File menu in the Recorder window, choose Open.

A list of Recorder files is presented.

2 Double-click DAILY.REC.

Run the macro

▶ Press CTRL+D.

This is the shortcut key for the macro. The Calendar schedule prints.

Close the applications and restore Program Manager

When you have finished working with Recorder, you should close it. Closing Recorder removes it from the desktop.

1 Click the Recorder icon.

The Control menu appears.

2 Click Close.

   Recorder closes.

3 Double-click the Control-menu box in Calendar's window.

   Calendar closes.

4 Double-click the Program Manager icon.

   The Program Manager window is restored.

One Step Further

In this exercise you create a macro that opens the correct Calendar file and prints the current day's schedule.

Create the macro

1. Start Calendar and Recorder.
2. Minimize the Program Manager window.
3. Create a macro named Print Daily Schedule that uses the CTRL+B shortcut key.
4. Press Start to begin recording.
5. From the Calendar File menu, choose Open.
6. Double-click the WIN31SBS folder in the directories box.
7. Double-click MYCAL.CAL.
8. From the File menu, choose Print.
9. Click OK.
10. From the File menu, choose Exit.
11. Press CTRL+BREAK.
12. Save the macro with the name PRINTDAY.REC in the WIN31SBS subdirectory.

If you want to continue to the next lesson

1. Close Recorder.
2. Close Calendar.
3. Restore the Program Manager window.

If you want to quit Windows for now

1. Click on the Program Manager window.
2. Double-click the Control-menu box in the Program Manager window.
3. When the message "This will end your Windows session" appears, click OK or press ENTER.

Lesson Summary

To	Do this
Calculate values in Calculator	Start Calculator, type or click numbers, and choose an action, such as add or equals.
Use memory to store and retrieve values	Use Calculator to calculate values, and use the M+, MS, MR, and MC buttons to add to, store to, recall from, and clear memory.
Display the system date and time	Start Clock.
Keep the clock on top of all windows	From the Control menu in Clock, choose Always On Top.
Enter an appointment	Click on a time interval and type the appointment information.
Enter an appointment at a specific time	From the Options menu, choose Special Time and type the new time. Click Insert.
Add a note or reminder	Click in the scratch pad area and type the text.
View a specific date	From the Show menu, choose Date and type the specific date to view. Be sure to use "/" to separate the numbers in the date. Click OK.
Set or clear an alarm	Click the appropriate appointment and then choose Set from the Alarm menu.
Make an alarm sound early	Click the appropriate appointment, then choose Controls from the Alarm menu. Type the number of minutes (from 1-10) in the box. Click OK.
Change the view of the schedule	From the View menu, choose Month or Day.
Mark a specific day	From the Options menu, choose Mark, then click one or more of the Symbol boxes. (The symbol is displayed only in the Monthly view.)
Record a macro	Start (or activate) the application in which you will record the keystrokes. Start (or activate) Recorder. From the Macro menu, choose Record. Type a name and a shortcut key. Perform your actions. When you have completed the steps, press CTRL+BREAK. Choose Save Macro.
Play back a macro	Start (or switch to) Recorder. Start (or activate) your application. If you choose the shortcut key method, press the shortcut key. If you choose the macro name method, switch to Recorder and highlight the macro name. Choose Run from the Macro menu.

To	Do this
Modify a macro	Choose Properties from the Macro menu. Change the properties of the macro and click OK.

Special Calculator Keys To	Choose this key
Clear the entries	C
Clear the last entry	CE
Clear the last digit	Back
Enter a number	Any number
Change a number's sign	+/-
Enter a decimal point	. [period]
Add a number	+
Subtract a number	-
Multiply a number	*
Divide a number	/
Calculate the square root	sqrt
Calculate the percentage	%
Calculate the inverse	1/x
Calculate the result	=

Special Calculator Memory Keys To	Choose this key
Add a number into memory	M+
Store a number into memory (and clear the current contents of memory)	MS
Retrieve a number from memory	MR
Clear memory	MC

For more information on	See the *Microsoft Windows User's Guide*
Calculator, Clock, Calendar, or Recorder	Chapter 12, "Accessories"

Preview of the Next Lesson

In the next lesson, you learn how to use Notepad to create and edit text files. You learn how to identify text files, and learn why Notepad is used to work with them. You create a special daily log file using Notepad so you can keep track of your daily tasks. You also use Cardfile to create and edit a personal address list. You learn how to manage separate address lists, and how to merge them together.

Using Notepad and Cardfile

In this lesson you use Notepad to create and edit text files. You learn how to identify text files, and learn why Notepad is used to work with them. You create a special daily log file using Notepad so you can keep track of daily tasks. You also use Cardfile to create and edit a personal address list. You learn how to manage separate address lists, and how to merge them together.

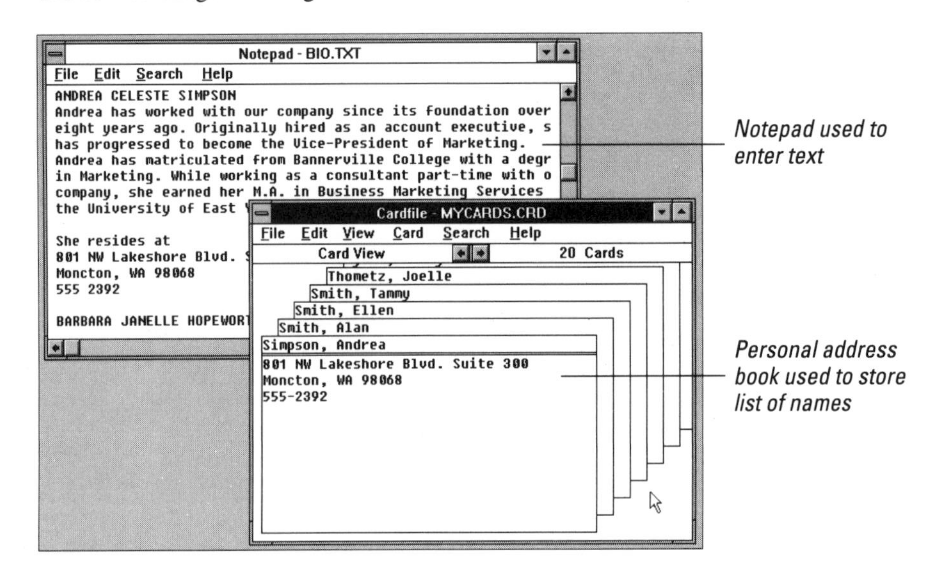

This lesson explains how to do the following:

- Use Notepad
- Use Cardfile

Estimated lesson time: 35 minutes

Using Notepad

You use Notepad to review and edit short *text files,* such as memos or notes. A text file contains only letters, numbers, and other characters found on most keyboards. It does not contain special characters or formatting codes that are used in many files such as word processing documents or spreadsheet files. Text files often have the TXT extension, although other extensions such as ASC and PRN can also be used.

Unlike a word processor, Notepad does not automatically *wordwrap* a text file. That is, Notepad does not insert a line break when you type past the right margin. You must press ENTER at the end of each line to insert a line break.

Caution Do not use Notepad to modify a non-text file, such as COMMAND.COM or FORMAT.EXE. Using Notepad to modify the contents of a non-text file will corrupt the file and make it unusable. If you see odd characters or black rectangles in a file you opened with Notepad, close the file *without* saving it.

Starting Notepad

In these next exercises, you use Notepad to manage the contents of a text file. You open a text file and view its contents. You learn to use Clipboard to copy and paste text from one part of the document to another. You print the file to the default printer.

Open Notepad

1 Find the Notepad icon in the Accessories group.

2 Double-click Notepad.

Notepad icon

The application starts. The Notepad window is displayed on the screen.

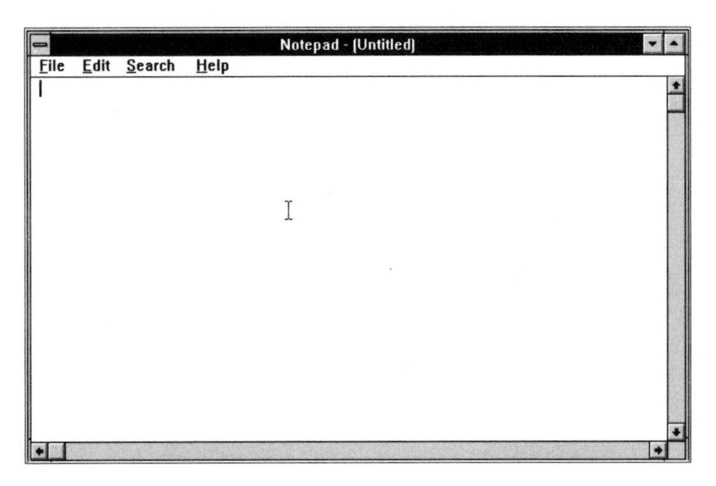

3 Click the Maximize icon in the Notepad window.

Notepad expands to fill the screen.

Create a text file

You create a text file by typing in the window. (Remember, you must press ENTER at the end of each line.)

1 Type **Things to do on Monday**: ENTER ENTER.

2 Type * TAB **Go to cleaners** ENTER.

3 Type * TAB **Purchase stamps** ENTER.

4 Type * TAB **Pick up milk and bread at grocery store** ENTER.

5 Type * TAB **Deposit weekly paycheck** ENTER.

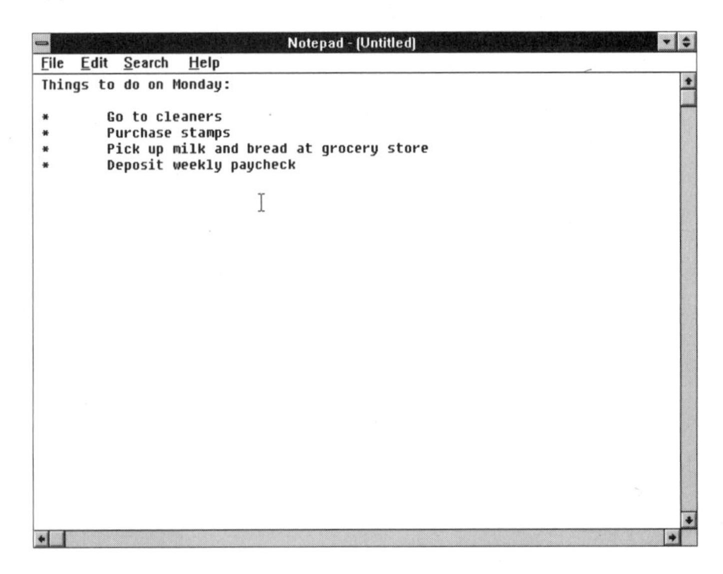

Save the text file

When you have finished entering your text, you can save your file. Notepad adds the TXT extension to any file you save.

1 From the File menu, choose Save.

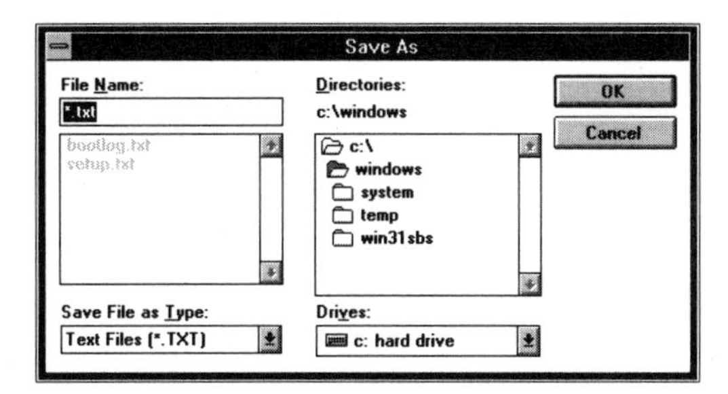

2 In the File Name box, type **MYLIST**

3 Double-click the WIN31SBS folder icon.

Double-clicking sets the default directory to the WIN31SBS subdirectory.

4 Click OK.

Notepad adds the TXT extension when you save the file.

Open a text file

You can use Notepad to open and edit an existing text file.

1 From the File menu, choose Open.

Notepad defaults to show only files with the TXT extension.

2 Double-click LIST.TXT.

This is a file copied to the WIN31SBS subdirectory when you installed the practice files in "Getting Ready." The file opens.

Save with a new name

You use the Save As command to give your existing file a new name. You might want to rename a file before you save it so you can keep the original file intact.

1 From the File menu, choose Save As.

2 In the File Name box, type **NEWLIST**

3 Click OK.

This saves the file with a new name.

Editing Text

You can insert, replace, and delete text in your Notepad file. As in other Windows applications, you select the text you wish to edit.

Remove a word

1 In the fifth line, double-click *grocery*.

2 From the Edit menu, choose Delete.

The word is removed from the file.

Use Undo

You can use Undo to reverse the results of the last action. The Undo command is a feature of many Windows applications.

1 From the Edit menu, choose Undo.

The word *grocery* is replaced.

2 Press DEL.

This is an alternate method to remove text. You can also press BACKSPACE.

Add a line of text

1 In the sixth line, click before the asterisk.

You add a new line of text at this position. By placing the insertion point before the asterisk, you force the new line to begin there.

2 Type * TAB **Go to bank** ENTER.

Using the Clipboard

You can cut, copy, and paste information using the Clipboard. Windows uses the Clipboard (a special place in memory) to store this information temporarily, and keeps it there until you place something else there or until you quit Windows.

Note You do not see the contents of the Clipboard when you cut or paste information onto it.

When you place information, such as text or graphics, onto the Clipboard, you can insert it into other documents (as long as the document can accept the information). In the following exercises, you learn to use the Clipboard to copy and move text from one location to another in the same document.

Copy vs. Cut

See Lesson 11, "Integrating Windows-Based Applications," to learn how to copy and paste text between different applications.

You use one of two methods to place information onto the Clipboard. The Copy command puts a copy of the selected information onto the Clipboard, and leaves the selected information in the document. You use Copy when you have information you would like to use in another part of your document, but you do not want to remove the original information.

The Cut command removes the selected information from the document and places it onto the Clipboard. You use Cut when you have information you want to move from one place in a document to another.

Note Copying or cutting information onto the Clipboard replaces the existing contents of Clipboard. However, pasting information from the Clipboard does not clear the contents. You can paste the contents of Clipboard as many times as you wish.

Copy text

In this exercise, you copy information from one place in the document and paste it into another.

1 Double-click the word *Report* in the tenth line.

2 From the Edit menu, choose Copy.

The selected text is copied onto the Clipboard.

3 Click just after the word *Procedures* in the eleventh line.

4 From the Edit menu, choose Paste.

The Paste command inserts the information at the insertion point. Note that the two words are joined together, because there is no space between the words.

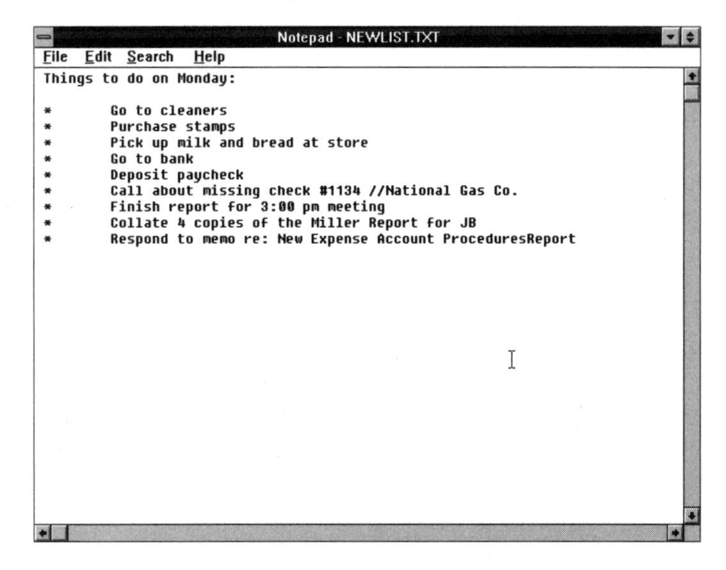

5 Click between the *s* in *Procedures* and the *R* in *Report.*

This places the insertion point between the two words.

6 Press SPACEBAR.

The two words are separated by a space.

Move text

In this exercise you move text from one position in the list to another.

1 Click before the asterisk in the sixth line.

2 Drag straight down to the eighth line.

Do not include the text in the eighth line. Compare your selection to this picture.

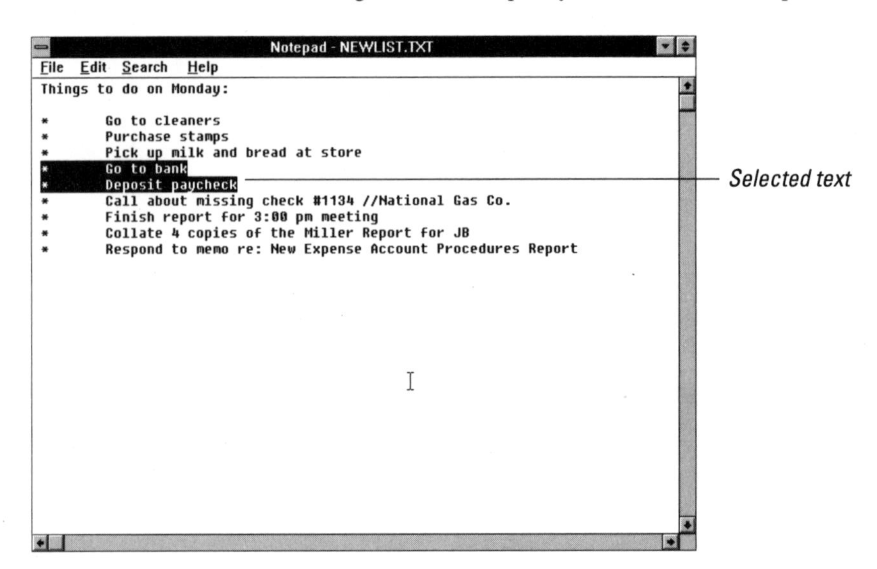

3 From the Edit menu, choose Cut.

The line of text is removed from Notepad and placed onto the Clipboard.

4 Click before the asterisk in the third line.

This line currently has the first task on your list.

5 From the Edit menu, choose Paste.

The line of text is pasted from the Clipboard and placed at the insertion point.

Save the file

You should save your file after you make changes to it.

▶ From the File menu, choose Save.

Print text files

Notepad can print text files to your default printer. (You chose the default printer when you first set up Windows. You will learn more about how to choose a default printer in Lesson 12, "Using the Control Panel.")

▶ From the File menu, choose Print.

Notepad prints the file to the default printer.

Using a Daily Log

You can use Notepad to keep track of your daily tasks by creating a *log file*. Each time you open this log file, Notepad inserts the current time and date at the end of the file. The insertion point automatically moves to the end of the file for you to type any new information. You can use this log file to keep track of the start date and start time of each new task.

Notepad uses the marker .LOG to identify this log file. This entry must be typed as the first entry in a log file. It must be on a blank line, start with a period, and be in capital letters.

1. From the File menu, choose New.
2. At the left margin of the first line, type **.LOG**

   Make sure to type this in all capital letters.
3. From the File menu, choose Save.
4. In the File Name box, type **DAILYLOG**
5. Click OK.

Retrieve the daily log file

You must open the log file for Notepad to insert the current date and time.

1. From the File menu, choose Open.
2. Double-click DAILYLOG.TXT.

   The file is opened. Notepad inserts the current date and time, and moves the insertion point to the end of the file.
3. Type **Wrote memo to Kelly** ENTER.
4. Type **Finished budget proposal** ENTER.
5. Type **Called Leigh about the Wallerman account** ENTER.
6. From the File menu, choose Save.

   Notepad saves the file.

Open the file again

1. From the File menu, choose Open.
2. Double-click DAILYLOG.TXT.

   The file is opened again. Note that the date and time are inserted below the text you typed in step 3, and the insertion point is placed below this new date and time entry at the end of the file.

3 Type **Returned call to Terry** ENTER.

4 From the File menu, choose Save.

Notepad saves the file.

Close Notepad

You can close Notepad when you have finished working with your text file. Closing Notepad removes it from the desktop, and makes more memory available for other applications.

▶ Double-click the Control-menu box in the Notepad window.

Notepad closes.

Using Cardfile

Cardfile is an accessory you use to store information such as names, phone numbers, addresses, or customer information. This information is stored on *cards* that are similar in design to index cards. Cardfile stores the information as two parts: the top line, or *index line*, and the contents of the remainder of the card (below the index line). Cardfile alphabetizes the cards using the index line of the card. Usually you enter names as last name first, followed by first name, but you can use any order you wish, as long as it makes sense to you. You can enter up to 39 characters in the index line, and up to 11 lines of text on the card itself.

In the following exercises, you create a personal address list using Cardfile. You insert, duplicate, edit, and delete cards in this list.

Start Cardfile

1 Find the Cardfile icon in the Accessories group.

2 Double-click Cardfile.

Cardfile icon

Cardfile starts, and the window appears on the screen.

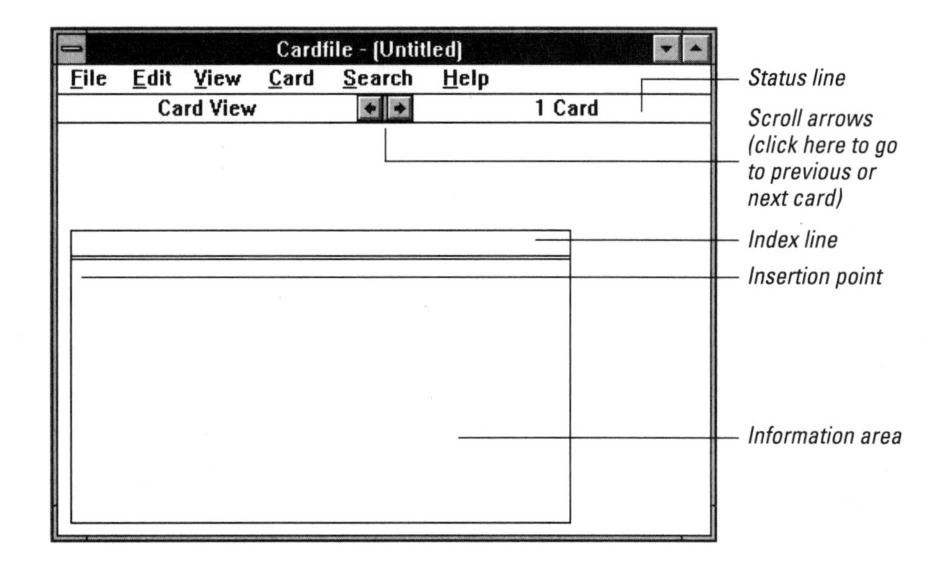

3 Click the Maximize icon of the Cardfile window.

The Cardfile window expands to fill the screen.

Building Your Cardfile

It's easy to create your own personalized Cardfile list. The structure of the program mimics a simple manual system using index cards.

You build a new Cardfile list in two steps. Because Cardfile always starts a new list with one blank card, you begin by typing the index line and the card contents for this blank card. After you type the information for the first card, you continue your list by adding new cards.

Enter the first card

You create the first entry by adding text to the blank card.

1 From the Edit menu, choose Index.

You use this command to edit the index line of the current card.

2 Type **Smith, Ellen** and click OK.

3 Type **123 Elm St.** ENTER
Moncton Bay, WA 98068 ENTER
555-6975

Add new cards

When you add a new card, you enter identifying information on the index line. After the index line is complete, you enter the text for the card contents.

1 From the Card menu, choose Add.

   The index line box appears.

2 Type **Bell, Frank** and click OK.

3 Type **1172 Pine St.** ENTER
   Moncton Bay, WA 98068 ENTER
   555-3398.

4 From the Card menu, choose Add.

5 Type **Moreton, John** and click OK.

6 Type **236 S. Oak** ENTER
   Moncton Bay, WA 98068 ENTER
   555-1802.

Duplicate an entry

You use the Duplicate feature to copy the current card onto another card. This is useful when you have several entries in a row that are similar to each other.

Note Any action, such as Delete or Duplicate, works on the active or *front* card.

---

1 From the Card menu, choose Duplicate.

   The current card for John Moreton is duplicated.

2 From the Edit menu, choose Index.

   The index line for the duplicate card is displayed.

3 Type **Moreton, Jerry** and click OK.

4 Select the phone number.

5 Type **555-3956**

Save a Cardfile list

You should save your Cardfile list frequently. The first time you save your list, you give it a name. Cardfile adds the CRD extension to this name.

1 From the File menu, choose Save.

2 In the File Name box, type **MYCARDS**

3 Double-click the WIN31SBS folder icon.

   Double-clicking sets the default directory to the WIN31SBS subdirectory.

4 Click OK.

   Cardfile adds the CRD extension when you save the file.

Working with Cardfile

After your Cardfile list is prepared, you can quickly open, use and modify the list. Commands let you quickly jump to or search for a card. You can easily modify the cards as information changes.

Change the view

You can change the display of your Cardfile list from the usual single card to an alphabetic list of the index line. This is useful when you want to see how many cards you have on your list.

1 From the View menu, choose List.

Cardfile displays the cards by their index lines only.

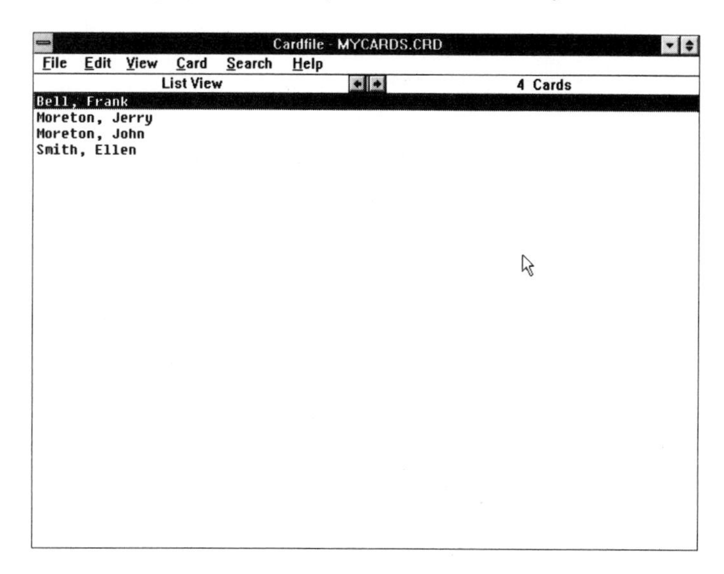

2 From the View menu, choose Card.

Cardfile displays the list a single card at a time.

Open a Cardfile list

You can open and edit an existing Cardfile list. Cardfile shows all the files with the CRD extension.

1 From the File menu, choose Open.

2 Double-click CARDLIST.CRD.

This is a file you copied to the WIN31SBS subdirectory when you installed the practice files in Lesson 1, "Getting Started with Windows."

Merge an address list

You use the Merge feature to combine two or more separate Cardfile lists into one. This is useful when you maintain separate lists for different activities, but would like to prepare one master list.

1 From the File menu, choose Merge.

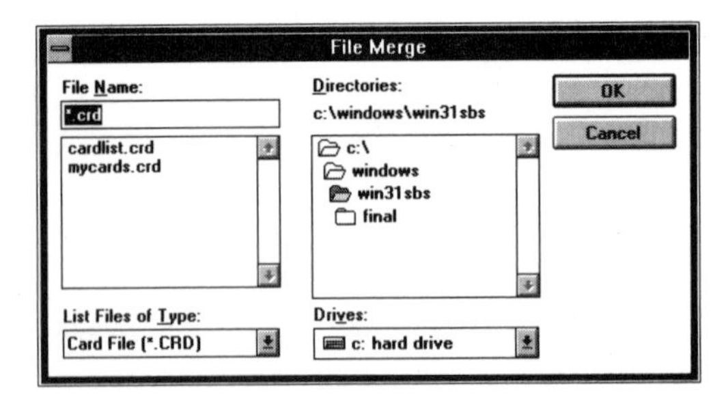

2 Double-click MYCARDS.CRD.

The cards you entered are merged into the current list.

Replace a Cardfile list

You can replace an existing Cardfile list with an updated list by saving the current file with a new name. If the new name matches the existing filename, Cardfile replaces the disk file with the file you currently have open.

1 From the File menu, choose Save As.

2 In the File Name box, type **MYCARDS**

3 Click OK.

A dialog box appears, asking you to confirm replacing the existing file.

4 Click Yes.

The disk file is replaced by the new file that you created when you merged MYCARDS.CRD and CARDFILE.CRD together.

Scroll through a Cardfile list

You can scroll through the list with the scroll arrows or the keyboard. You can also bring a card to the front by clicking it.

Tip If you are in the List view, you can also use the scroll bars.

1 Click the right arrow in the status line.

The next card appears.

2 Click the left arrow in the status line.

The previous card appears.

3 Click the index line for Berwick, Ann.

Clicking the index line brings that card to the front. The card for Ann Berwick appears.

Go to a card

You use the Go To command to find a card based on the information in the index line.

1 From the Search menu, choose Go To.

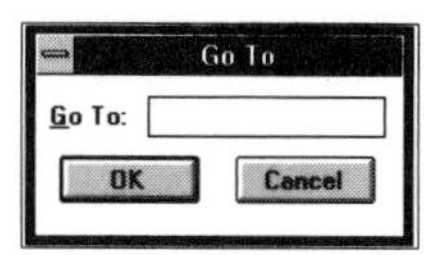

2 Type **Smith** and click OK.

The card for Alan Smith appears.

Find a card

You use the Find command to find a card based on the information on the card, not in the index line.

1 From the Search menu, choose Find.

2 Type **Riverview** and click Find Next.

The first card after the current card containing *Riverview* appears. The dialog box remains on the screen so you can continue your search.

3 Click Find Next.

The next card containing *Riverview* appears.

4 Click Cancel to stop the search.

Modify an index line

You modify the index line when you want to change a name or index entry.

1 Click the card for Deloral, Tom.

2 From the Edit menu, choose Index.

3 Type **D'Loralle, Tom** in the index line.

4 Click OK.

Modify the contents of a card

1. Click on the index line for Eastman, Sharon.
2. Select the city name Riverview.
3. Type **Moncton**
4. Select the ZIP Code.
5. Type **98069**
6. Select the phone number.
7. Type **555-7990**

Delete a card

In this exercise you will delete the card for Andrew Hollingsworth from your Cardfile list.

Caution When a card is deleted, there is no way to restore it. Be sure to save your Cardfile list before deleting any cards. That way, you can recover your work if you delete a card accidentally.

1. From the File menu, choose Save.
2. Click the card for Andrew Hollingsworth to bring it to the front.
3. From the Card menu, choose Delete.

   A dialog box appears for you to confirm the action.
4. Click OK.

   The card is deleted.
5. From the File menu, choose Save.

One Step Further

In this exercise, you use Notepad to examine a file containing text to be used in Cardfile. You create a new entry in Cardfile based on the information from Notepad.

1. Start Notepad.
2. Open the file BIO.TXT from the WIN31SBS subdirectory.

   This is a file copied to your WIN31SBS subdirectory when you installed your practice files in "Getting Ready."
3. Scroll through the file to view the information on Andrea Simpson. Notice that it contains information showing her phone number and address.
4. Create a new entry for Andrea Simpson in Cardfile using the information in the BIO.TXT file.

5 Save the Cardfile as ANDREA.CRD to the WIN31SBS subdirectory.
6 Open the Cardfile MYCARDS.CRD from the WIN31SBS subdirectory.
7 Merge it with the Cardfile ANDREA.CRD from the WIN31SBS subdirectory.
8 Save the Cardfile MYCARDS.CRD.

If you want to continue to the next lesson

1 Double-click the Control-menu box in the Notepad window.
2 Double-click the Control-menu box in the Cardfile window.

If you want to quit Windows for now

1 Switch to the Program Manager.
2 Double-click the Control-menu box in the Program Manager window.
3 When the message "This will end your Windows session" appears, click OK or press ENTER.

Lesson Summary

To	Do this
Create a text file	Open Notepad and enter text.
Remove a character, word, or phrase	Select the information and choose Delete from the Edit menu.
Undo a previous command or action	Choose Undo from the Edit menu.
Move or copy text	Select the text, choose Cut or Copy from the Edit menu, move the insertion point to the new location, and choose Paste from the Edit menu.
Create a daily log file	Create a new document and type .LOG as the first entry on a blank line. Save the document, and reopen it. Each time you open it, Notepad inserts the current date and time, and moves the insertion point to the end of the file.
Create a Cardfile list	Start Cardfile and edit the index line for the first blank card. Type information on this card. To insert more cards, choose Add from the Card menu. Type an entry for the index line, and then type information on the card.
Bring a card to the front	Click on the scroll arrows or scroll bar until the card appears. If you can see the card's index line on the screen, you can click on it to quickly bring it to the front.

To	Do this
Edit an index line	Bring the desired card to the front. Choose Index from the Edit menu, and replace or retype the information.
Edit a card	Bring the desired card to the front. Replace or retype the information.
Duplicate a card	Bring the desired card to the front. Choose Duplicate from the Card menu and then edit the information on the duplicate card.
Change the view of the card list	Choose Card or List from the View menu.
Merge two address lists	Open the file you want to merge with, choose Merge from the File menu and double-click the name of file to be merged.
Go to a card (by index information)	Choose Go To from the Search menu, enter the information, and click OK.
Find a card (by card information)	Choose Find from the Search menu, enter the information, and click OK.
Delete a card	Bring the desired card to the front. Choose Delete from the Card menu.

To	See the *Microsoft Windows User's Guide*
Set up a printer	Chapter 6, "Print Manager"
Select a default printer	Chapter 6, "Print Manager"

For more information on	See the Microsoft Windows User's Guide
Notepad	Chapter 12, "Notepad"
Cardfile	Chapter 12, "Cardfile"

Preview of the Next Lesson

In the next lesson you use Write to create and edit longer documents and memos. You learn how to change the format of a document by adjusting paragraph spacing, tabs, and page margins.

Using Write

In this lesson you learn how to use Write to create and edit longer documents. You learn how to cut, copy, and paste text. You also learn how to change the layout of your document by adjusting tabs, line spacing, and page margins.

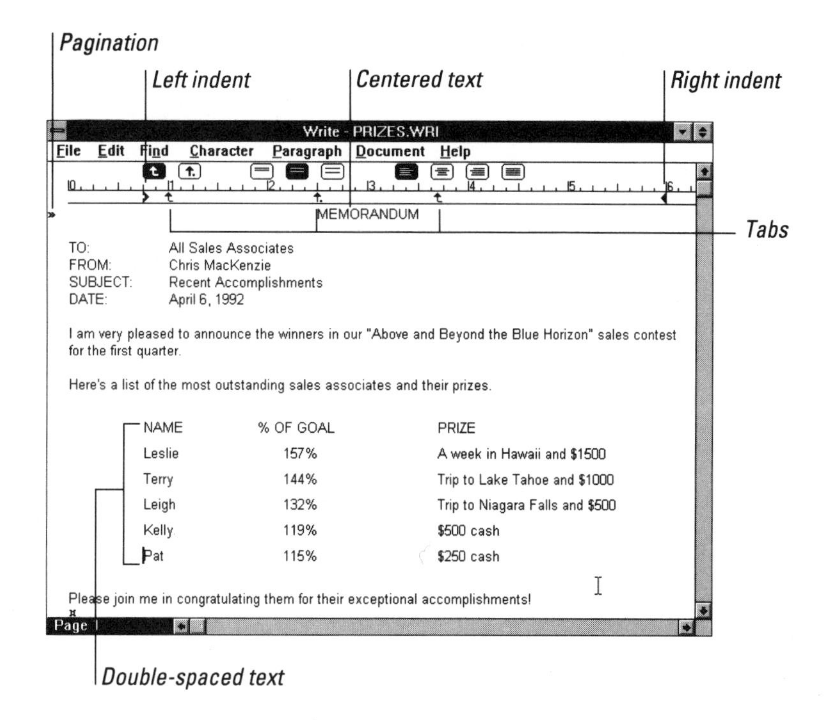

This lesson explains how to do the following:

- Use Write to create a document
- Edit, delete, copy, cut, and paste text
- Format the page layout of a document
- Save, retrieve, and print a document

Estimated lesson time: 40 minutes

Creating Documents with Write

You use Write to create documents of any size, from short notes to elaborate memos and reports. These documents can use other formatting features, such as indents, centered lines, italic, double-spacing, and tab stops.

Note The other Windows accessory used to create documents, Notepad, does not use these special effects. It creates and edits only plain text files. Although it is possible to use Write to create and edit plain text files, it is often easier to use Notepad.

Start Write

1 Find the Write icon.

The Write icon is in the Accessories group in the Program Manager.

Write icon

2 Double-click the Write icon.

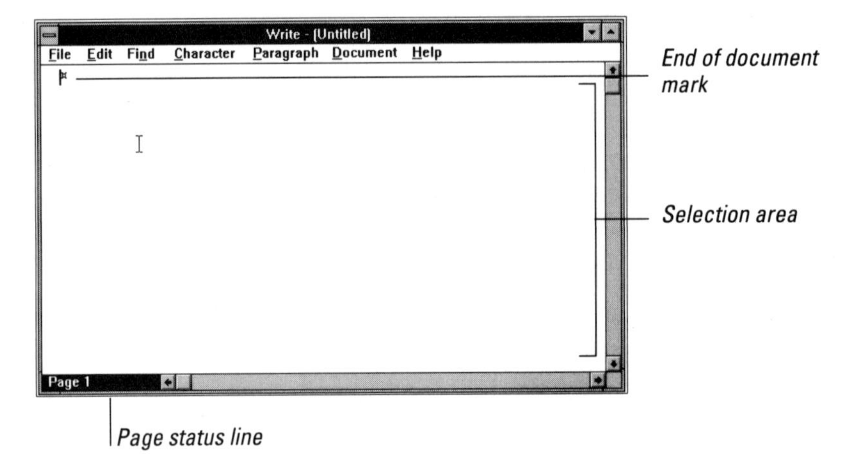

3 From the Control menu, choose Maximize.

Creating a Simple Document

Each time you start Write, it creates a new document. When you are ready to write, simply begin typing. As you reach the end of the line, Write automatically *wordwraps*; that is, it breaks the line near the right margin and moves it down to the next line.

Tip Use the New command on the File menu to create a blank document if you have a document currently loaded in Write.

▶ Type the following text. Do not press ENTER until you are instructed to do so.

`To most people, the term "outdoors" means "where you go camping." But to increasing numbers of people, the outdoors is becoming part of their home. From potted plants to room-sized terrariums, a green environment is becoming a popular addition to one's living space.` ENTER ENTER

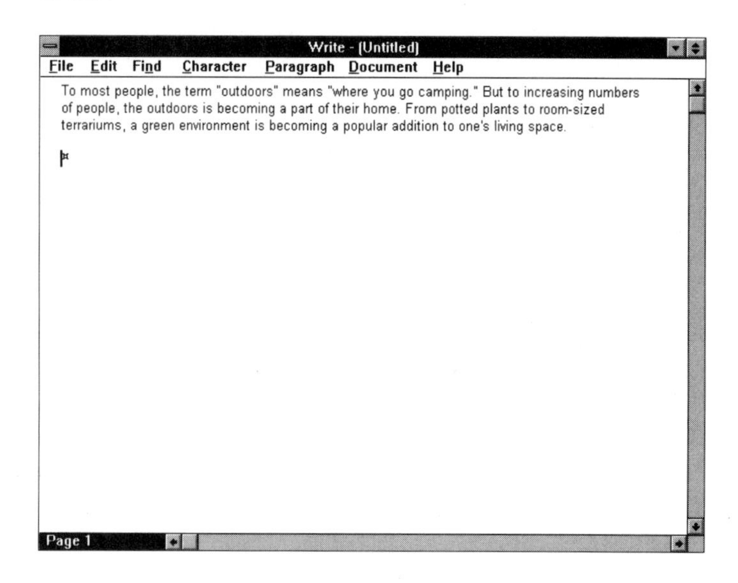

Save a document

1. From the File menu, choose Save.
2. In the File Name box, type **OUTDOORS**
3. Double-click the WIN31SBS folder icon.

   Double-clicking sets the default directory to the WIN31SBS subdirectory.
4. Click OK.

   Write assigns the WRI extension when you save the file.

Retrieve a document

1. From the File menu, choose Open.
2. Double-click ADVENTUR.WRI.

   This is a longer file you use to practice moving through a document. Opening this document closes the OUTDOORS.WRI document.

Rename a document

1. From the File menu, choose Save As.
2. In the File Name box, type **MYTRIP** and click OK.

   A copy of ADVENTUR.WRI is saved as MYTRIP.WRI, and ADVENTUR.WRI closes. You now have two copies of the same document on your hard disk with different names.

Basic Editing

Write can easily handle basic editing tasks. You edit in two steps. First, you select text, and then you make changes using the insert, cut, copy, and paste commands on the Edit menu. When you cut or copy text, Windows stores the text onto the Clipboard.

Select text

Because you must select text before you can edit it, you explore several ways to select text in a Write document in this exercise.

1. Click before the word *my* in the first line and drag to the word *together*.

   You can select several characters, words, lines, and paragraphs by dragging the mouse.
2. Double-click the word *Vacation* in the title.

   The word and the space following are selected.
3. Click in the selection area next to the first paragraph starting with *For years my family...*

   The selection area is the blank area to the left of each line of text in the Write window.
4. Double-click in the selection area next to the first paragraph starting with *For years my family...*

   The paragraph is selected.
5. Press CTRL and click anywhere in the selection area.

   The entire document is selected.
6. Click immedately to the left of the word *Dad* in the first line of the first paragraph, hold down SHIFT, and click to the right of the period ending this sentence.

   The entire sentence is selected.

Tip You can use selection techniques to select any quantity of text, not just sentences.

---

7. Click in the first sentence.

   Clicking anywhere in the text cancels the previous selection.

Insert text

You insert text by first clicking in the text to establish the insertion point. After you set the insertion point, you begin typing. Any text to the right of the new text is moved to the right. Write adjusts line breaks as necessary to keep all the text in the margins.

1 Click to the left of the word *years* in the first sentence of the first paragraph.

2 Type **many** and press SPACEBAR.

The word *many* is inserted before the word *years*. The existing text is moved to the right.

Replace text

You replace text by first selecting it. Any new text you type replaces the selected text.

1 Select the word *yearly* in the first line of the second paragraph.

2 Type **annual** and press SPACEBAR.

The word *annual* replaces the word *yearly*. Selecting a word and then typing over it replaces the word. This feature is called *typeover*.

Delete text

You can delete unwanted text either a single letter at a time, or by selecting the text and then choosing to delete it.

1 Double-click the word *River* in the sixth line of the second paragraph to select it.

2 Press DEL.

The word is deleted.

3 Press BACKSPACE.

The extra space is deleted. You can delete text using either DELETE or BACK-SPACE.

Cut and paste text

In the next exercise you practice cutting and pasting text, two more editing functions that you use frequently.

1 Select the last sentence in the third paragraph, *It all started so quietly*.

Make sure you do not select the return at the end of the line.

2 From the Edit menu, choose Cut.

Write removes the sentence, and places it on the Clipboard.

3 Click just before the first sentence in the fourth paragraph.

Write always pastes text at the insertion point. Be sure you place your insertion point where you want to paste the new text.

4 From the Edit menu, choose Paste.

5 Press SPACEBAR.

You press SPACEBAR because your text did not include the space needed to separate the two words.

Copy and paste text

In the next exercise you practice copying and pasting text.

1 Select the phrase *Vacation in France* in the first paragraph.

2 From the Edit menu, choose Copy.

The text is copied onto the Clipboard.

3 Select the phrase *Tour of Tours* in the third paragraph.

4 From the Edit menu, choose Paste.

The text is pasted into the document, replacing the selected text.

Save the document

Save your documents frequently. When you save the document, Write collects all the information in the document, including any changes, and makes sure the disk file is properly updated.

▶ From the File menu, choose Save.

Changing the Format of a Document

You can adjust the page margins, tabs, or paragraph specifications of a document. You can use menu commands and dialog boxes to make these format changes, or you can display and use the Ruler, which shows the current margin and tab settings and lets you adjust these format settings using the mouse.

Display the Ruler

1 From the Document menu, choose Ruler On.

Choosing this command *toggles* the display of the Ruler. That is, if the Ruler display was turned off, it is now turned on. If it was turned on, it is turned off.

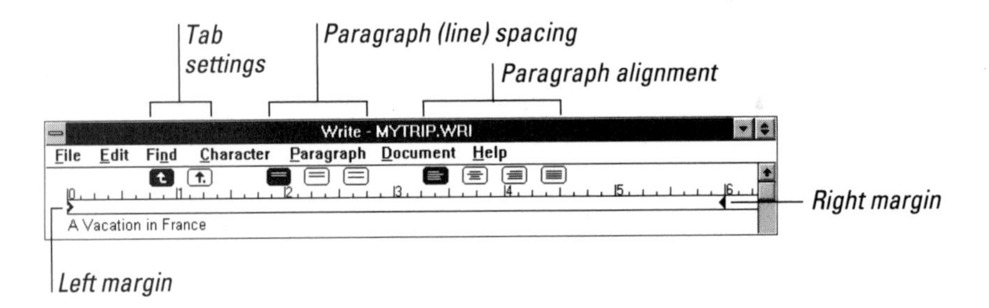

Change the page margins

1 From the Document menu, choose Page Layout.

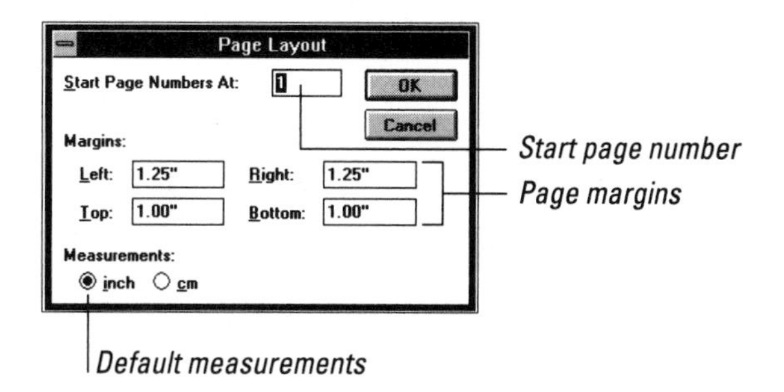

2 Click the Left box under the word Margins and select the text 1.25".

3 Type **1.5**

4 Click the Right box under Margins and select the text 1.25".

5 Type **1.5**

6 Click the Top box under Margins and select the text 1.00".

7 Type **1.5**

8 Click the Bottom box under Margins and select the text 1.00".

9 Type **1.5** in the Bottom box under Margins.

10 Click OK.

The entire document reformats to the new margins.

Change the paragraph alignment

When you want to modify the appearance of a paragraph, you change the paragraph alignment. You can align the text to the left margin (the default alignment), to the right margin, evenly between both margins (justified), or centered between both margins.

1 Hold down CTRL and click in the selection area.

The entire document is selected.

2 From the Paragraph menu, choose Centered.

Because every paragraph is selected, every paragraph in the document is centered.

3 Click the Justified alignment button on the Ruler.

Every paragraph is justified. Using the icons on the Ruler has the same effect as using the commands in the Paragraph menu.

4 Click in the first line of the document.

This deselects the document, and places the insertion point in the the first line of the document.

5 Click the Centered alignment button on the Ruler.

You do not need to select a paragraph to change its alignment. If no text is selected, Write acts on the paragraph containing the insertion point.

Changing Indents

Write formats the text of your document to fit between the left and right margins. You can override these left and right margins for a paragraph by setting an *indent*. An indent is used to make a temporary change to your page margins for a selected paragraph. For example, you can use an indent to force every paragraph to be indented one inch from each margin, or to format a paragraph so that the first line of each paragraph is indented a half-inch.

Set a first-line indent

In this exercise you format the paragraphs so that each has a first-line indent.

1 Hold down CTRL and click in the selection area.

This selects every paragraph in the document.

Triangle

2 Click on the left triangle on the Ruler.

The left margin mark (the triangle) has a small dot on it. This dot is the symbol used to represent the first-line indent.

3 Drag the dot to the right to the half-inch mark on the Ruler.

4 Release the mouse.

Every paragraph has a half-inch indent set from the left margin.

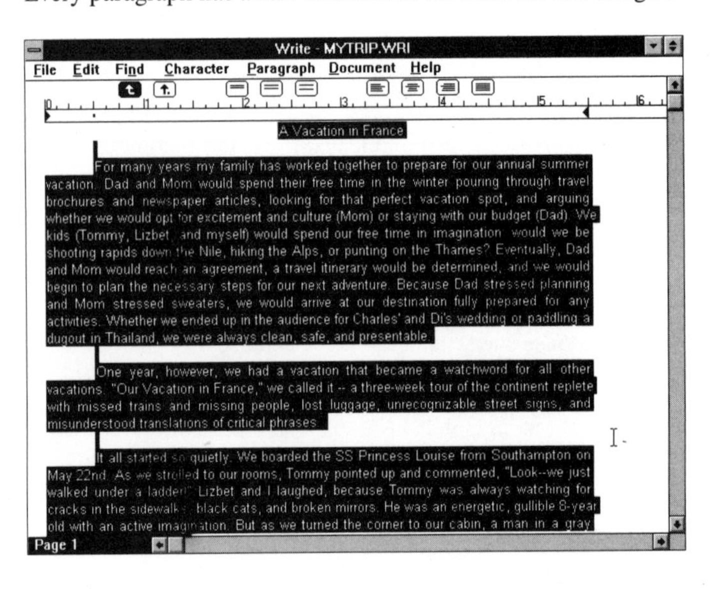

5 Click on the title.

The title does not need an indent.

6 From the Paragraph menu, choose Indents.

The Indents dialog box appears.

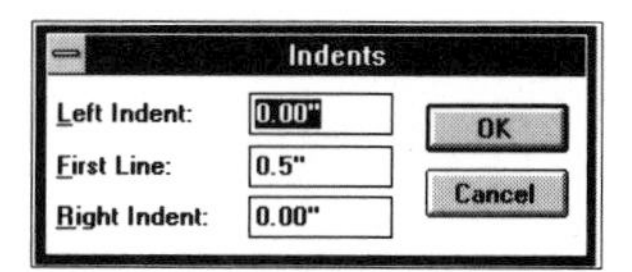

7 Click in the First Line box and select the text 0.5".

8 Type **0**

This is an alternate way to set the paragraph indent.

9 Click OK.

Change the left and right indents

1 Click in the first paragraph.

This is the paragraph below the title *Our Vacation in France.*

2 Drag the left triangle on the Ruler over to the half-inch mark.

3 Drag the right triangle on the Ruler over to the 5-inch mark.

This sets a 1-inch right indent for the paragraph.

Set the line spacing

Write has three options for line spacing. You can format your document so it has a single space (the default line spacing), one and a half spaces, or two spaces between each line of text.

1 Hold down CTRL and click in the selection area.

The entire document is selected.

Double-space button

2 Click on the double-space button on the Ruler.

The entire document is double-spaced.

3 From the Paragraph menu, choose 1½ Space.

The entire document now has one and a half lines of space between each line.

Using Tabs and Tab Stops

Tabs are special characters you use to control the alignment of text in a table of numbers or a list. Each time you press TAB, Write inserts a tab character and moves the cursor to the next *tab stop*. These tab stops are points in the paragraph at which you want to align the text. You insert tab stops using the Tabs command on the Document menu, or by clicking on the Ruler at the point where you want to insert a tab stop. Each time you click on the Ruler, Write places a tab stop, and shows the tab stop as a *tab mark*.

Write supports left tabs (the default tab setting) and right (decimal) tabs. Write has default tab stops every one-half inch, but you can insert other tabs stops. You can place up to 10 tab stops in the document.

Note Tab stops apply to the entire document.

Set tab stops with the ruler

You can quickly set tab stops by clicking on the Ruler. Write sets a tab stop wherever you click.

1 Press CTRL+END to move to the end of the document.

Your new tab stop settings affect the layout of the table of numbers at the end of the document.

Left tab mark

2 Click on the 4-inch mark on the Ruler.

This inserts a left tab mark (an upward-pointing arrow with a small hook) on the Ruler. The left tab is the default tab style.

3 Click the right/decimal tab mark on the Ruler.

You choose the tab style you want before you click on the Ruler.

Right/decimal tab mark

4 Click on the 2-inch mark on the Ruler.

This inserts a right tab mark (an upward-pointing arrow with a decimal point) on the Ruler. When you press TAB and type a number, it is aligned to the decimal point.

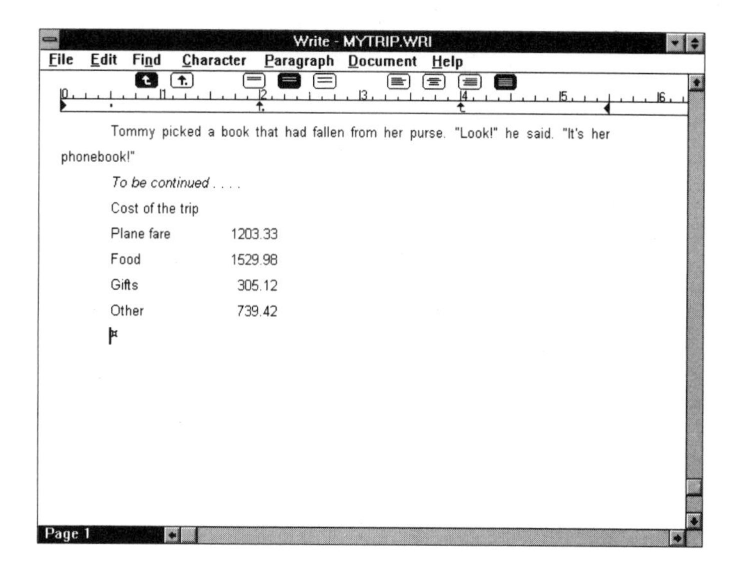

5 Click on the 4.5-inch mark on the Ruler.

This inserts a right tab mark on the Ruler.

Set and edit tab stops with the menu

Use the menu when you want to set or move a tab stop to a precise position.

1 From the Document menu, choose Tabs.

The Tabs dialog box appears.

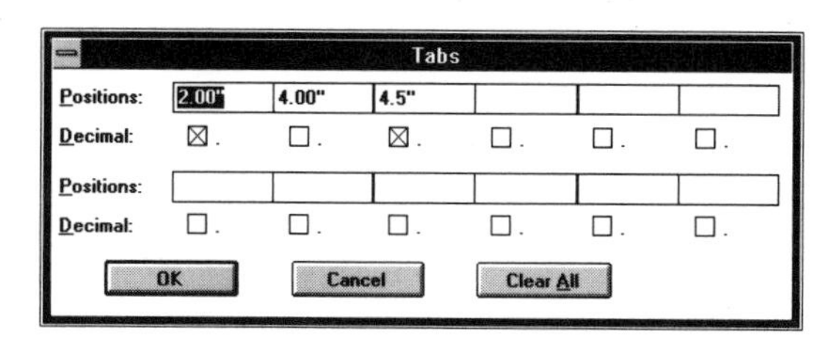

2 Select the text 2.00" and type **3.125**

This moves the tab stop at the 2-inch mark to the 3.125-inch mark.

3 Select the text 4.00" and type **3.67**

This moves the tab stop at the 4-inch mark to the 3.67-inch mark.

4 Click OK.

Remove tab stops with the ruler

You can remove tabs stops that are incorrectly placed by dragging them away from the Ruler.

▶ Drag the 3.67" tab away from the Ruler.

The tab stop is now removed.

Remove tab stops with the menu

You can also remove tab stops using the menu. This is useful if you have several tab stops that are placed closely together and you cannot easily remove one by dragging it away from the Ruler.

1 From the Document menu, choose Tabs.

2 Select the text 4.50" by dragging it with the mouse.

3 Press DELETE.

You can also press BACKSPACE.

4 Click OK.

5 Press CTRL+HOME.

This moves the cursor to the top of the document.

Printing a Document

Write can print documents to your default printer. You can choose the number of copies and the range of pages you want to print.

Print the file

1 From the File menu, choose Print.

The Print dialog box appears.

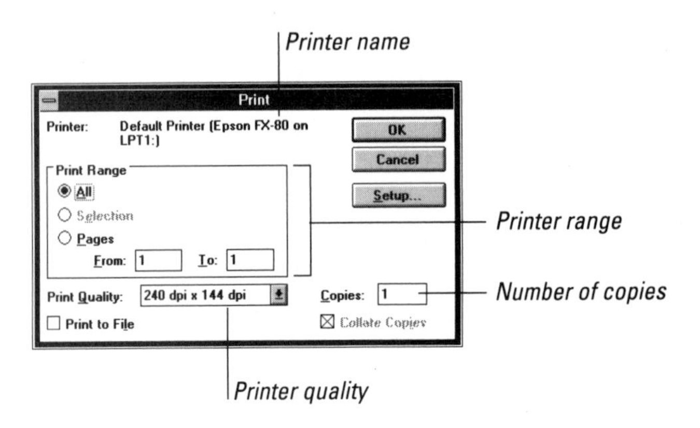

2 Click OK.

The document prints. After printing the document, the » character (a double chevron) appears in the left margin at the beginning of the document. The » character marks the start of the first page.

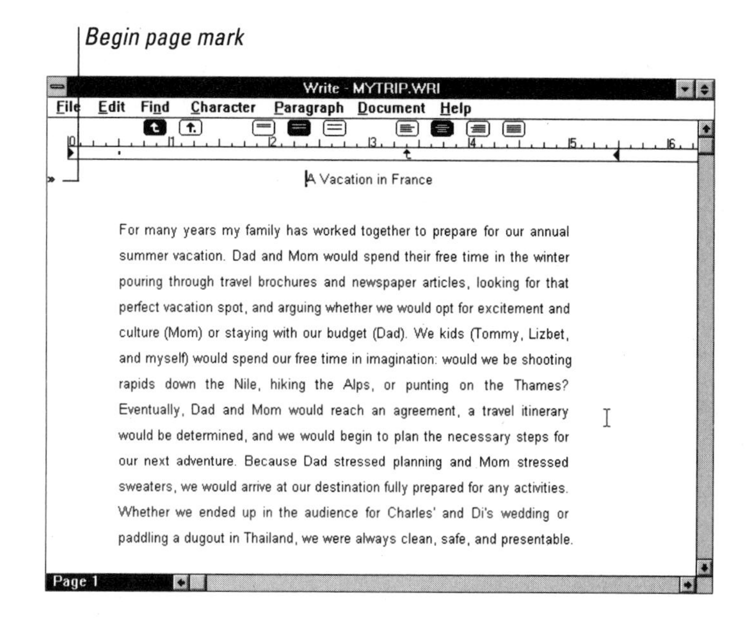

3 From the File menu, choose Print.

4 In the Copies box, type **2**

5 Click the Pages button.

6 In the From box, type **2**

7 Click OK.

This prints two copies of the document starting with the second page. You do not need to fill in the To box, because this document has only two pages.

Using Page Breaks

Write automatically breaks the document into separate pages when you print it. This process, called *pagination*, places a » character in the left margin at the beginning of each new page. If you want to override Write's page breaks, or add extra breaks, you can insert your own page breaks by putting the insertion point at the desired location and then pressing CTRL+ENTER. Each time you press CTRL+ENTER, Write displays the page break as a dotted line that runs across the width of the application's window.

Insert a page break

1 Press CTRL+END to move to the end of the document.

2 Click to the left of the phrase *Cost of the Trip*.

3 Press CTRL+ENTER.

Write inserts a page break above the line where you clicked with the mouse. This page break is displayed as a dotted line.

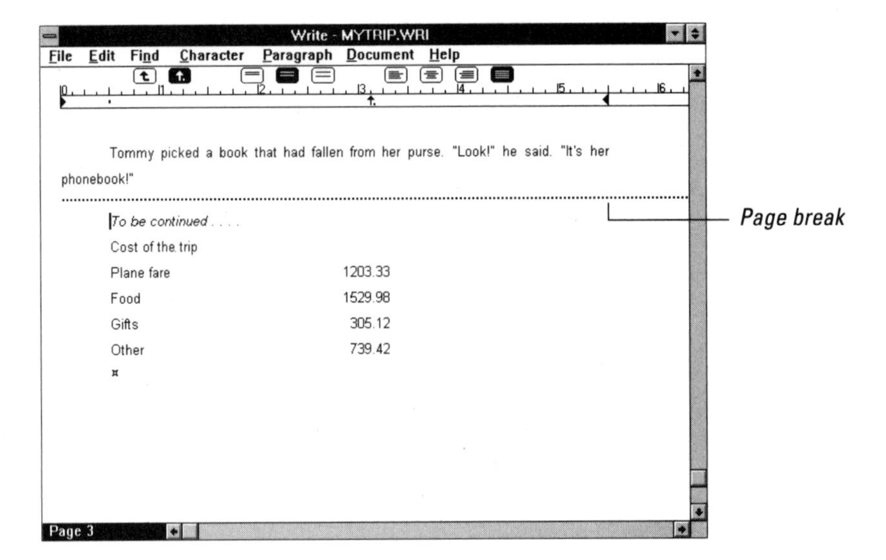

Repaginate a document

When you want Write to recalculate where page breaks occur, you repaginate the document. This is useful when you want to check whether a page break occurs in an odd part of a document (such as between a headline and a following paragraph).

1 From the File menu, choose Repaginate.

The Repaginate dialog box appears.

2 Click the Confirm Page Breaks box to place an X in it.

Clicking the Confirm Page Breaks box makes Write stop at each proposed page break for you to confirm its placement. If you did not click the Confirm Page Breaks box to place an X in it, Write would repaginate the entire document without showing you each page break.

3 Click OK.

Write begins calculating page breaks based on the length of the printed page, and displays the first line where it calculates a page break should be inserted. Write also displays the Page Break dialog box, which you can use to confirm the placement of the page break or to move the page break to another line.

4 Click Confirm.

Write inserts a page break and moves to the next place that it calculates it should insert another page break.

5 Click the Up button three times.

6 Click Confirm.

7 In the Page Break dialog box, click Keep.

This keeps the page break you inserted manually.

Print the file

After you have inserted and modified page breaks, you can see the results when you print the file.

1 From the File menu, choose Print.

2 Click OK.

Save the file

▶ From the File menu, choose Save.

Collapse Write to an Icon

▶ From the Control menu in the Write window, choose Minimize.

The Write window is reduced to an icon.

One Step Further

In this exercise you write a memo. After you create the memo, you practice setting tabs. You change the appearance of the document using formatting commands.

1 Double-click the Write icon.

2 From the File menu, choose New to create a new document.

3 Type the following text. Do not press ENTER until instructed to do so.

`MEMORANDUM` ENTER ENTER

`To:`	TAB	`Kelly Leighton`	ENTER
`From:`	TAB	`Lee Taylor`	ENTER
`Date:`	TAB	`(Today's date)`	ENTER
`Subject:`	TAB	`Bonus checks`	ENTER ENTER

`The following people are to receive bonus checks in their next pay envelopes for their suggestions entered into the "Total Quality Management" contest:` ENTER ENTER

`Bonus Amounts:`	ENTER		
`Terry Jackson`	TAB	`$145.50`	ENTER
`Jay Alton`	TAB	`$135.66`	ENTER
`Lindsey Walker`	TAB	`$172.30`	ENTER
`Pat Weyland`	TAB	`$142.50`	ENTER ENTER

`Please post this notice for all employees to see.` ENTER ENTER

4 Center the title MEMORANDUM.

5 Set left tab stops after the To/From/Date/Subject headings at the 1-inch mark.

6 Select the paragraphs containing the employee names, and set right/decimal tab stops at the 3.5-inch mark for the bonus amounts.

7 Indent the paragraphs containing the employee names 1 inch from the left margin. Compare your work with the picture below.

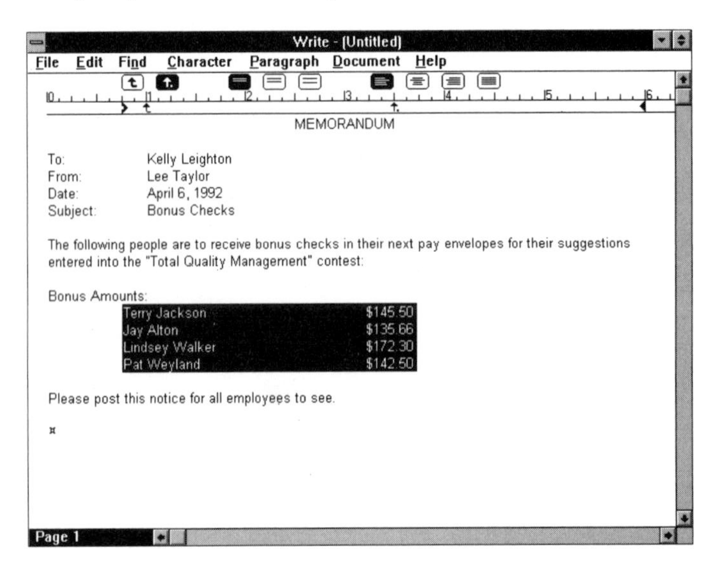

8 Save the file as MYMEMO in the WIN31SBS subdirectory.

If you want to continue to the next lesson

▶ Double-click the Control-menu box in the Write window.

If you want to quit Windows for now

1 Double-click the Control-menu box in the Program Manager window.

2 When the message "This will end your Windows session" appears, click OK or press ENTER.

Lesson Summary

To	Do this
Enter text	Position the insertion point and begin typing.
Save a document	From the File menu, choose Save. (If you have not saved the file before, type a filename in the box and click OK.)
Save a document with a new name	From the File menu, choose Save As. Type a filename in the box. Click OK.
Open a document	From the File menu, choose Open. Then either highlight a filename and click OK *or* double-click a filename.
Select a word	Double-click on a word.
Select a line	Click in the selection area.
Select a sentence	Click at the beginning of the sentence, hold down SHIFT, and then click at the end of the sentence.
Select a paragraph	Double-click in the selection area.
Select the entire document	Hold down CTRL and click in the selection area.
Select several letters, words, lines, or paragraphs	Click at the beginning of the text block, hold down SHIFT, and then click at the end of the text block.
Cancel a selection	Click anywhere in the document.
Insert text	Click in the document and begin typing.
Cut text	Select text and choose Cut from the Edit menu.
Copy text	Select text and choose Copy from the Edit menu.
Paste text	After placing text on the Clipboard with Cut or Copy, choose Paste from the Edit menu.
Remove text	Select text and choose Cut from the Edit menu. *or* Select text and press DEL or BACKSPACE.
Change the page margins	Choose Page Layout from the Document menu. Change the page margins by replacing the current values. Click OK.
Change the paragraph alignment	Select the paragraph or paragraphs to be changed. From the Paragraph menu, choose Centered, Left, Right, or Justified. *or* Select the paragraph or paragraphs to be changed. Then click the appropriate alignment button.

To	Do this
Change the paragraph indent	Select the paragraph or paragraphs to be changed. From the Paragraph menu, choose Indents. Change the indent value. Click OK. *or* Select the paragraph or paragraphs to be changed. Drag the left triangle on the Ruler to the right. A dot appears after you start dragging.
Change the line spacing	Select the paragraph or paragraphs to be changed. From the Paragraph menu, choose the appropriate spacing. *or* Select the paragraph or paragraphs to be changed. Click the appropriate button on the Ruler.
Set tabs stops	Select the paragraph or paragraphs to be changed. From the Document menu, choose Tabs. Type the appropriate number in the Tab boxes. Click Decimal to make a tab a right-aligned tab. Click OK. *or* Select the paragraph or paragraphs to be changed. Click the Left or Right Tab button on the Ruler.
Remove a tab	Select the paragraph or paragraphs to be changed. From the Document menu, choose Tabs. Select the box containing the tab you wish to clear, and press DEL. Click OK. *or* Select the paragraph or paragraphs to be changed. Drag the tab marker away from the Ruler.
Insert a page break	Click in the left-most end of the desired line and press CTRL+ENTER.
Print a document	From the File menu, choose Print. Change the appropriate settings, and click OK.
Repaginate a document	From the File menu, choose Repaginate. Click the Confirm Page Breaks box. At each page break, click the Up or Down button to move the page break. Click Confirm when the page break is in the desired location.
Collapse Write to an icon	From the Control menu choose Minimize. *or* Click the Minimize icon.
Restore Write from an icon	Click the Write icon, and choose Restore from the Control menu. *or* Double-click the Write icon.

For more information on	See the *Microsoft Windows User's Guide*
Using Write	Chapter 9, "Write"

Preview of the Next Lesson

In the next lesson you learn how to use Paintbrush to create a simple logo. You create a business logo consisting of a circle with a horizontal rectangle across its middle, and you also draw some freehand spirals. By adding and changing color, you can make your logo more interesting. To complete the lesson, you add text to the graphic and change its color and position.

Using Paintbrush

Paintbrush is a colorful and capable application. You can create original artwork and move it into many other Windows applications. You can also use Paintbrush to resize and edit art copied from other documents or sources. Paintings can be created and saved in either the widely used PCX format or the Windows BMP format. For the adventurous, the One Step Further section at the end of the chapter shows how to use the BMP format to create new "wallpaper" for your Windows desktop.

In this lesson, you use Paintbrush to create a simple logo. You add color and text to the logo then save and print the result.

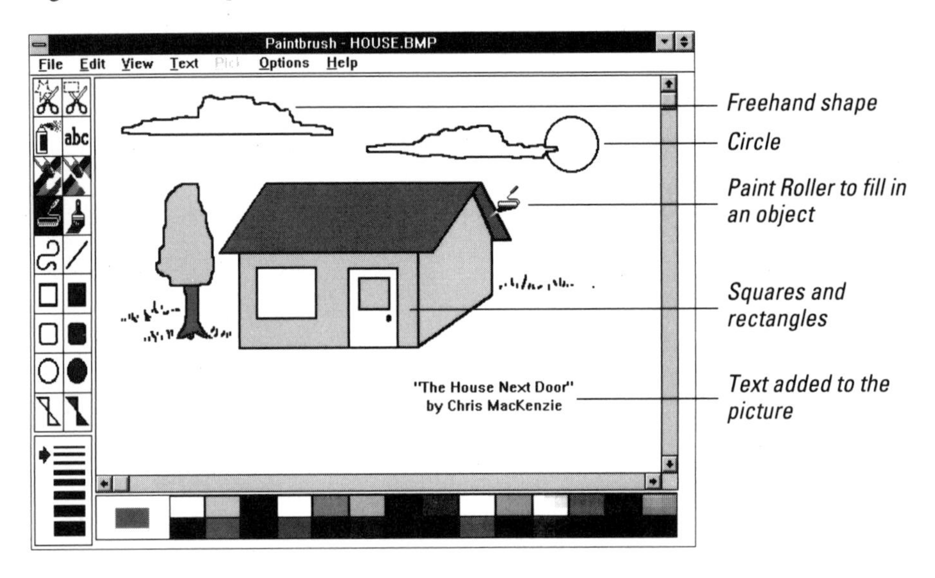

This lesson explains how to do the following:

- Start Paintbrush
- Create a simple graphic
- Add color to a graphic
- Add text to a graphic
- Save and retrieve a graphic
- Print a graphic

Estimated lesson time: 35 minutes

Starting Paintbrush

Paintbrush is useful for drawing simple pictures, such as logos or sketches. You can also edit existing pictures, which are available from many sources.

Paintbrush is designed to work best with the mouse, although you can use some keyboard equivalents. In this section, you use the mouse for drawing and editing a picture.

1 Find the Paintbrush icon in the Accessories group in the Program Manager.

Paintbrush icon

2 Double-click the icon.

The Paintbrush application starts.

3 Click the Maximize button in the Paintbrush window.

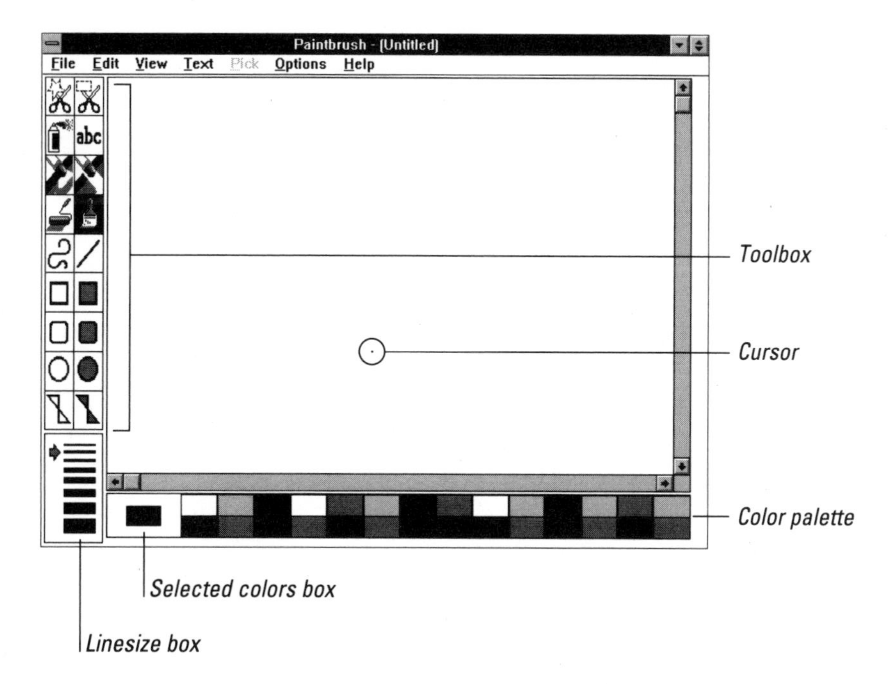

An Introduction to the Paintbrush Tools

You use the tools in the Toolbox to create or edit your picture. Clicking to select a tool determines the function of your mouse. For example, you use the Brush tool to draw freehand lines, and you use the Erase tool to remove selected areas of your picture.

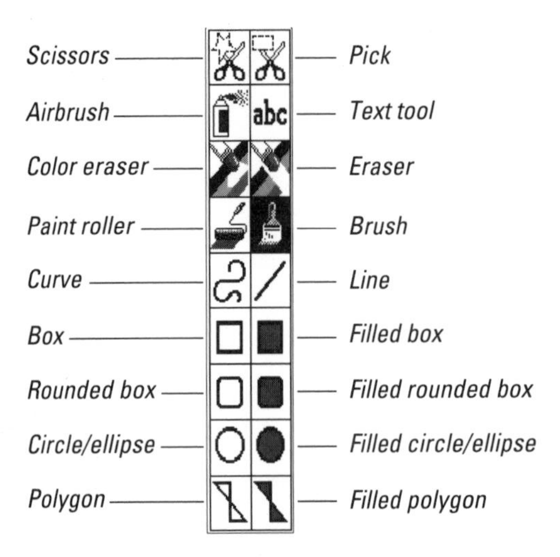

You select a tool by clicking it with the mouse. In some cases, the mouse pointer changes its shape depending upon the tool you clicked. For example, clicking the Paint Roller tool changes the mouse pointer to look like a paint roller.

Select tools

In this exercise you practice selecting the tools in the Toolbox.

1 Click the Scissors tool and move the pointer into the drawing area.

Notice that the mouse pointer is shaped like a pair of cross-hairs.

2 Click the Paint Roller tool and move into the drawing area.

The mouse pointer is now shaped like a paint roller.

3 Click the Brush tool and move the mouse pointer into the drawing area.

The mouse pointer becomes a small dot when you move it into the drawing area.

Using the Select Color box

Some of the Paintbrush tools are affected by changes to the colors selected in the Select Color box. Paintbrush uses the foreground color to draw the outline of a hollow object, such as a box. If you choose a tool that creates a filled object, such as the Filled Circle/Ellipse tool, the Paintbrush fills the object with the foreground color, and uses the background color to draw the outline for the object.

The Select Color box near the lower-left corner of the Paintbrush window shows the two colors available for drawing. The outer color is the background color, and the inner color is the foreground color.

You choose the colors using the right and left mouse buttons. Clicking a color on the palette with the *left* mouse button selects the foreground color. Clicking a color on the palette with the *right* mouse button selects the background color.

Note Unlike some Windows applications, Paintbrush uses both the right and left mouse buttons to support separate actions.

Select the colors

In this exercise you change the colors used for the foreground and background.

1. Click the yellow color with the left mouse button.

   The Select Color box immediately displays the new color in the foreground box.

2. Click the light blue color with the left mouse button.

   Light blue replaces the yellow.

3. Click the dark red color with the right mouse button.

   The Select Color box shows a box filled with light blue, framed in dark red.

4. Click the white color with the right mouse button.

   White replaces the red as the background color.

5. Click the black color with the left mouse button.

   The colors are reset to the default.

Sizing the Picture

Before you begin drawing your first picture, determine its size. The default size is based upon the type of display and amount of available memory you have in your computer. You can adjust this size so your picture is big enough for your needs, yet sized appropriately. You adjust the size of your graphic with choices in the Image Attributes dialog box. If you make a mistake, you can use the Default button to reset the picture to the original size.

Tip Size your picture so that there is very little wasted space. When you save a picture, the entire image area is saved. If you make a small picture in a large area, the saved file includes all the unused area.

You can also adjust the default measurement system used in the dialog boxes as well as the use of color or black-and-white. However, clicking the Default button does not reset these choices; you must reset them manually.

Adjust the size of the picture

1 Choose Image Attributes from the Options menu.

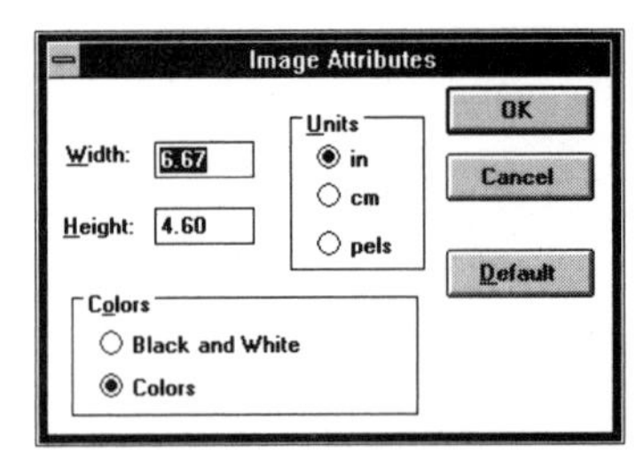

2 If necessary, click "in" (inches) under Units.

This sets the measurement system to inches.

3 Type **2** in the Width box.

4 Type **2** in the Height box.

5 Click OK.

Paintbrush uses this size as the default for all new pictures, as well as for the current picture.

Viewing the Cursor Position

You can display the position of the cursor in the Paintbrush picture. The cursor position is displayed as a set of two numbers, showing how far down and to the right the cursor is from the top left corner. These two numbers (or coordinates) show the distance in *picture elements*, or *pels* (also known as *pixels*). A standard VGA screen is 640 pels wide by 480 pels tall. Displaying the cursor position makes it easier for you to determine an object's exact dimensions.

Note If you are more comfortable drawing your picture without using the cursor position, you can skip this step.

---

1 From the View menu, choose Cursor Position.

The cursor position display shows in a small window that appears near the upper-right corner.

2 Move the mouse pointer to position 100, 100.

Notice the changes in the cursor position box.

Creating a Simple Graphic

In the next exercise you create a logo consisting of a circle with a horizontal rectangle across its middle. You also draw two spirals in the lower section of the picture.

Create a graphic

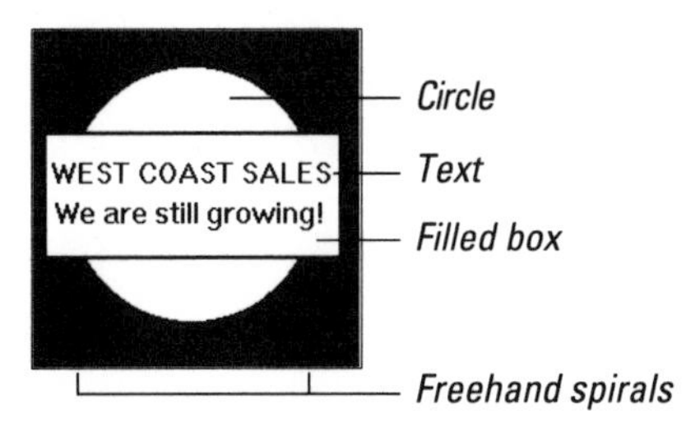

Note You can draw without using the cursor position to mark the beginning and end of each shape. However, try to make your picture match this illustration.

Hollow Oval tool

1. Click the Hollow Oval tool.
2. Move the pointer to position 20, 20 (in the upper-left corner of the drawing area) and click the left button.
3. Hold down SHIFT and drag to position 170, 170 (in the lower-right corner).

   The SHIFT key constrains the oval to a perfect circle. If the circle is not exactly where you want it to be, choose Undo from the Edit menu and try again.

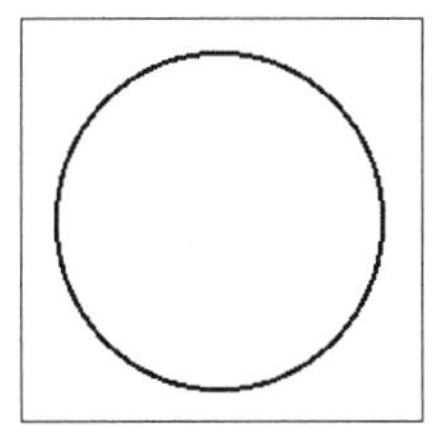

Brush tool

4. Click the Brush tool.
5. Move to position 40, 160 and draw a counterclockwise spiral that matches this illustration.

6. Move to position 150, 160 and draw another spiral, this time clockwise.

Filled Rectangle tool

7. Click the Filled Rectangle tool.

   This tool draws a black box with a white border.

Note You must use the Filled Rectangle tool to create a rectangle that covers other objects.

8 Drag from position 10, 60 to position 180, 130 to create a rectangle.

Changing the Colors in the Picture

Because you chose the filled rectangle, the rectangle covers the circle. However, the colors are *reversed*; that is, the inside is black, while the outside is white. You need to reverse the colors to create a hollow rectangle.

Revise the picture

▶ Choose Undo from the Edit menu.

Choosing Undo removes the rectangle from the picture.

Select the colors

1 Click the color white with the left mouse button.

This sets the the foreground color (the inside color for filled objects). Notice the change that occurs in the Select Color box.

2 Click the color black with the right mouse button.

This sets the color for the background (the border for filled objects). Notice the change that occurs in the example in the Select Color box.

3 Drag from the position 5, 60 to 185, 130 to create a rectangle that partially covers the existing circle.

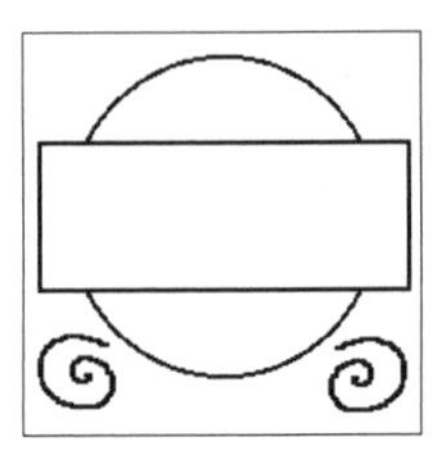

Adding Color to the Graphic

You use the Paint Roller tool to add color to an empty area of your graphic. Usually, this tool is used to color in a hollow polygon or the background of the picture, but if you are careful, you can also use it to change the color of an object's outline. The foreground color in the Select Color box is the color used by the Paint Roller.

Note Be sure the area you fill is closed (that is, the outline of the object should be solid). Otherwise, paint "leaks" from the area to be filled to the rest of the picture. If this happens, use the Undo command to remove the unwanted color.

Color the circle yellow and the background red

Paint Roller tool

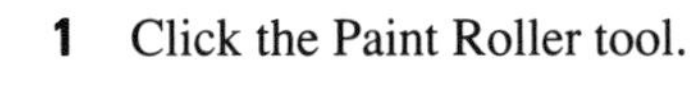

1 Click the Paint Roller tool.

   The mouse pointer changes its shape to that of a paint roller.

2 Click the color yellow with the left mouse button.

   The foreground color is set to yellow.

3 Click the hollow area of the upper part of the circle.

   The hollow area fills with yellow.

4 Click the hollow area of the lower part of the circle.

5 Click the color red with the left mouse button.

6 Click the background of the graphic.

   The background fills with red.

Adding Text to the Graphic

To add text, click in the picture with the text tool, and begin typing. Paintbrush, unlike Write, does not support wordwrap, so you must press ENTER at the end of each line. The text can be edited with the BACKSPACE key until you switch to another activity. After the text is in place, it behaves like a graphic. You can change its color or position using tools from the Toolbox, but the only way to change the text is to delete the text block and create a new one.

Add text

Text tool

1 Click the text tool.

2 Click at position 20, 80.

This sets the location where text will appear.

3 Type **WEST COAST SALES** ENTER.

4 Type **We are still growing**! ENTER

5 Click the color blue with the left mouse button.

The text changes to blue.

Moving the Text

You can move any object in your picture to another location by selecting it with the Scissors or Pick tool. After you select the object, you can move it to another location by dragging with the mouse.

Use the Scissors tool to select an irregular shape or section of the picture. Use the Pick tool to select a rectangular section of the picture. Paintbrush surrounds the selected area with a dotted line. This selected area is called a *flexible box*, because you continually change its size as you drag the mouse.

After you have selected the object, you move it with either the left or right mouse buttons. When you move an object, Paintbrush fills its former position using the background color.

Tip The left and right mouse buttons move the object, but the results are often different. If you use the left mouse button to move the object, the selection is moved as a transparent object. That is, the underlying colors and objects might show through after the move. If you use the right mouse button, the selection is moved as an opaque object. That is, the selection replaces any underlying colors and objects. However, you might not see a difference if the selection's colors are similar to the underlying colors.

Reset the colors

In this exercse you reset the colors to the default colors.

1 Click the black color with the left mouse button.

2 Click the white with the right mouse button.

Select and move the text

Pick tool

1 Click the Pick tool.

2 Use the left mouse button to draw a rectangle around the text.

This selects the text inside the dotted lines.

3 Using the left mouse button, drag the text until it is centered in the hollow rectangle.

The text is in its new location.

Save the picture

Save your work periodically when working with Paintbrush.

1 Choose Save from the File menu.

The File Save dialog box appears.

2 In the File Name box, type **MYLOGO**

3 Double-click the WIN31SBS folder icon.

This sets WIN31SBS as the default subdirectory.

4 Click OK.

Paintbrush adds the BMP extension when you save the file.

Open a picture

You can open a picture for further editing.

1 From the File menu, choose Open.

A list of available files with the BMP extension appears. Open LOGO.BMP if you did not complete the previous exercises. If you did, use MYLOGO.BMP.

2 Double-click MYLOGO.BMP or LOGO.BMP.

The picture opens.

Save a picture with a new name

You can save a picture with a new name. If the new name matches an existing filename, Paintbrush replaces it with the picture currently in the drawing area.

1 From the File menu, choose Save As.
2 Type **NEWLOGO** in the File Name box.
3 Click OK.

Printing a Picture

When you have completed your picture and saved any changes, you are ready to print.

1 Choose Print from the File menu.
2 Click Proof in the dialog box.

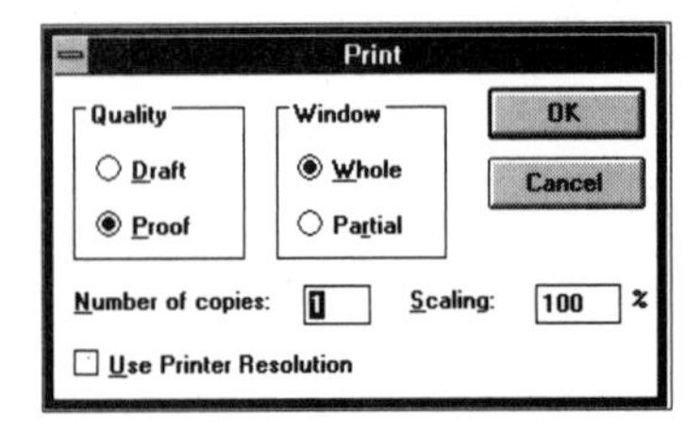

This prints the picture with the best resolution. The Draft option prints the picture faster, but with less detail.

3 Click OK.

The picture begins printing.

One Step Further

In this exercise, you draw a picture of several balloons using the Filled Oval tool and the Brush tool. In Lesson 12 you learn to use this picture as the background pattern on your Desktop.

1 Create a new picture that is 160 by 240 pels.
2 Save the file as BALLOONS.BMP.
3 Use the Filled Oval tool to draw seven ovals. Select a different fill color for each oval, and stack them so the ovals look like a group of balloons.
4 Use the Brush tool to draw strings that appear to dangle from each balloon.

Your picture probably resembles the example on the next page.

5 Save the picture again.

6 Produce a hard copy with your printer. Choose Draft for the print resolution.

If you want to continue to the next lesson

▶ Double-click the Control-menu box in the Paintbrush window.

If you want to quit Windows for now

1 Double-click the Control-menu box in the Program Manager window.

2 When the message "This will end your Windows session" appears, click OK or press ENTER.

Lesson Summary

Tool	Use to
Scissors	Define a free-form cutout.
Pick	Define a rectangular cutout.
Airbrush	Spray foreground color dots.
Text tool	Enter text.
Color Eraser	Change foreground color to background color.
Eraser	Change to background color.
Paint Roller	Fill a closed shape with the foreground color.
Brush	Draw freehand shapes and lines in the foreground color.
Curve	Draw curved lines in the foreground color.
Line	Draw straight lines in the foreground color.
Box	Draw hollow rectangles in the foreground color.

Tool	Use to
Filled Box	Draw filled rectangles that use the foreground color for the fill and the background color for the border.
Rounded Box	Draw hollow rectangles with rounded corners in the foreground color.
Filled Rounded Box	Draw filled rectangles with rounded corners that use the foreground color for the fill and the background color for the border.
Circle/Ellipse	Draw hollow circles in the foreground color.
Filled Circle/Ellipse	Draw filled circles that use the foreground color for the fill and the background color for the border.
Polygon	Draw hollow polygons in the foreground color.
Filled Polygon	Draw filled polygons that use the foreground color for the fill and the background color for the border.
Draw a graphic object	Click the appropriate tool, and then drag with the mouse.
Change a color	Click the palette display (for outside or inside), and then click a color.
Move a graphic element (transparent)	Click the Pick tool, draw a box around the element, and then drag with the left mouse button.
Move a graphic element (opaque)	Click the Pick tool, draw a box around the element, and then drag with the right mouse button.

For more information on	See the *Microsoft Windows User's Guide*
Choosing commands and working in dialog boxes	Chapter 1, "Using Menus and Dialog Boxes"
Installing and selecting a printer	Chapter 6, "Printers"

Preview of the Next Lesson

In the next lesson you learn to integrate Windows applications by cutting and pasting information, such as text or graphics, from one Windows application into another. You use this technique to copy a picture from Paintbrush and paste it into a document in Write. You also learn to use the Task Manager to select, manage, and close any open Windows application.

Integrating Windows-Based Applications

In this lesson you learn how to work with several Windows-based applications at the same time. Windows can run many applications simultaneously, so that you can view and edit information from a variety of sources. You can start several applications and use the Task List to select, manage, and close these applications. You can also cut and paste information, such as text or graphics, from one Windows application into another.

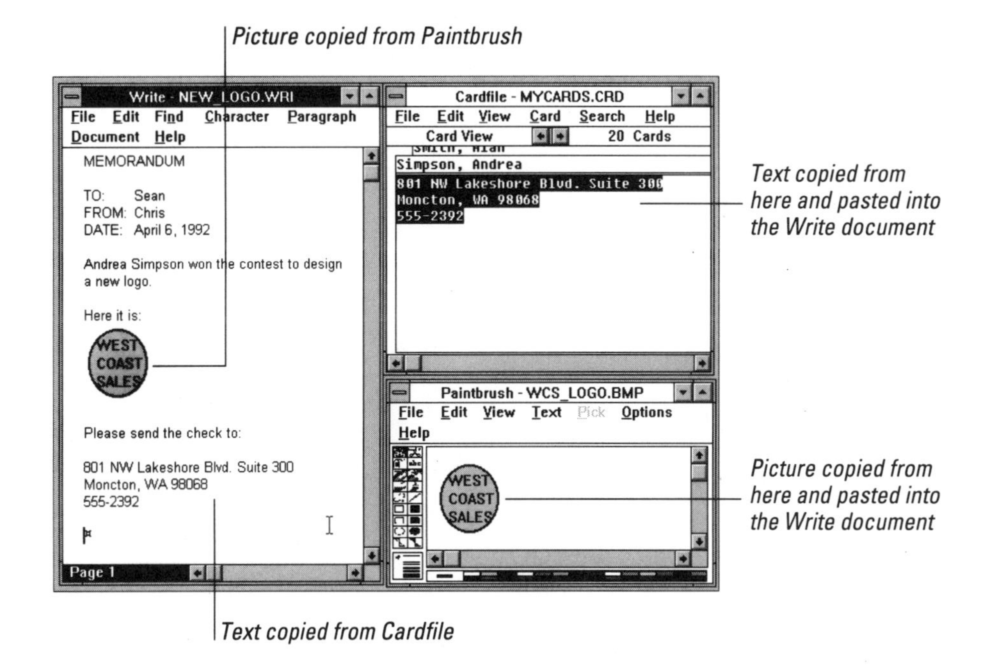

This lesson explains how to do the following:

- Use the Task List to manipulate applications
- Paste an address from Cardfile into Write
- Paste a graphic from Paintbrush into Write

Estimated lesson time: 35 minutes

Using the Task List

You can run many different applications at the same time in Windows. Each application runs in its own window. You can switch to any open application by clicking in its window. However, you might find it confusing to keep track of how many applications you have open at the same time. Often, one application's window covers another application. This makes it difficult to find the "hidden" applications.

You can use the Task List to select and manage any application. The Task List is an application that is always running anytime you are working with Windows. You use the Task List to switch to an application, to size the windows of all the open applications, or to arrange the icons of the minimized applications. You can also use the Task List to close any Windows application.

There are several ways to bring the Task List window to the foreground. You can:

- Choose Switch To from the Control-menu box of any window.
- Press CTRL+ESC.
- Double-click the desktop. (The desktop is the area behind all windows.)

There are also several ways to make an open application active. You can:

- Click its window (if it is visible).
- Select its name from Task List and click the Switch To button.
- Double-click its name from Task List.
- Press ALT+ESC, and then press enter.
- Press ALT+TAB until the application is active.

Tip If you hold down SHIFT when starting an application, Windows places it on the desktop as an icon, rather than running it as a window. This helps to manage the desktop when many applications are open at the same time.

Start several applications

In this exercise you start several applications as icons.

1. Hold down SHIFT and double-click Notepad in the Accessories Group.

   Notepad is started, but is minimized as an icon on the Desktop.

2. Hold down SHIFT and double-click Write in the Accessories Group.
3. Hold down SHIFT and double-click Cardfile in the Accessories Group.

   The three applications are now started and are placed as icons on the desktop.

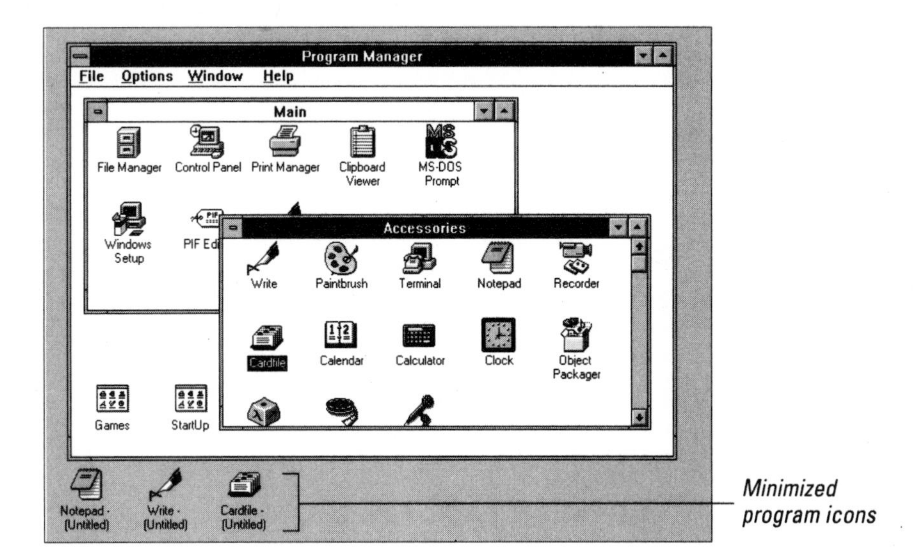

4 Click the Minimize button in the Program Manager window.

Use Task List to switch among applications

In this exercise, you explore several ways to display the Task List window.

1 Double-click anywhere on the desktop.

   The Task List window appears where you double-click.

2 Press ESC.

   The Task List window closes.

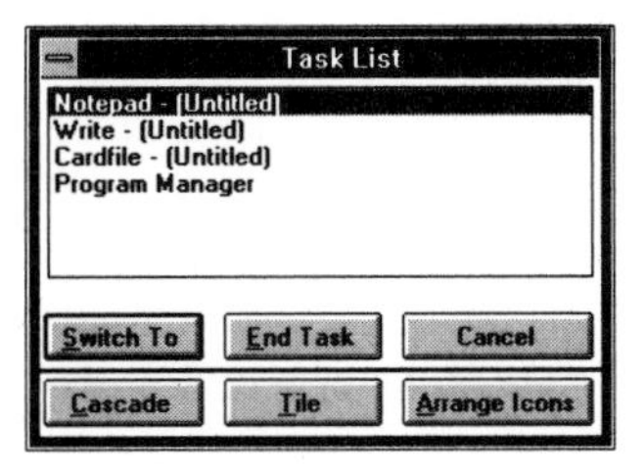

3 Press CTRL+ESC.

   The Task List window appears again. (You can also choose Switch To from the Control menu.)

4 Click Write from the names in the Task List.

5 Click the Switch To button.

   The Write window appears.

6. Hold down ALT and press TAB.
7. Continue holding down ALT and press TAB repeatedly.

   The names and icons of other running applications appear consecutively in the middle of your screen.
8. Press ALT+TAB until Cardfile appears.

   After you release ALT+TAB, the application opens.

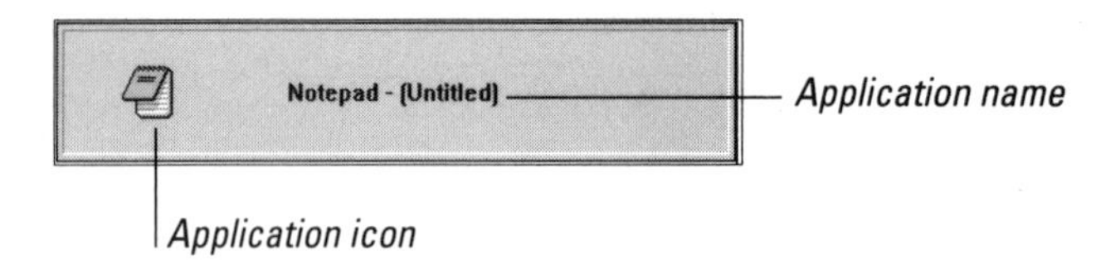

Manage applications

In this exercise, you use the Task List to arrange applications on the screen.

1. Press CTRL+ESC.
2. Click Cascade.

   The open windows are arranged as stacked windows. The most recently used application, Cardfile, is the top window.
3. Press CTRL+ESC.
4. Click Tile.

   The two open windows are arranged as tiles so that each is the same size. The most recently used application, Cardfile, is the left-most window.

Close applications

You can use the Task List to close applications.

1. Press CTRL+ESC.
2. Select the name Notepad in the Task List.
3. Click End Task.

   Windows briefly displays the Notepad window and then closes Notepad.

Working with Cardfile and Write

You can cut and paste text between most Windows-based applications. For example, you might have a set of names in a Cardfile list that you want to incorporate into a Write document. Or, you might have a name and address in a Write document that you need to add to a Cardfile list. You share information using the Copy and Paste commands on the Edit menu.

In these next exercises you copy and paste information between two applications, Write and Cardfile. You use the Task List to switch from one application to another.

Tip Open the applications that you will be using before you begin to cut and paste information. After the applications are open, use the Task List's Tile command to display and arrange the application windows on the desktop.

Arranging multiple applications

In this exercise you use the Task List to arrange the two open applications, Write and Cardfile.

1 Press CTRL+ESC.

2 Click Tile.

The two applications, Write and Cardfile, appear side by side on the desktop. Tiling these applications helps you to see where you are copying from in Cardfile, and where you are copying to in Write.

Open the Cardfile list

In this exercise, you open the Cardfile list you created in Lesson 7.

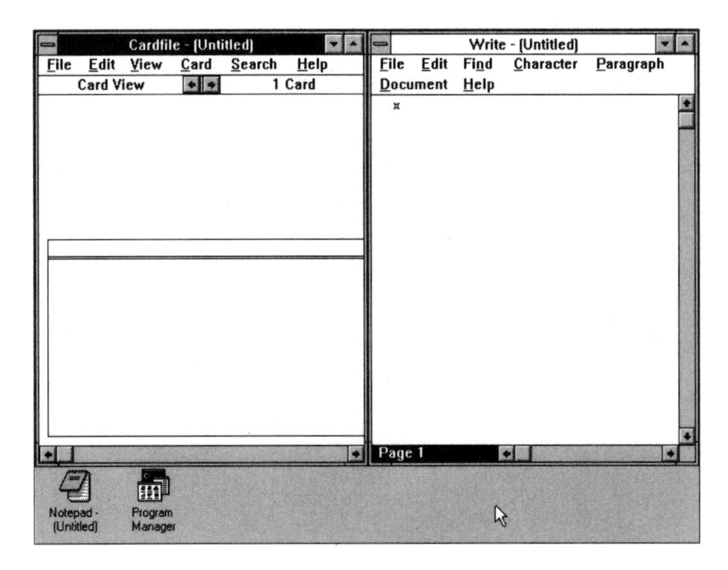

1 Click in the Cardfile window.

2 Choose Open from the File menu.

3 Double-click the WIN31SBS folder icon.

4 Double-click MYCARDS.CRD.

Copy the information to the Clipboard

1 Go to the card for Jerry Moreton.

Click on the right arrow in the status line until his card is the active card.

2 Select all the text on his card by dragging with the mouse.

3 From the Edit menu, choose Copy.

A copy of the information on Jerry's card is placed on the Clipboard.

Paste the information into Write

1 Click the Write window.

2 Type the following in a blank document. Do not press ENTER until instructed.

`Fran,` ENTER ENTER

`Here's the information you requested on Jerry Moreton. I am also enclosing a sample of the artwork.` ENTER ENTER

3 From the Edit menu, choose Paste.

The information from Cardfile is pasted into the Write document at the location of the insertion point.

4 Press ENTER twice.

This adds two new blank lines at the end of the document.

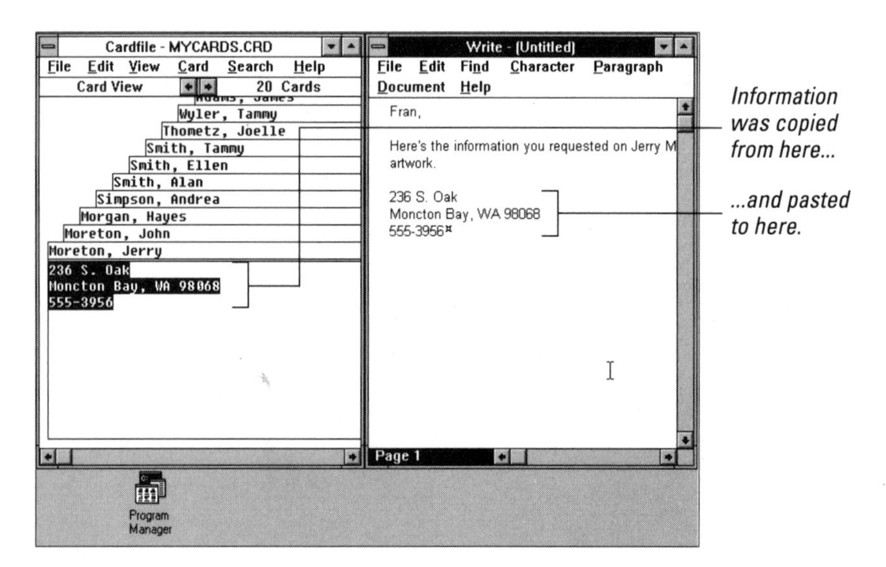

Save the Write document

1 Choose Save from the File menu.

2 Double-click the WIN31SBS folder icon.
3 Type **JERRY** in the File Name box.
4 Click OK.
5 Click the Minimize icon in the Cardfile window.

Change the configuration of Program Manager

In this exercise you change the options in Program Manager so that its window automatically shrinks when you start a new application You also change the options so that these settings are saved when you quit Windows. Automatically minimizing the Program Manager window helps you to reduce screen clutter without having to manually minimize Program Manager. Saving the option ensures that Windows works the same way the next time you start Windows.

1 Press ALT+TAB until the Program Manager window appears.
2 Open the Options menu.

   A list of options appears.

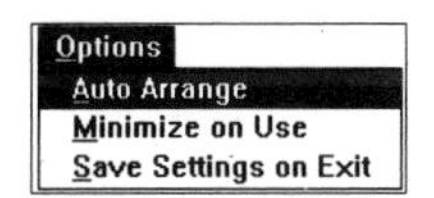

3 Choose Minimize On Use.

   This option changes the configuration of Program Manager so that each time you start an application, the Program Manager window shrinks to an icon.

4 Open the Options menu again.

   Notice that the Minimize On Use option has a check mark next to its name. This check mark shows that this option is selected.

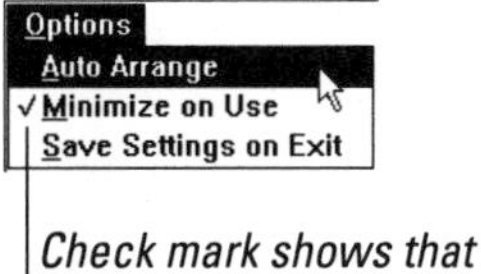

Check mark shows that the option is selected

5 Choose Save Settings On Exit.

   This option will save all your Windows settings, such as the size and position of the Program Manager and group windows, when you quit Windows. When you next restart Windows, your screen will look the same as the last time you used Windows.

Working with Paintbrush and Write

You can cut and paste graphic information between many Windows applications. These graphics come from a variety of sources, such as Paintbrush.

Set up the applications

In this exercise, you start Paintbrush and then arrange the open applications so that they are tiled. Tiling the two applications helps you to see where the source graphic is and where you want to place it into the target document.

1 Double-click Paintbrush in the Accessories group.

Paintbrush starts. Notice that Program Manager automatically shrinks to an icon.

2 Press CTRL+ESC to bring up the Task List.

3 Choose Tile.

Write and Paintbrush are tiled on the desktop.

Open the graphic file

In this exercise, you open the file MYLOGO.BMP you created in Lesson 9.

1 Click anywhere in the Paintbrush window to make it active.

2 Choose Open from the File menu.

3 Double-click the WIN31SBS folder icon.

4 Double-click MYLOGO.BMP.

Copy a graphic from Paintbrush into Write

In this exercise, you select the graphic and paste it onto the Clipboard. After you switch to Write, you paste it at the end of the existing document.

1 Use the Scissors tool to select the entire graphic.

2 From the Edit menu, choose Copy.

3 Click in the Write window to make it active.

4 Click the mouse pointer under the last line of text in the document.

This places the insertion point in the blank line under the text.

5 From the Edit menu, choose Paste.

Windows pastes the graphic into the Write document at the insertion point.

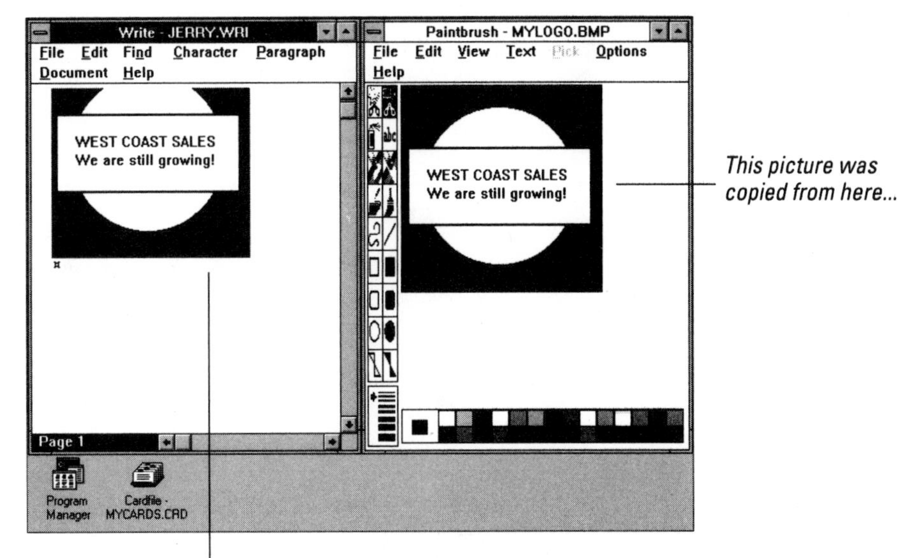

This picture was copied from here...

...and pasted to here.

Close unused applications

After you have copied the information from an open application, close the unused application. Closing the application increases the available memory for other Windows applications.

1 Press CTRL+ESC to open the Task List.

2 Select the name Paintbrush in the Task List.

3 Click End Task.

  Windows closes Paintbrush.

4 Press CTRL+ESC to open the Task List again.

5 Select Cardfile.

6 Click End Task.

  Windows closes Cardfile.

Move the graphic

You can change the placement of the graphic in the Write document using the Move Picture command. You can only move the graphic horizontally with this command. If you want to move the graphic to another position in the document, you must cut and paste it.

1 Click the Maximize button in the Write window.

2 Click the graphic to select it.

3 From the Edit menu, choose Move Picture.

The cursor changes to a double box.

4 Drag the graphic about 1 inch to the right.

You can move the graphic left or right only on the same line. You cannot move it up or down.

5 Click the mouse.

When you click the mouse button, Move Picture command stops and the graphic remains in its new position.

Size the graphic

You change the size of the graphic with the Size Picture command.

1 Click the graphic to select it.

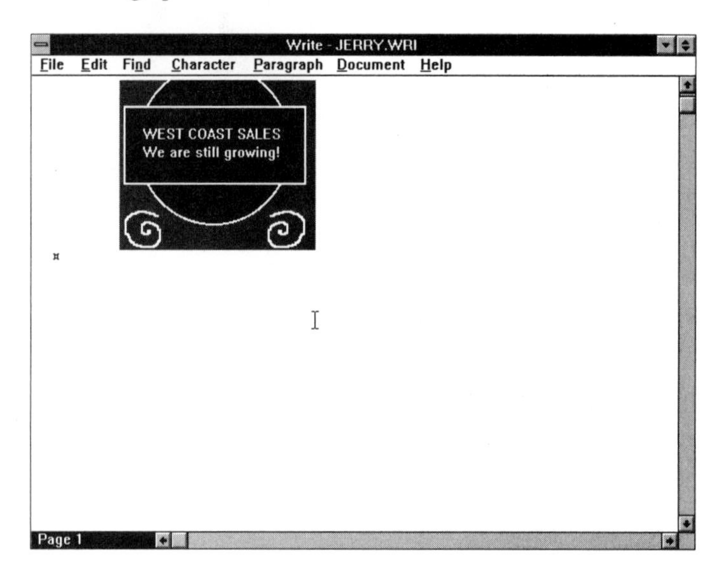

2 From the Edit menu, choose Size Picture.

The mouse pointer changes to a double box.

3 Move the mouse pointer down and to the left, about an inch below the bottom of the logo.

This stretches the graphic to a larger size.

4 Click the mouse button.

When you click the mouse button, the graphic stays at its new size.

5 Choose Save from the File menu.

If you want to continue to the next lesson

1. Choose Exit from the File menu in Write.

   Write closes.

2. Click the Cardfile icon.

   The Control menu appears.

3. Click Close.

   Cardfile closes.

4. If Windows displays a message asking you if you want to save changes in any application, click No.

5. Double-click the Program Manager icon.

   The Program Manager window is restored.

If you want to quit Windows for now

1. Double-click the Control-menu box in the Program Manager window.

2. When the message "This will end your Windows session" appears, click OK or press ENTER.

One Step Further

In this exercise you practice your skills learned in this lesson. You copy a map drawn in Paintbrush and paste it into a Cardfile list.

First you start Paintbrush and Cardfile, and open the file MAP.BMP.

1. Start Paintbrush and Cardfile.
2. Minimize the Program Manager window.
3. Press CTRL+ESC and click the Tile button.
4. Click in the Paintbrush window and open the file MAP.BMP in the C:\WINDOWS\WIN31SBS subdirectory.
5. Click the Pick tool (it looks like a pair of scissors cutting out a box), and drag around the map to select it.
6. Choose Copy from the Edit menu.

   A copy of the map is put onto the Clipboard.

Next you open the MYCARDS.CRD file and paste the map onto the card for Hayes Morgan.

1. Click in the Cardfile window and open the file MYCARDS.CRD in the C:\WINDOWS\WIN31SBS subdirectory.
2. Scroll to the card for Hayes Morgan.
3. Choose Picture from the Edit menu.

   You must switch from Text to Picture in Cardfile before you paste in a graphic image.
4. Choose Paste from the Edit menu.

   The copy of the map from Paintbrush is pasted onto the card for Hayes Morgan. The picture covers the address information on the card.
5. Drag the picture over to the right until the address information for Hayes Morgan reappears.
6. Choose Save from the File menu in Cardfile.

   The file is saved.
7. Double-click the Control-menu box in Cardfile.

   Cardfile closes.
8. Double-click the Control-menu box in Paintbrush.

   Paintbrush closes.
9. Double-click the Program Manager icon.

   The Program Manager window is restored.

Lesson Summary

To	Do this
Cut and paste text between applications	Start both applications. Select the text you want to copy in the source application. From the Edit menu choose Copy. Click the other application's window, and click the place in the document where you wish the new text to be inserted. From the Edit menu choose Paste.
Cut and paste graphics between applications	Start both applications. Select the graphic in the source application. From the Edit menu choose Copy. Click the other application's window, and click the place in the document where you want to insert the new graphic. From the Edit menu choose Paste.
Move a graphic to the left or right in Write	Select the graphic. From the Edit menu choose Move Picture. Move the mouse pointer left or right, until the graphic is in the position you wish. Click the mouse to set it in place.
Size a graphic in Write	Select the graphic. From the Edit menu choose Size Picture. Move the mouse pointer until the graphic is the size you wish. Click the mouse to confirm the new size.

For more information on	See the ***Microsoft Windows User's Guide***
Copying text	Chapter 9, "Write"
Copying graphics	Chapter 10, "Paintbrush"

Preview of the Next Lesson

In the next lesson, you learn how to use the Control Panel to customize your Windows environment. You select and change your screen colors, and learn how to create your own custom color scheme. You choose a background picture for your Desktop, one of which is the Paintbrush drawing you created previously. You also use the Control Panel to change the date and time of your computer's internal clock.

Part 5

Customizing Your Work Environment

Using the Control Panel

The Control Panel customizes your Windows environment. This lesson shows you how to select and change your screen colors, and how to create your own custom color scheme. You use a picture as the background for your desktop, and change the date and time of your computer.

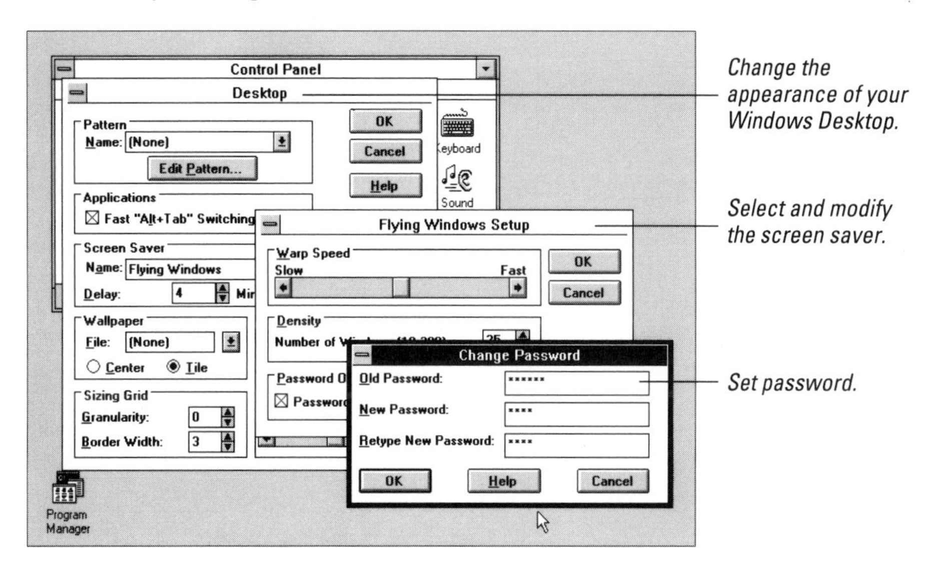

This lesson explains how to do the following:

- Start the Control Panel
- Set up a color scheme
- Set up and configure the Desktop
- Set the date and time

Estimated lesson time: 45 minutes

Starting the Control Panel

The Control Panel customizes the operation and appearance of Windows. The Control Panel is a window consisting of a collection of utilities to set your screen colors, modify the appearance of your desktop, and change the date and time. (You can also modify other features of Windows using the Control Panel. Some of these are discussed in Lesson 13, "Fonts and Basic Printing," while others outside the scope of this book are described in your Windows documentation.)

The Control Panel Icons

The Control Panel contains about one dozen icons, depending upon your type of machine and how you initially installed Windows. Each icon represents a utility that can change an aspect of your Windows environment.

Start the Control Panel

1 Find the Control Panel icon.

The Control Panel is in the Main group.

2 Double-click the Control Panel icon.

Control panel icon

The Control Panel is displayed on the desktop. Because you selected Minimize On Use in Lesson 11, the Program Manager window shrinks to an icon. Reducing Program Manager to an icon lets you see more of the desktop, so you can see how changes you make with the Control Panel affect the desktop and other Windows elements, such as the scroll bars or window borders.

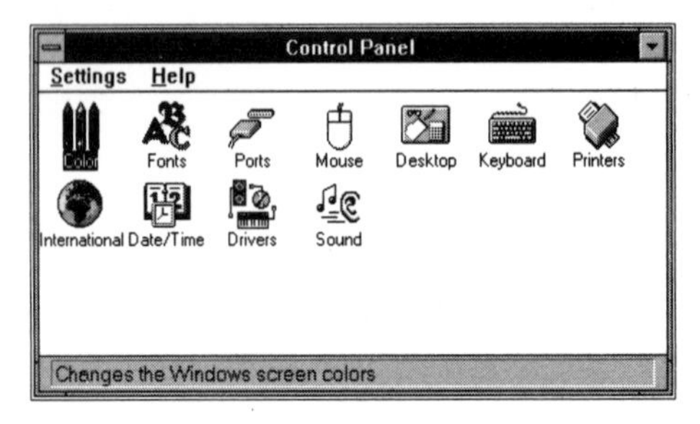

Check the functions of the icons

Each icon runs a different utility. If you are not sure what the icon does when it runs, you can click the icon with the mouse. When you do, a short phrase describing the purpose of the selected icon appears in the bottom line of the Control Panel window.

1 Click the Mouse icon.

The phrase "Changes settings for your mouse" is displayed at the bottom of the Control Panel.

2 Click the International icon.

The phrase "Specifies international settings" is displayed at the bottom of the Control Panel.

Customizing Your Display

You use several of the icons in the Control Panel to customize your Windows environment. The Color icon changes your color scheme, and the Desktop icon selects a background picture or design.

Modifying Screen Colors

Each Windows element, such as the scroll bars or window borders, is assigned a color from the *color palette*. The collection of these colors assigned to each object is called the *color scheme*.

As a convenience, color schemes can be saved and selected by name. Each Windows element is initially colored using the default color scheme named "Windows Default." You can select a different color scheme by selecting one of the named color schemes, or you can create your own by choosing a selection of colors for the Windows elements from the color palette. After you select new colors, you can name and save your settings as a new color scheme.

If you do not have a color monitor

Windows has several color schemes that are designed for use on monochrome or LCD (liquid crystal display) screens. These color schemes work best with the absence of a color display. Choose one of these color schemes, such as "Monochrome" or "LCD Default Screen," if the default color setup is not satisfactory. If your display can display multiple shades of gray, your screen element shows a selection of grays.

Select the color scheme

You create or select a different color scheme from the choices displayed in the Color dialog box. Each predefined color scheme is listed in the Color Schemes box.

1 Find the Color icon in the Control Panel.

This icon is a group of three crayons.

Color icon

2 Double-click the Color icon.

The Color dialog box appears.

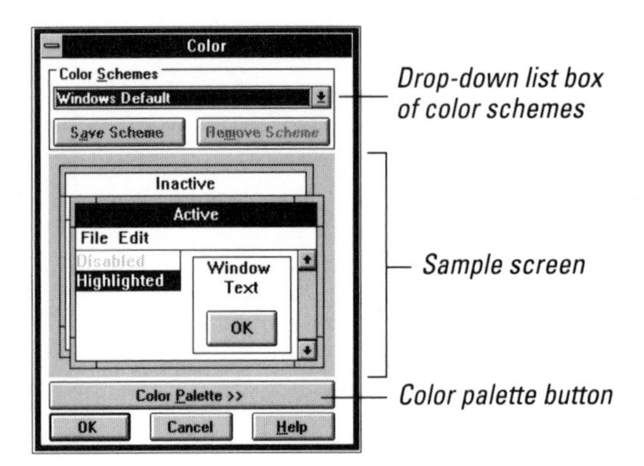

3 Click the down arrow on the right side of the Color Schemes box.

A list of color schemes appears. The current color scheme in the Color Schemes box shows Windows Default.

4 Click Arizona in the Color Schemes box.

The screen colors in the sample screen are set to the colors used in the Arizona color scheme.

5 Click the down arrow on the right side of the Color Schemes box.

6 Scroll down and click Fluorescent.

7 Click the down arrow on the right side of the Color Schemes box.

8 Scroll up and click Windows Default.

9 Click OK at the bottom of the dialog box.

The Color dialog box closes. The screen colors are set to the Windows Default color scheme.

Expand the color dialog box

You change the color of the screen elements using the Color utility; however, you must first *expand* the Color dialog box using the Color Palette button to change individual elements to other basic and custom colors. The expanded Color dialog box shows the selection of choices available in the Color Palette.

1 Double-click the Color icon.

2 Click the Color Palette button.

This button expands the Color dialog box to reveal settings for basic and custom colors.

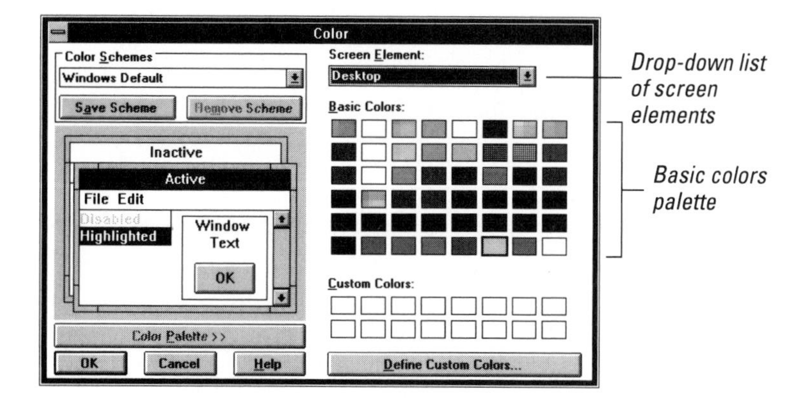

Change the color palette

There are two methods for selecting a different color for a screen element. You can select a screen element by clicking it in the sample screen box. After you have selected the element, click a color in the Basic Colors palette. The selected element is set to this color. This is often the fastest way to change the color of a screen element. However, you might have difficulty selecting the smaller screen elements such as the shadow or highlight on the "OK" button using this procedure.

To select these smaller screen elements, you can select them by name from the list in the Screen Element box. Click the name of screen element you wish to change and then click the color that you want for that screen element.

Tip The sample screen shows the current color scheme. The changes you make affect this color scheme. You might want to select an existing color scheme that has most of the colors set to the settings you want before you start changing the colors of the screen elements. This saves the time it takes to select and change the color of every screen element.

---

1. Click the active title bar in the sample screen.

   The phrase in the Screen Element box should say "Active Title Bar." If it says "Active Title Bar Text," click the title bar again until the phrase says "Active Title Bar."

2. Click the third square from the right in the top row.

   The title bar is now set to a medium blue.

3. Click the down arrow to the right of the Screen Element box.

   A menu of screen elements appears.

4. Scroll up to find Desktop.
5. Click Desktop.

6 Click the fourth square from the left in the top row.

The Desktop is set to a light green.

7 Click OK.

The Color dialog box closes.

Creating a New Color Scheme

The new color scheme you have selected sets the colors for the screen elements. You might want to switch to another color scheme, however. If you do, your custom color scheme will be replaced by the new color scheme, and your original custom color scheme will be lost. To save yourself the time of re-creating your color scheme, you can save it as a name. Name any new color scheme you want to keep as soon as you are satisfied with your color selections.

The name you choose appears at the bottom of the current list of color scheme names. You can choose it just as you would any of the predefined color schemes. Be careful when you choose a name for your custom color scheme. If the one you choose matches an existing color scheme, that one will be replaced with your new color scheme.

Create a custom color scheme

In this exercise you create a custom color scheme and give it a new name.

1 Double-click the Color icon.

Notice that the name of the current color scheme is blank. Whenever you have changed a screen element, the name of the color scheme is blank. Also, notice that the Save Scheme button is disabled (it appears dimmed). This button is enabled only when you have expanded the Color dialog box.

2 Click the Color Palette button.

3 Click the Save Scheme button.

The Save Scheme dialog box appears.

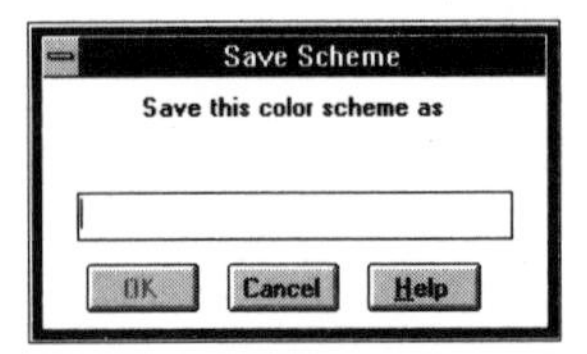

4 Type **My Colors** in the box and click OK.

Examine the new color scheme

1 Click the down arrow to the right of the Color Schemes box.

A list of color scheme names appears. Notice that your new color scheme appears at the bottom of the list.

2 Click Wingtips.

The screen colors are set to shades of brown and gray.

3 Click the down arrow to the right of the Color Schemes box.

4 Click My Colors.

The screen colors reset to your custom color palette.

5 Click OK.

The Color dialog box closes.

Remove a color scheme

You can remove a color scheme using the Color dialog box. Be sure that you never plan to use it again. So many color selections are involved that after a color scheme is removed, it cannot easily be re-created.

Note Skip this exercise if you want to keep your custom color scheme.

---

1 Double-click the Color icon.

2 Click the color scheme My Colors.

This step ensures you select the correct color scheme to remove. When you open the drop-down list, the list box covers the Remove Scheme button.

3 Click the color scheme My Colors again.

This step closes the list and leaves the color scheme My Colors selected.

4 Click the Remove Scheme button.

A dialog box appears for you to confirm the deletion.

5 Click Yes.

The color scheme is removed. Windows resets the color to the previous scheme on the list, Wingtips.

Reset the color scheme

1 Click the down arrow to the right of the Color Schemes box.

2 Scroll up to find Windows Default.

3 Click Windows Default.

4 Click OK.

The Color dialog box closes. The screen colors reset to the Windows Default color scheme.

Modifying the Appearance of the Desktop

You can change the way your desktop looks by using the Desktop icon in the Control Panel. You can set a new design for the desktop, or choose a picture to be used as a background. You can also choose a screen saver to turn off the display of your monitor after a specified time.

Set the screen pattern

The default desktop is a solid color that you set using the Color icon in the Control Panel. You can change the appearance of your desktop by replacing the solid color with a *pattern*. A pattern is a small design that is repeated many times on your desktop to form an intricate mosaic.

1 Find the Desktop icon in the Control Panel.

Desktop icon.

2 Double-click the Desktop icon.

The Desktop dialog box appears.

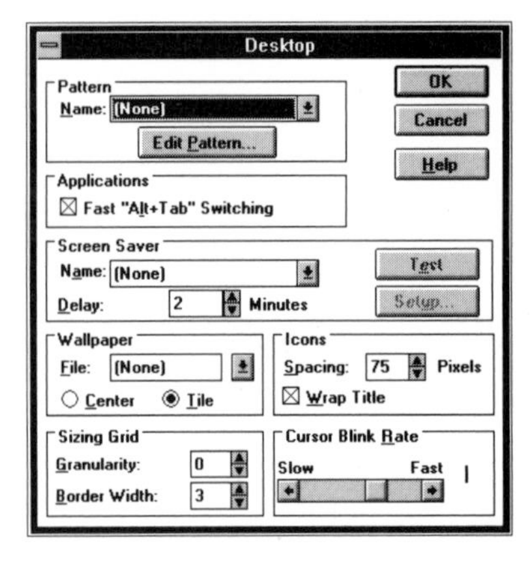

3 In the box named Pattern, click the down arrow to the right of the Name box.

A list of patterns appears. The word (None) is highlighted because there is no pattern selected.

4 Click the pattern named Boxes.

5 Click OK.

The desktop pattern changes to a series of tiny boxes.

Create a new pattern

You can create your own pattern for the Desktop. Your pattern can be as simple or as complex as you wish, as long as it fits into a block eight pels high and eight pels wide. After you have created your pattern, you must save it with a name. If you choose an existing pattern name, your new pattern replaces the existing pattern.

1 Double-click the Desktop icon.

2 Click the Edit Pattern button.

The Edit Pattern dialog box appears. Note that the sample to the left shows the results of editing the pattern. Click in the area to the right to create the pattern. Each time you click in the area to the right of the pattern, the current block (representing one pel) changes to its opposite color. Because the current pattern is "Boxes," your new pattern is based on its design. To start with a blank design, choose "(None)" as the pattern before you click Edit Pattern.

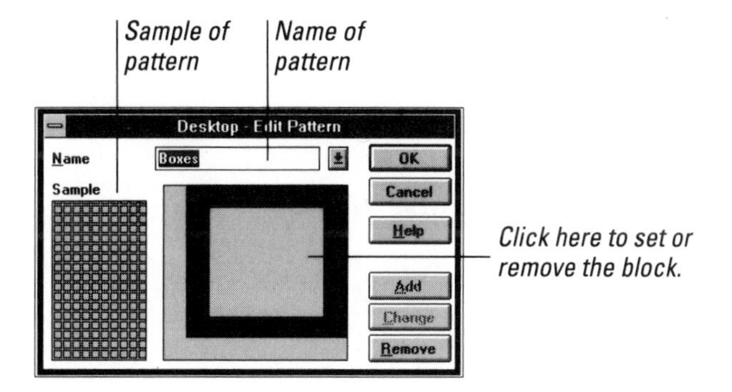

3 Type **My Boxes**

This is the new name for your pattern.

4 Click several times in the pattern area with the mouse to create your own pattern.

5 Click the Add button.

The pattern is added to the list, and becomes the selected pattern.

6 Click OK.

The Edit Pattern dialog box closes.

7 Click OK.

The Desktop dialog box closes. The new pattern appears on your Desktop.

Remove a pattern

When you have a pattern you no longer want, you can remove it from the Patterns list in the Desktop dialog box.

Note Skip this exercise if you want to keep your pattern.

---

1. Double-click the Desktop icon.
2. Click Edit Pattern.
3. Click My Boxes.

   This ensures that you have selected the correct pattern.
4. Click Remove.

   A dialog box appears asking you to confirm the removal.
5. Click Yes.

   The pattern is removed.
6. Click OK.

   The Edit Pattern dialog box closes.
7. Click OK.

   The Desktop dialog box closes.

Setting the Wallpaper

You can customize your desktop to display a picture as background *wallpaper*. The wallpaper can be any picture that is formatted as a Paintbrush file. This picture cannot be larger than the current screen. Windows comes with many files to use for wallpaper. These files are contained in the \WINDOWS subdirectory. You can also use other pictures, as long as they are not larger than the current screen.

Note It is possible to set the desktop to display both a pattern and a wallpaper. However, the picture you select as wallpaper is displayed on top of the design you select as a pattern. In this case, you cannot see the pattern except as the background of applications that are shrunk to icons on the desktop.

If the wallpaper is fairly small, you can *tile* it. Tiled wallpaper is repeated so that no extra space remains on the desktop. Unusual and interesting patterns can develop when you tile wallpaper. If the wallpaper is large, so that it does not look good when it is tiled, you can center it on the Desktop. Any extra space around the wallpaper is filled with the desktop color.

Center the wallpaper

1. Double-click the Desktop icon.
2. In the Wallpaper box, click the down arrow next to the File drop-down list box.

   A list of available wallpaper is displayed. The word (None) is highlighted because no wallpaper is selected.

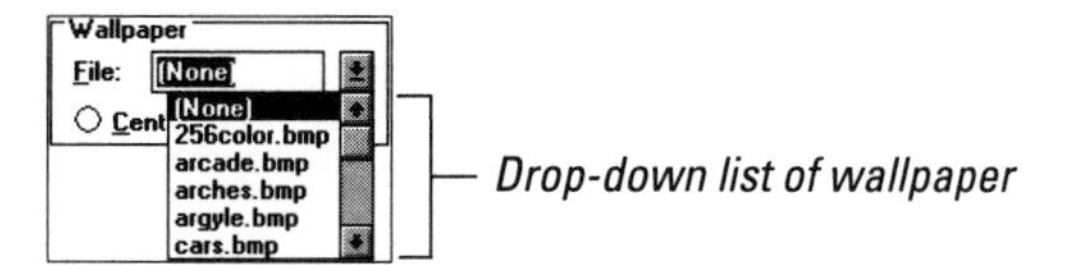

Drop-down list of wallpaper

3 Scroll down and click TARTAN.BMP.
4 Click Center.
  This centers the wallpaper on the desktop.
5 Click OK.
6 Move the Control Panel if necessary to see the centered wallpaper.
  The Desktop shows the wallpaper.

Tile the wallpaper

1 Double-click the Desktop icon.
2 Click the down arrow next to the File drop-down list box in the box named Wallpaper.
3 Click CARS.BMP.
4 Click Tile.
  This repeats the picture to fill the desktop.
5 Click OK.
  The Desktop fills with a pattern that looks like parked cars.

Reset the desktop

You can reset the desktop so no wallpaper is used. If you run low on memory in Windows, reset your wallpaper to "(None)." Removing the wallpaper saves memory that can be used by other applications.

Note Skip this exercise if you want to keep your wallpaper.

---

1 Double-click the Desktop icon.
2 Click the down arrow next to the File box under Wallpaper.
3 Scroll up to find (None).
4 Click (None).
  This removes the wallpaper.
5 Click OK.

Using a Screen Saver

Many Windows elements are displayed in the same place in each application. For example, the Control-menu box, the Minimize and Restore icons, and the scroll bars are always displayed in the same areas of the screen. After much time has passed, these images might permanently mark the screen as "ghost images." (This is true of any application that displays information in the same area for extended periods of time.)

You can avoid this damage by using a *screen saver*. A screen saver is an application that blanks the screen after a predetermined amount of time of inactivity. Many screen savers also include some type of moving graphic or pattern, so that you are reminded that the computer is still turned on.

A screen saver can also include a password option. After a passworded screen saver has taken control of the computer and is displaying its moving graphic or pattern, no one can regain use of the computer while it is still turned on without typing the correct password.

The Windows screen saver is an option you set using the Desktop icon on the Control Panel. Windows comes with several screen savers. You can customize many of these screen savers to suit your own preferences.

Select a screen saver

1 Double-click the Desktop icon.

2 Click the down arrow to the right of the Name drop-down list box in the box named Screen Saver.

A list of screen savers appears. The current screen saver is (None).

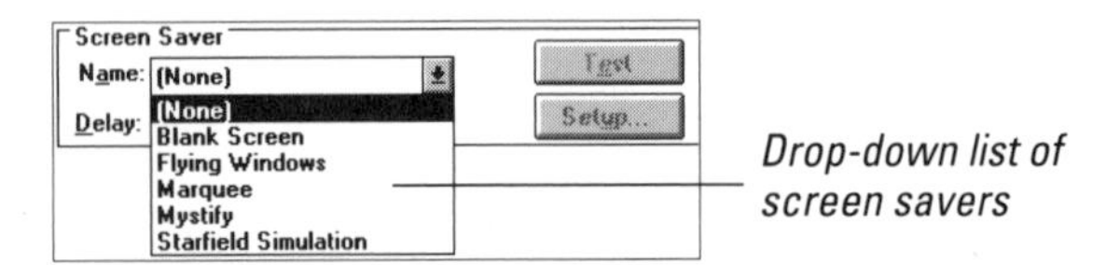

Drop-down list of screen savers

3 Click Flying Windows.

This sets the screen saver to the Flying Windows moving graphic.

4 Click Test.

The Flying Windows screen saver appears. It remains on the screen until you press a key or move the mouse.

5 Move the mouse.

The Flying Windows screen saver disappears.

Change the delay time

You can determine the number of minutes to elapse during a period of inactivity before the screen saver will take control of the computer. You can set this delay from one to 99 minutes.

1. Click the up arrow next to the Delay text box.

   The number of minutes increases by one.

2. Hold down the mouse button on this up arrow.

   The number of minutes begins to increase.

3. Double-click in the Delay text box.
4. Type **5** in the Delay text box.

   You can enter a value from 1 to 99 minutes.

5. Click the down arrow once.

   Clicking the up or down arrow is an alternate way to change the number of minutes that elapse before the screen saver begins.

Configure the screen saver

Many screen savers have options, such as the number of graphic images displayed or the speed at which the graphic images move. You configure these options by clicking the Setup button.

1. Click the Setup button.

   The Flying Windows Setup dialog box appears.

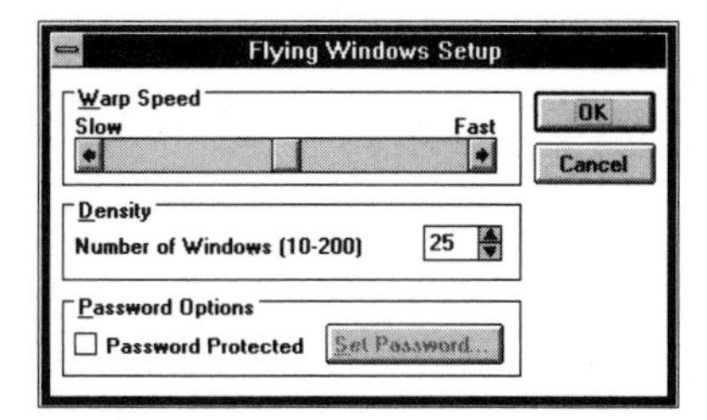

2. Move the scroll box on the Warp Speed scroll bar to the right.

   This scroll bar is used to control the speed of flight for the Flying Windows.

3. Double-click in the Density box and type **50**.

   This sets the number of graphic images to 50.

4. Click OK.

5 Click Test.

The Test button makes the screen saver appear immediately. Notice that more graphic images appear than before, and they move faster.

6 Move the mouse to turn off the screen saver.

Set the password

You can set a password so that no one can regain control of Windows until either the correct password is used or the current password is removed.

Caution Any word you choose as you password is *encrypted*, and appears only as a series of asterisks when you type it in a dialog box. Write the new password down and put it in a safe place, away from a casual observer. If you forget your password, there is no way in Windows to unlock the computer.

If you are entering a password for the first time, simply type it in the dialog box. If you are changing your password, you must enter your old password first, and then enter a new password.

Note A password is not a replacement for good security procedures. A skilled Windows user can defeat a password.

Your password can be any short word or phrase you wish. You can mix letters and numbers. Windows ignores upper or lower case for the password.

1 Click Setup.

The Flying Windows Setup dialog box appears.

2 Click the Password Protected check box under Password Options.

You must click this box to enable the password protection.

3 Click Set Password.

The Change Password dialog box appears. (Note that because this is the first time a password is set, the Old Password box is disabled.)

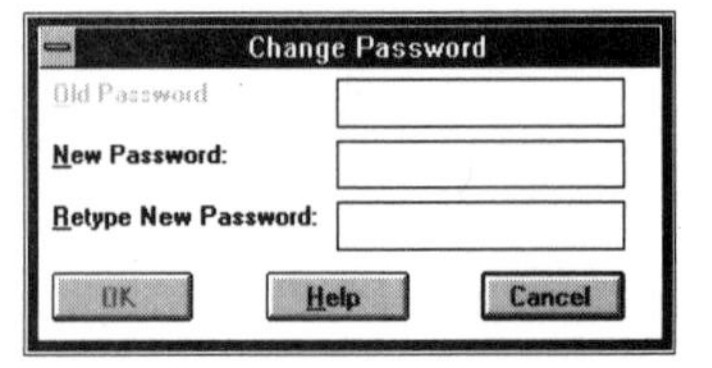

4 Type **Secret** in the New Password box.

This is the new password. Note that asterisks appear instead of the word when you type in the box.

5 Type **Secret** in the Retype New Password box.

You must confirm the new password by retyping it.

6 Click OK.

7 Click OK.

Test the password

In this exercise you test the password. Check that it works by first using the correct password. Test it again by using the wrong password.

1 Click Test.

The screen saver reappears.

2 Move the mouse.

A dialog box appears for you to type the password.

3 Type **Secret** in the Password box and click OK.

Because this is the correct password your screen redisplays the Desktop dialog box.

4 Click Test.

This time use the wrong password for a demonstration of the security feature of the password.

5 Move the mouse.

6 Type **Testing** in the Password box and click OK.

This is the wrong password, but you are simply testing the security of the password system. A dialog box appears, warning that you used the wrong password.

7 Click OK.

8 Move the mouse and type **Secret** in the Password box.

This is the correct password.

9 Click OK.

Your screen re-displays the Desktop dialog box.

Disable the password

You can disable the password when you no longer need to keep your computer secure.

Note Skip this exercise if you want to keep your password.

---

1 Click Setup.

2 Click the Password Protected check box to remove the X in the check box.

This disables the password protection.

3 Click OK.

Remove the screen saver

You can disable the screen saver feature by choosing (None) from the list of screen savers.

Note Skip this exercise if you want to keep your screen saver.

---

1 Click the down arrow next to Name under Screen Saver.

2 Click (None).

Choosing (None) disables the screen saver.

3 Click OK.

The Desktop dialog box closes.

Setting the Date and Time

The date and time are set using the Date/Time icon in the Control Panel.

1 Find the Date/Time icon.

Date/time icon

2 Double-click the Date/Time icon.

The Date & Time dialog box appears.

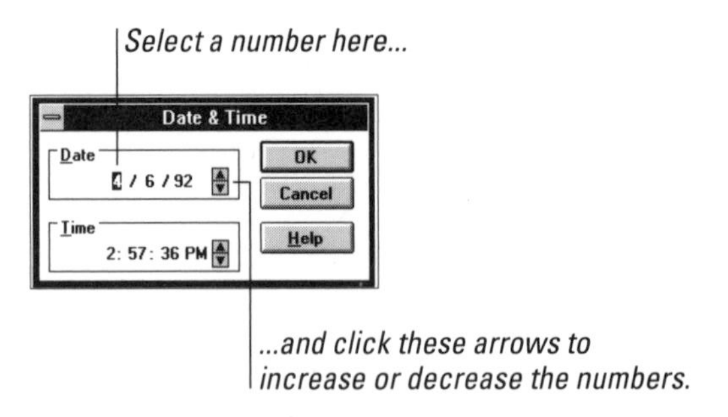

3 Select the digits for the month in the box named Date.

4 Click the up arrow next to the Date.

The date advances by one month.

5 Click the down arrow.

6 Select the digits for the hour in the box named Time.

7 Type **8**

The hour is set to eight o'clock.

8 Click the appropriate arrow next to the Time until the hour is reset to the current time.

This is an alternate way to change the number.

9 Click OK.

Any changes are accepted and the dialog box closes.

Close the Control Panel

▶ Double-click the Control-menu box in the upper-left corner of the Control Panel window.

The Control Panel closes.

One Step Further

In this exercise you use a Paintbrush picture as your wallpaper. After you examine the effect of using the Picture, you reset the wallpaper to (None).

1 Double-click the Program Manager icon.

The Program Manager window is restored.

2 Double-click the Control Panel icon in the Program Manager window.

The Control Panel window appears. Because you set the Program Manager window to minimize automatically, the Program Manager window shrinks to an icon.

3 Double-click the Desktop icon in the Control Panel.

The Desktop dialog box appears.

4 Select the current name in the File drop-down list box under Wallpaper.

5 Type **C:\WINDOWS\WIN31SBS\MYLOGO.BMP**

This is the location and file name of the Paintbrush file you created previously.

6 Click OK.

Because you clicked the Tile button earlier in this lesson, the file MYLOGO.BMP is tiled on the Desktop.

7 Open Desktop again and click the arrow in the File box.

The drop-down list of pattern names appears.

8 Scroll up and click (None).

This resets the wallpaper patter to (None).

9 Click OK.

This removes the wallpaper.

If you want to continue to the next lesson

▶ Double-click the Program Manager icon.

The Program Manager window is restored.

If you want to quit Windows for now

1 Double-click the Program Manager icon.

The Program Manager window is restored.

2 Double-click the Control-menu box in the Program Manager window.

3 When the message "This will end your Windows session" appears, click OK or press ENTER.

Lesson Summary

To	Do this
Check the function of an icon in the Control Panel	Click on the icon and view the bottom of the Control Panel.
Choose an existing color scheme	Double-click the Color icon. Click the down arrow under Color Scheme, and click one of the color schemes. Click OK.
Create a new color scheme	Double-click the Color icon. Click Color Palette. Click the screen element you want to change, then click the color you want. Click OK. *or* Click the down arrow under Screen Element and click the name of the screen element. Then click the color you wish. Click OK.
Save a new color scheme	Double-click the Color icon. Click Color Palette and make the changes to the color scheme. Click Save Scheme and type a new name. Click OK.
Remove a color scheme	Double-click the Color icon. Select a color scheme from the Color Scheme list. Click Remove Scheme. Click OK. Click OK again.
Set the screen pattern	Double-click the Desktop icon. Click the down arrow to the right of the Name box under Pattern. Click a pattern name and click OK. Click OK again.

To	Do this
Create a new screen pattern	Double-click the Desktop icon. Click Edit Pattern. Click in the sample area to turn on or turn off the blocks. Type a name for the pattern. Click Add. Click OK. Click OK again.
Remove a screen pattern	Double-click the Desktop icon. Click the down arrow to the right of the Name box under Pattern. Click a pattern name and click Edit Pattern. Click Remove. Click Yes. Click OK. Click OK again.
Select a wallpaper	Double-click the Desktop icon. Click the down arrow next to File under Wallpaper. Click a wallpaper. Click Tile or Center. Click OK.
Select a Paintbrush picture as wallpaper.	Double-click the Desktop icon. Type a filename (including the extension BMP) in the box next to File under Wallpaper. Click Tile or Center. Click OK.
Reset the wallpaper	Double-click the Desktop icon. Click the down arrow next to File under Wallpaper. Click (None). Click OK.
Select a screen saver	Double-click the Desktop icon. Click the down arrow to the right of Name under Screen Saver. Click a screen saver. Click OK.
Test a screen saver	Double-click the Desktop icon. Click the test button. To restore the screen, move the mouse or press any key. If necessary, type the password in the Password box. Click OK.
Change the delay time for a screen saver	Double-click the Desktop icon. Click the up or down arrows next to Delay to set the time from 1 to 99 minutes. *or* Double-click the Desktop icon. Select the time in the Delay box, and type a new number from one to 99. Click OK.
Configure the screen saver	Double-click the Desktop icon. Click Setup. Adjust any scroll boxes in the scroll bars. Change any values in the boxes. Click OK. Click OK again.
Set a password for a screen saver	Double-click the Desktop icon. Click Setup. Click the Password Protect box to place a check mark in the box. Click Set Password. Type the current password (if any) in the Old Password box. Type the new password in the New Password box. Retype this password in the Retype Password box. Click OK. Click OK again.
Disable the password for a screen saver	Double-click the Desktop icon. Click Setup. Click the Password Protect box to remove the check mark. Click OK. Click OK again.

To	Do this
Remove the screen saver	Double-click the Desktop icon. Click the down arrow next to Name under Screen Saver. Click (None). Click OK.
Set the date and time	Double-click the Date/Time icon. Select the digits you want to change in the date or time. Click the up or down arrows. Click OK.

Preview of the Next Lesson

In the next lesson you learn how to identify and use fonts to enhance your documents. By choosing different fonts and sizes, you can change the look and emphasis of the text in your document. You also learn how to change the attributes of your text by enhancing your text with bold and italic type. Identification and use of TrueType fonts are explained, and printer setup and configuration is introduced.

Fonts and Basic Printing

When creating a document in a Windows application, you can use a variety of fonts and special characters to create just the look you want. Changing the printing options can dramatically affect the look of your document. In this lesson you learn how to identify and use fonts to enhance your documents. You also change the attributes of your text by enhancing it with bold and italic type. You learn how to identify and use TrueType fonts. This lesson also explains how to set up and configure your printer.

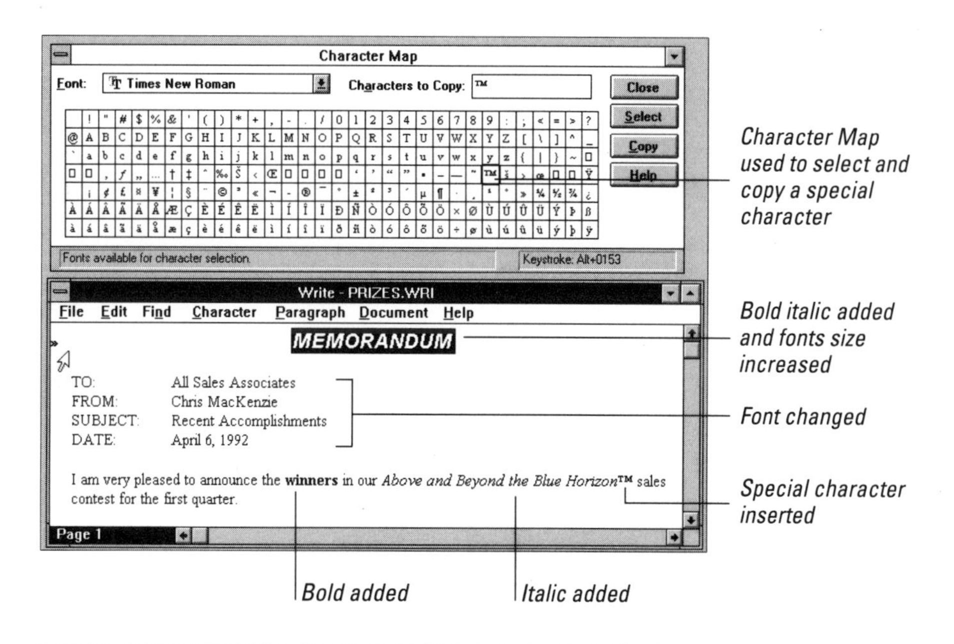

This lesson explains how to do the following:

- Review the installed fonts in Windows
- Select and use fonts in a document
- Work with TrueType fonts
- Use Character Map to find and paste special characters
- Set up and configure a printer
- Modify the printer configuration
- Use the Print Manager

Estimated lesson time: 45 minutes

What is a Font?

A *font* is the set of characters that are formatted in the same typeface (such as Courier), style (such as italic), and size. Characters formatted in a font appear in a similar fashion on your screen as when printed to your printer. Each font has its own *name*, such as Arial, Times New Roman, or Wingdings. This name is used to identify and select the font.

You can alter the *size* or *style* of any font. The size of a font is measured in points, with one *point* (or *pt*) equal to approximately 1/72 of an inch. You generally use a 10- or 12-point font for basic text, and larger fonts for headlines and titles. You can also alter the style of font with bold, italic, or underline styles for emphasis or special effects.

Identifying the Installed Fonts in Windows

You use the Fonts icon on the Control Panel to identify the installed fonts in Windows. You can also use the Fonts icon to install or remove fonts (explained in your Windows documentation).

Open the fonts dialog box

1 Double-click the Control Panel icon.

This icon is in the Program Manager Main group.

2 Locate the Fonts icon.

3 Double-click the Fonts icon.

The Fonts dialog box appears.

Fonts icon

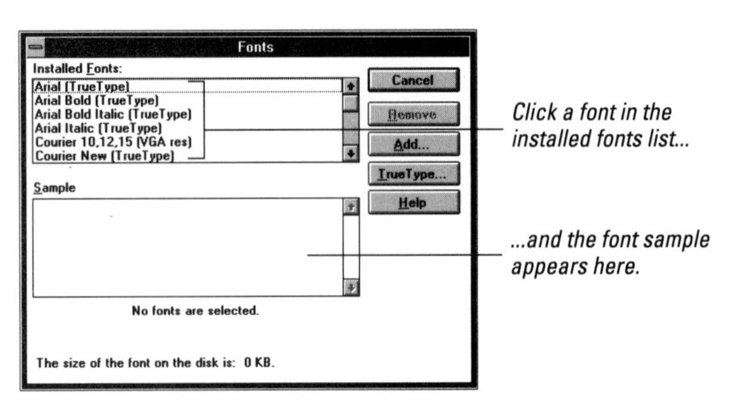

Click a font in the installed fonts list...

...and the font sample appears here.

View the installed fonts

You can view a sample of the installed fonts by clicking on the name of the font. The Fonts dialog box displays the selected font in the sample box. Viewing the fonts helps you to see what kinds of fonts are available, and also lets you see how they would look if used in a document.

1 Click Arial (TrueType).

   A sample of the font appears. Notice that the word *TrueType* is a part of its name. You learn about TrueType fonts later in this lesson.

2 Scroll down the list and click Roman.

   A sample of the font appears.

3 Click Cancel.

   The Control Panel closes dialog box.

4 Click the Minimize icon on the Control Panel window.

Using Fonts in a Document

The Windows Setup program copies several fonts for use with your applications. You usually have three different types of fonts installed in Windows. In these next exercises, you explore the types of fonts used in Windows.

Start Write

You use Write to examine the effect of font changes upon a copy of a document you created previously in this book.

1 Double-click the Program Manager icon on the desktop.

2 Find the Write icon in the Accessories group in the Program Manager window.

3 Double-click Write in the Accessories group.

4 Choose Open from the File menu.

5 Double-click the WIN31SBS directory icon.

6 Double-click MYTRIP.WRI.

   This is the file you worked with in Lesson 9.

7 Choose Save As from the File menu.

8 Type **MYTRIP13** in the Filename box.

   This saves the file with a new name.

9 Click OK.

Using TrueType Fonts

A *TrueType* font is identical both on the screen and on the printed document. Unlike the other two types of fonts, TrueType fonts can be reduced or enlarged to any size without distortion on the screen.

TrueType is a new feature of Windows 3.1, which comes with five standard TrueType fonts, named *Arial*, *Courier New*, *Times New Roman*, *Symbol*, and *Wingdings*. TrueType fonts display a "TT" symbol next to their names in a font list in many applications.

Although you can format your document with as many fonts as you wish, it is a good idea to use as few fonts as necessary in your documents. The more fonts you use on a page, the slower that page prints.

Format the text using TrueType

In this exercise you examine the effect of formatting a document with TrueType fonts.

1. Hold CTRL and click in the selection area of the MYTRIP13.WRI document.

   The selection area is the blank area to the left of the document in the Write window. Clicking here while holding down CTRL selects the entire document. You change the font, size, and style of selected text.

2. Choose Fonts from the Character menu.

   The Font dialog box appears.

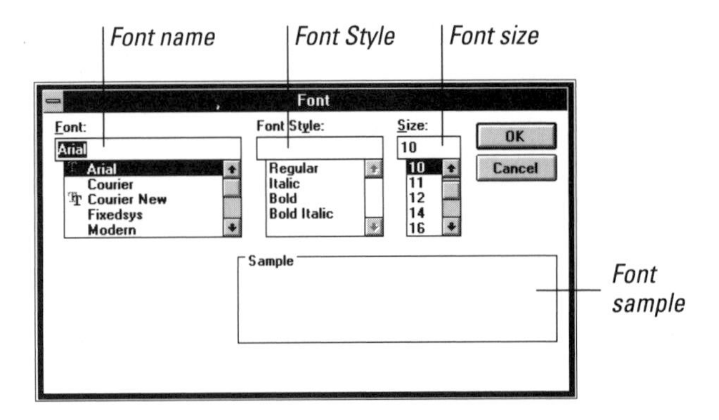

3. Scroll down in the Font name box and click Times New Roman.

   Note that this font name has the symbol "TT" next to its name. The description below the sample box also states that this is a TrueType font.

4. Click OK.

   All the text in the entire document is changed to Times New Roman.

5. Click in the selection area to the left of the first line.

   The title, *A Vacation in France*, is selected.

6. Choose Fonts from the Character menu.

7. Scroll up in the Font Name box and click Arial.

   This is another TrueType font.

8 Click OK.

The text is changed to Arial.

Size the font

One advantage TrueType fonts have over other fonts is that they can be enlarged or reduced without distortion. In this exercise you examine the results of changing the size of the text.

1 Select "A Vacation in France" and choose Fonts from the Character menu.

2 Click 18 in the Size box.

This selects 18 pt for the size of the text.

3 Click OK.

The text is enlarged to 18 pt.

Set the font style

You can change the emphasis of a document by changing the style of the font. Most fonts include three styles: bold, italic, and underline.

1 Select the phrase *SS Princess Louise* in the fourth paragraph.

2 Choose Fonts from the Character menu.

3 Click Italic in the Font style box.

The text is italicized.

4 Click OK.

Using Screen Fonts

A *screen font* (also called a *raster font* or *bitmapped font*) is used for displaying text on the screen, and is designed for optimal display at your screen's resolution. Screen fonts are different from TrueType fonts, because they are available in only a limited number of sizes, and they do not look good when enlarged or reduced.

Select a screen font

1 Double-click in the selection area to the left of the second paragraph.

The entire paragraph is selected.

2 Choose Fonts from the Character menu.

3 Scroll up to find Roman PS.

Note that the font name shows a small printer icon next to it. The description under the sample area shows more information about this font.

4 Click OK.

The selected text is set to the new font. Notice that the screen appearance of this paragraph, which is now set to a screen font, is different from the text in the next paragraph, which is still set in a TrueType font.

Using Plotter Fonts

A *plotter font* (also called a *vector font* or *stroke font*) is used for displaying text on the screen that needs to be enlarged or reduced to another size, or for printing text on a plotter. Like TrueType fonts, plotter fonts can be scaled to any size without too much distortion. However, the display quality of a plotter font is not as high as TrueType fonts.

Select a plotter font

1 Double-click in the selection area of the first line of text.

2 Choose Fonts from the Character menu.

3 Scroll up and click Modern.

This is a plotter font. The font name shows no icon next to it.

4 Click OK.

Using Only TrueType Fonts

In many cases, TrueType fonts are the easiest kind of font to use. TrueType fonts ensure that what you see on the screen matches what you see on the printed document. You can enlarge and reduce TrueType fonts without the distortion that would occur if you tried to use a screen font. You can also use TrueType fonts on a variety of printers.

You can set an option in the Control Panel so that only TrueType fonts are displayed in a font list in all applications. By restricting your use of fonts to only TrueType fonts, you ensure that your documents on screen match the quality of the printed output.

Switch to the Control Panel

You use the Fonts icon on the Control Panel to set the option that restricts the font list to displaying only TrueType fonts.

▶ Press ALT+TAB until the Control Panel appears.

Set only TrueType fonts

1 Double-click Fonts.

2 Click the TrueType button.

The TrueType dialog box appears.

3 Click the box for Show Only TrueType Fonts in Applications.

4 Click OK.

5 Click Close.

Switch to Write

▶ Press ALT+TAB until the Write window appears.

Format text

1 Press CTRL+END.

This keystroke shortcut moves to the end of the document.

2 Select the text from *Cost of the trip* to *739.42*.

3 Choose Fonts from the Character menu.

A list of available fonts appears. Notice that there are only TrueType fonts in this list.

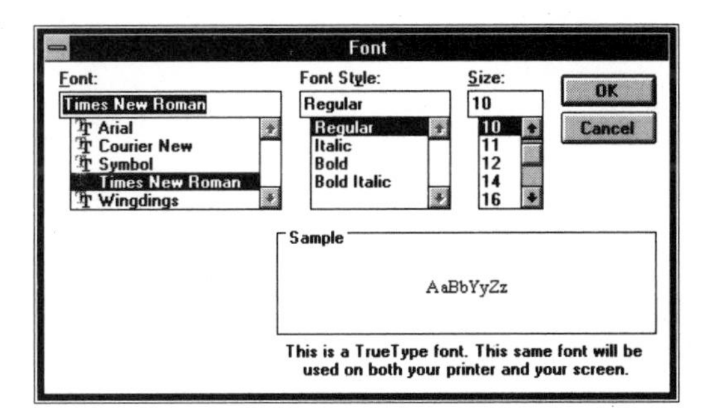

4 In the Font Name box click Arial.

5 Click Bold under Font Style.

6 Click 14 under Size.

7 Click OK.

The text is set to the new font, size, and style.

Make all fonts available

1 Press ALT+TAB until the Control Panel appears.

2 Double-click Fonts.

3 Click TrueType.

4 Click the box next to Show Only TrueType Fonts in Applications to remove the check mark.

This restores the default Windows settings.

5 Click OK.

6 Click Close.

7 Click the Minimize icon on the Control Panel window.

Using Character Map

As you work with your Windows applications, you might find that you need to insert a special character, such as π, ¢ or ½, into a document. Although these special characters are included with most fonts, they are not found on the standard keyboard.

The Character Map accessory gives you an easy way to find and insert these special characters into a document. You use Character Map to view every character available within a selected font and to choose special characters from that font. After you chose the characters, you can switch to your document and paste them in.

Start Character Map

1 Find the Character Map icon.

   Character Map is found in the Accessories group in the Program Manager.

Character map icon

2 Double-click the Character Map icon.

   The Character Map window appears.

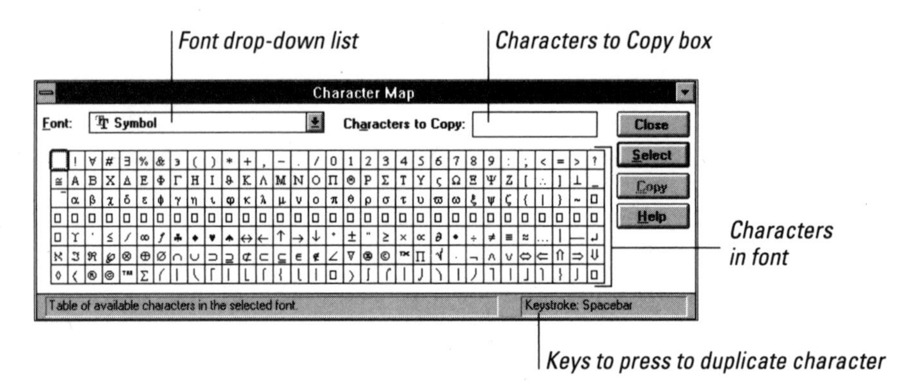

Select a font

You can select the font you want to use with Character Map. You can choose the same font as the one you are using in your document, or you can choose a font with special characters, such as Symbol or Wingdings.

1 Click the down arrow next to Font.

   A list of font names appears. If this is your first time using Character Map, the font name shows Symbol.

2 Scroll down and click Wingdings.

The characters displayed change to the Wingdings font. The Wingdings font is a collection of special symbols you use to add emphasis in a document.

3 Scroll up and click Times New Roman.

The characters displayed change to the Times New Roman font. This is a font used in many documents for body text.

Select a character

You select a character in the Character Map you want to paste into your document by clicking it with the mouse. If you click and hold the mouse button, a larger view of the character pops up. Once you find the character you want, you can either double-click to select it, or click Select. The selected character appears in the Characters to Copy box. Click Copy to place the character on Clipboard.

In this exercise you locate the "£" symbol, used to identify currency amounts as British pounds. You paste this character onto Clipboard for use in another application.

1 Click the fourth character in the fifth row.

This is the "£" character. A larger image of the character briefly appears.

2 Click Select.

The character is placed in the Characters to Copy box.

3 Click Copy.

The character is copied to the Clipboard.

4 Double-click the Control-menu box in the Character Map window.

Character Map closes.

Paste the character into a document

You use the Paste command to insert the characters you placed on the Clipboard from Character Map. In this exercise, you paste the "£" character into the Write document so that the costs of the trip are expressed in British pounds.

1 Press ALT+TAB until the Write document appears on the screen.

2 Click immediately to the left of the number 1203.33.

This is the amount listed for Plane Fare.

3 Choose Paste from the Edit menu.

The "£" character is inserted.

4 Press SPACEBAR.

Pressing SPACEBAR separates the currency symbol from the number.

5 Choose Save from the File menu.

6 Click the Minimize button on the Write window.

Setting Up and Configuring a Printer

When you first install Windows, you pick a printer to use with your applications. After you have installed Windows, however, you might want to modify the existing printer. You use the Printers icon on the Control Panel to select and change printers. You can also use the Printers icon to install a new printer (explained in your Windows documentation).

Because there are hundreds of brands and types of printers, this next section assumes that you installed an Epson FX-80 dot-matrix printer when you installed Windows. If you installed a different printer, you can still use this section to learn how to set up and configure your own printer, because many of the steps are similar no matter what brand of printer you have. Simply follow the steps, substituting your own printer name for the printer used in the example.

Switch to Control Panel

You use the Control Panel to modify your printer configuration.

1 Press ALT+TAB until the Control Panel appears.

2 Double-click Printers.

The Printers dialog box appears.

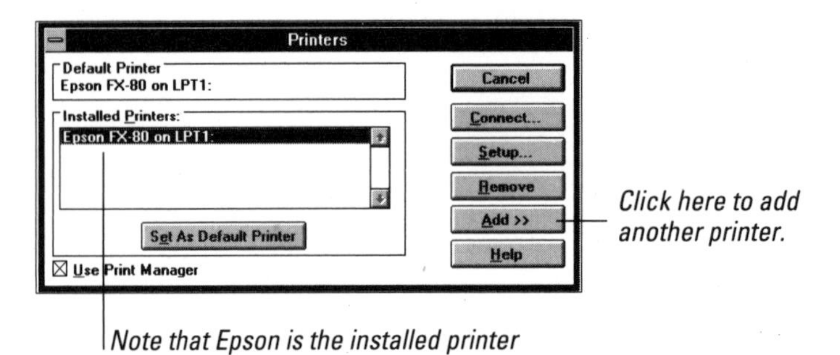

Click here to add another printer.

Note that Epson is the installed printer

Types of Connections

When you connected your printer to your computer, you used a cable to connect it to a *port* on the back of your computer. Your computer usually has two kinds of ports used to connect different types of devices, such as a mouse or a printer. These ports have abbreviated names, such as LPT1 (for Line Printer port number 1) and COM2 (for Communications port number 2). An LPT port is a parallel port, while a COM port is a serial port. Most printers use a parallel port, but some types, such as some PostScript printers, use a serial port. Consult your printer documentation if you are not sure which type your printer uses.

After the printer and computer are connected, you use the Control Panel to designate the port Windows uses to print documents.

Examine the printer connection

In this exercise you examine the connection for your Epson FX-80 printer.

1 Click Connect.

The Connect dialog box appears for the selected printer, the Epson FX-80. Notice that the printer is connected to the LPT1: port.

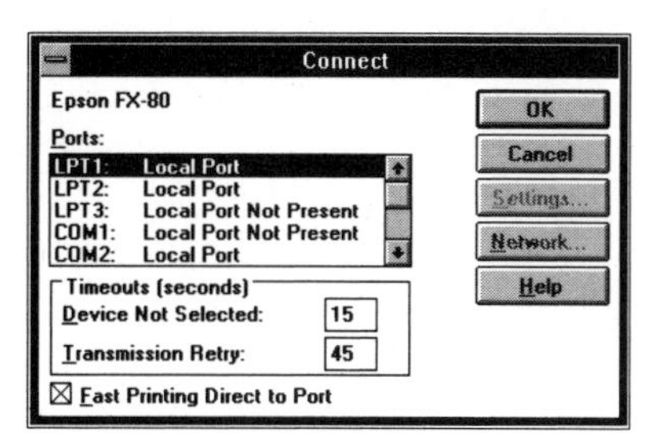

2 Click OK.

Modifying the Printer Configuration

You can change the settings for your printer so that you can use longer paper, better graphics printing, and so on. You make these changes using the Setup button in the Printers dialog box.

The options in the Setup dialog box vary from one brand of printer to another, reflecting the options available for each printer model. However, the steps you learn in the following exercise can help you to understand how to change the settings for your own printer.

Adjust the settings

1 Click Setup.

The FX-80 Setup dialog box appears.

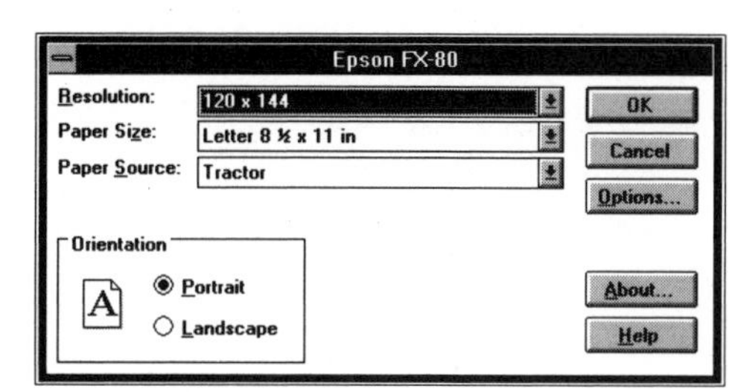

2 Click the down arrow next to Resolution.

A list of graphic resolutions appears. These values are used to calculate how many dots per inch print when the printer prints graphics. The greater the number, the finer the detail. However, the more dots per inch, the slower the graphic prints.

3 Click 240 x 144.

4 Click OK.

The dialog box closes.

If You Have More Than One Printer

You can choose which printer is used when an application prints. This printer, called the *default printer*, is used whenever you choose Print from a File menu. You can select any printer to be the default printer.

Set the default printer

1 Click the FX-80 printer.

2 Click Set As Default Printer.

From this point on, all documents will print to the Epson FX-80 printer unless otherwise specified.

Using Print Manager

Print Manager is a Windows application that manages how and when documents print. The application that wants to print a document sends the *print job* to the Print Manager, which then assigns the print job a place in its list of jobs to be printed, called the *print queue*. After the Print Manager accepts the print job, the application that sent the print job is free to work on another task.

You can change several features of Print Manager so that it better handles its tasks. However, you must enable Print Manager from the Control Panel before you can modify any Print Manager options.

Enable Print Manager

By default, Print Manager is enabled. However, in this exercise you examine settings in the Printers dialog box.

1 Click in the box next to the label Use Print Manager, if necessary, to place a check mark in the box.

The check mark shows that Print Manager is enabled.

2 Click Close to close the Printers dialog box.

Viewing Print Manager

After Print Manager is enabled, Windows uses it whenever a print job is sent to the printer. When the print queue is emptied, Print Manager closes.

You can start Print Manager yourself whenever you wish. You can use the Print Manager window to view the print queue, change the priority and order of the print jobs, and determine if Windows should alert you when a print job has failed.

Start Print Manager

1 Locate the Print Manager icon.

  Print Manager is in the Main group in the Program Manager.

Print Manager icon

2 Double-click the Print Manager icon.

  The Print Manager window appears on the Desktop.

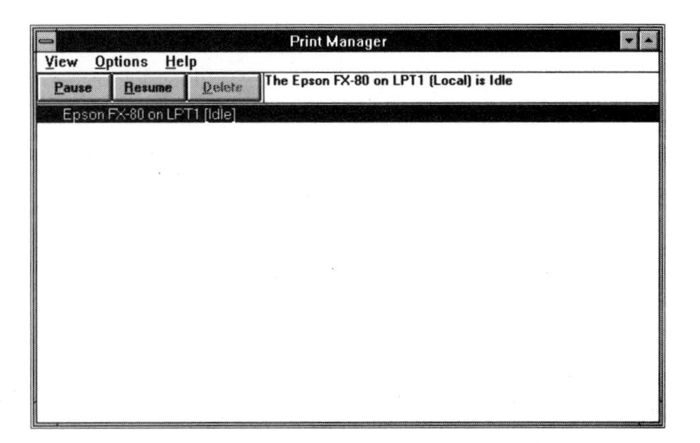

Print a file

In this exercise you print the Write document and examine the contents of the Print Manager window.

1 Press ALT+TAB until the Write window appears.

2 Choose Print from the File menu.

3 Click OK.

  A copy of the file is sent to Print Manager.

4 Press ALT+TAB until the Print Manager window appears.

  Notice the print job listed in the print queue under Epson FX-80.

Pause a printer

You can set Print Manager to hold (or pause) all print jobs by pausing the printer. This is useful if you notice that your printer is low on paper, or if you want to start a large number of jobs and want to wait until the end of the day to start printing.

Print Manager automatically pauses the print job whenever the printer is unavailable or *offline*, either due to an error or because the printer is disconnected from the computer. Usually, the solution is to add paper, or to check that the cable is connected, or to turn the printer on and *online*. When you correct the problem, you can resume the print job.

In this exercise you examine the results of pausing the print job.

1 Click the Epson FX-80 on LPT1 [Idle] in the Print Manager window.

Print Manager shows [Idle] next to the printer name when there are no active print jobs for your local printer.

2 Click Pause.

Print Manager pauses the Epson FX-80 printer queue. Notice the word *Paused* and a hand icon that appear next to the printer name.

Print a file

1 Press ALT+TAB until the Write window appears.

2 Choose Print from the File menu.

3 Click OK.

A copy of the file is sent to Print Manager.

Restart the print queue

You can resume a print job that has been paused, whether it was paused by you or by Print Manager. If the print job paused because of a problem, and that problem is not corrected, Print Manager pauses the print job again until the problem is corrected.

1 Press ALT+TAB until the Print Manager window appears.

Note that the Epson FX-80 printer shows a print job in its queue.

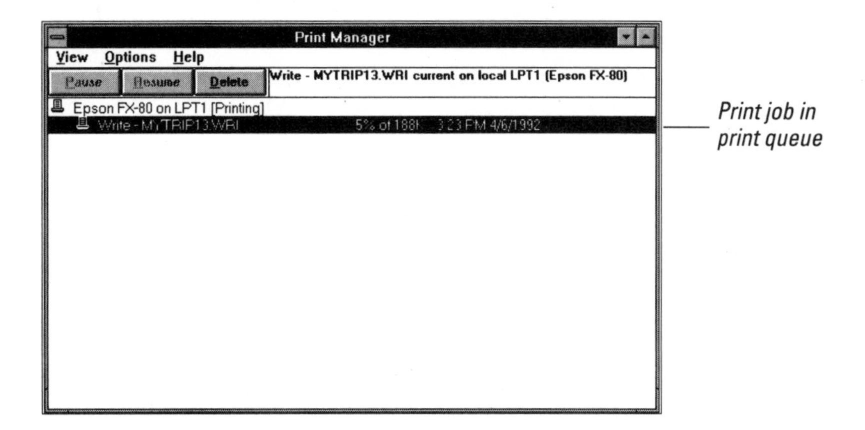

2 Click Resume.

This resumes the print job.

Set the priority

You can set the priority of Print Manager. That is, you can tell Windows to allow more time for the print jobs to print, and less time for the other applications to work, by changing the priority of the Print Manager to High, Medium, or Low. Using High Priority gives more time to your print jobs and less time for the other applications; it makes the print jobs print faster, but it causes other applications to work slower. You can also set the priority to be lower for print jobs. A lower priority for the print jobs prints them more slowly, but gives more time to your other applications.

1 Select the Options menu.

2 Choose High Priority.

This sets the Print Manager to the highest priority so that print jobs print quickly. However, this setting makes other applications work more slowly.

3 Select the Options menu.

4 Choose Medium Priority.

This sets Print Manager to the default priority.

Set the alert message

You can also determine how you should be notified when a print problem occurs. Print Manager can send you a message for any problems. Or, it can simply flash its title bar or icon. You can also set Print Manager so it never informs you of errors.

1 Select the Options menu.

2 Choose Alert Always.

This option sets Print Manager to display a message box whenever there is a printing problem. The message box pops up on top of any other open window.

Close the Print Manager

You do not need to leave the Print Manager application open, because Windows will restart it whenever you print. However, closing Print Manager cancels any pending print jobs.

1. Double-click the Control-menu box in the Print Manager window.
2. If necessary, click OK in the warning box.

   The warning box appears if you have any print jobs queued in the Print Manager when you close Print Manager.

One Step Further

In this exercise you change the page orientation of your printer from portrait (tall) to landscape (wide). Changing the orientation from portrait to landscape makes the print jobs print "sideways." You view how changing the orientation affects your Write document, and print the document in the landscape orientation.

1. Double-click the Printers icon in the Control Panel.
2. Click FX-80 on LPT1: to select it.
3. Click Setup.
4. Click Landscape under Orientation.
5. Click OK.
6. Click Close.

   The printer will now print sideways on the paper.
7. Press ALT+TAB until the Write document appears.

   The document reformats to fit the new page orientation.
8. Choose Print from the File menu and click OK.

   The print job is sent to the Print Manager, and the file prints.
9. Press ALT+TAB until the Print Manager window appears.

   You can review the progress of the print job by viewing the contents of this window.
10. Press ALT+TAB until the Control Panel window appears.
11. Click Setup in the Printers dialog box.
12. Click Portrait under Orientation.

    This sets the orientation to its default setting.
13. Click OK.
14. Click Close.

If you want to go on to the next lesson

1 Double-click the Control-menu box in the Control Panel window.

2 Press ALT+TAB until the Write document appears.

3 Choose Save from the File menu.

4 Double-click the Control-menu box in the Write window.

Write closes.

5 Press ALT+TAB until the Print Manager window appears.

6 Double-click the Control-menu box in the Print Manager window.

Print Manager closes.

7 Double-click the Program Manager icon to restore it to its former size.

If you want to quit Windows for now

1 Press ALT+TAB until the Program Manager window appears.

2 Double-click the Control-menu box in the Program Manager window.

3 When the message "This will end your Windows session" appears, click OK or press ENTER.

Lesson Summary

To	Do this
Review the characteristics of the currently installed fonts	Start the Control Panel. Double-click the Fonts icon. Click on a font name and examine its characteristics in the Sample box. Click Cancel.
Identify a TrueType font	Start the Control Panel. Double-click the Fonts icon. Click a font name and examine the description below the font name in the Sample box. (A TrueType font name includes the phrase "TrueType.") *or* Choose the Fonts dialog box in your document. Check for the "TT" symbol next to the font name.
Change fonts in a document	Select the desired text in your document. Choose the Fonts option (it might be its own menu item, or it might be on a menu such as the Character menu in Write). Click a font name. Click OK.
Change the font size	Select the desired text in your document. Choose the Fonts option (it might be its own menu item, or it might be on a menu such as the Character menu in Write). Click a font size, or type a font size in the box. Click OK.

To	Do this
Change the font style	Select the desired text in your document. Choose the Fonts option (it might be its own menu item, or it might be on a menu such as the Character menu in Write). Click a font style. Click OK.
Work only with TrueType fonts	Start the Control Panel. Double-click the Fonts icon. Click TrueType. Click the box next to Show only TrueType fonts in applications so that a check mark appears. Click OK.
Show all fonts	Start the Control Panel. Double-click the Fonts icon. Click TrueType. Click the box next to Show only TrueType fonts in applications so that the check mark is removed. Click OK.
Select and copy a special character to the Clipboard	Start Character Map. Click on the arrow next to the Font Name box and select a font. Click on a character. Click Select to copy it to the Characters to Copy box. Click Copy to place a copy on the Clipboard.
Paste a special character into a document	Use Character Map to select and copy a special character to the Clipboard. Switch to your document. Click in the text where you want to insert the character. Choose Paste from the Edit menu.
Tell Windows to which port your printer is connected	Start the Control Panel. Double-click the Printers icon. Click the desired printer. Click Connect. Click the proper port by name (LPT1:, for example). Click OK.
Configure your printer	Start the Control Panel. Double-click the Printers icon. Click the desired printer. Click Setup. Change the options in the printer dialog box (Portrait, for example). Click OK.
Select the default printer	Start the Control Panel. Double-click the Printers icon. Click the desired printer. Click Set As Default Printer. Click OK.
Enable the Print Manager	Start the Control Panel. Double-click the Printers icon. Click the box next to Use Print Manager so that a check mark appears. Click OK.
Disable the Print Manager	Start the Control Panel. Double-click the Printers icon. Click the box next to Use Print Manager so that the check mark is removed. Click OK.
Start Print Manager	Double-click Print Manager in the Main group in the Program Manager.
Pause a printer	Start Print Manager. Click on the printer and job name. Click Pause.

To	Do this
Restart a printer	Start Print Manager. Click on the printer and job name. Click Resume.
Set the priority of print jobs	Start Print Manager. Choose a priority (Low, Medium, or High) from the Options menu.
Set the alert message	Start Print Manager. Choose an alert message level (No Message, Flash If Inactive, Alert Always) from the Options menu.

Preview of the Next Lesson

In the next lesson, you learn how to manage MS-DOS–based applications. You learn how to start a non-Windows-based application in its own window. You create a special icon to handle a non-Windows-based application. You learn how to set the size of the non-Windows-based application.

Part 6

Using MS-DOS–Based Applications with Windows

Managing MS-DOS–Based Applications

The full power of Windows is available when you use programs designed specifically to use its graphical interface. However, many programs still in use are not written for Windows. These applications, called *MS-DOS–based applications* or *non-Windows-based applications*, are designed to be used with MS-DOS, the Microsoft Disk Operating System that runs nearly every PC.

Windows runs most MS-DOS–based programs. Although these programs cannot take full advantage of the rich graphical environment Windows provides, they can still operate properly on your computer. This lesson shows how to use MS-DOS–based applications with Windows.

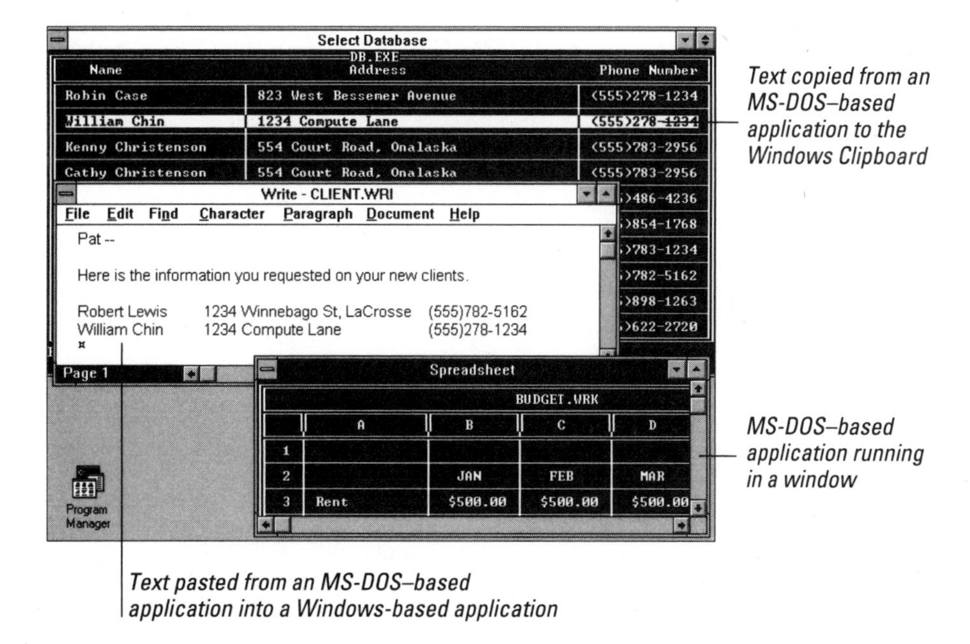

Text copied from an MS-DOS–based application to the Windows Clipboard

MS-DOS–based application running in a window

Text pasted from an MS-DOS–based application into a Windows-based application

---

This lesson explains how to do the following:

- Start an MS-DOS–based application
- Start multiple MS-DOS–based applications
- Switch between MS-DOS–based applications
- Quit an MS-DOS–based application

Estimated lesson time: 30 minutes

If You Have an 80286 Computer

You can run MS-DOS–based applications effectively with a computer containing an 80286 processor, but there are some limitations. You cannot cut and paste between an MS-DOS–based application and a Windows-based application. Also, with an 80286, whenever you switch from the MS-DOS–based application back to Windows, the MS-DOS–based application stops running until you return to it.

The remaining sections of this chapter require the use of Windows 386 enhanced mode, a feature not available for 80286-based computers.

Using 386 Enhanced Mode

In the 386 enhanced mode, Windows starts a new session of MS-DOS for each MS-DOS–based application. Each of these sessions is treated as if it were running in a separate computer. Windows provides each MS-DOS–based application with its own memory and workspace, and when you run an MS-DOS–based application, the application thinks it's the only application running on your system.

Because each MS-DOS–based application runs as a separate session, you can have several MS-DOS–based applications running at the same time, subject to the limitations of your computer's memory. This means that it is possible to use a spreadsheet program to calculate a budget, while a database updates the records for a payroll file.

Full Screen vs. Window

You can run these MS-DOS–based applications in one of two different modes. In the *full screen mode*, the MS-DOS–based application behaves as it would if it were running without Windows, and it takes control of the screen. If the MS-DOS–based application supports the use of a mouse, you can use the mouse to operate the menus and perform commands just as if you were running the application from MS-DOS.

Note Although the MS-DOS–based application seems to have taken control of the machine, the other Windows and MS-DOS–based applications are still running in the background, with Windows still in control of the system. You do not see Windows or the other applications, but they are still performing their work.

In the *window mode*—available only on 80386-based or higher computers—the MS-DOS–based application runs in a resizable window. You can move and size this window as you would with a standard Windows-based application. You can also cut and paste information between an MS-DOS–based application window and a Windows-based application running in another window.

Starting an MS-DOS–Based Application

You can start an MS-DOS–based application in several ways. You can install a program icon into a group in the Program Manager that simply starts the MS-DOS–

based application. You can install a program icon that uses a Program Information File (PIF) to start the application. (The use of a PIF is discussed in more detail in your Windows documentation.) Or you can use the Run command from the File menu in the Program Manager.

Set up a new group

In this exercise you set up a new program group to hold the program icons for your MS-DOS–based applications.

1. Choose New from the File menu in Program Manager.

   The New Program Object dialog box appears.
2. Click Program Group and click OK.
3. Type **MS-DOS Based Applications** in the Group Name box and click OK.

   The new program group window appears on your desktop.

Install the MS-DOS–based program icons

In this exercise you install two icons into the MS-DOS–based applications group. One program icon runs SHEET.EXE and the other runs DB.EXE.

1. Choose New from the File menu.
2. Click OK.
3. Type **Spreadsheet** in the Description box.
4. Type **SHEET.EXE** in the Command Line box.
5. Type **C:\WINDOWS\WIN31SBS** in the Working Directory box.

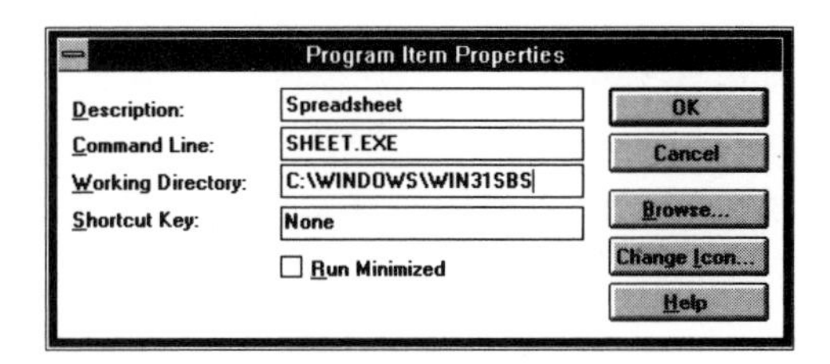

6. Click OK.

   The new program icon appears in the group window.
7. Choose New from the File menu.
8. Click OK.
9. Type **Database** in the Description box.
10. Type **DB.EXE** in the Command Line box.
11. Type **C:\WINDOWS\WIN31SBS** in the Working Directory box.
12. Click OK.

Start an MS-DOS–based application

In this exercise you start an MS-DOS–based application using the icons from the "MS-DOS Based Applications" group you just created.

▶ Double-click the Spreadsheet icon.

The SHEET.EXE application appears. This program represents a spreadsheet program runnning in an MS-DOS window.

BUDGET.WRK

	A	B	C	D	E	F
1						
2		JAN	FEB	MAR	APR	
3	Rent	$500.00	$500.00	$500.00	$500.00	
4	Insurance	$23.00	$23.00	$23.00	$23.00	
5	Food	$175.00	$175.00	$175.00	$175.00	
6	Utilities	$200.00	$200.00	$150.00	$100.00	
7	Automotive	$210.00	$210.00	$210.00	$210.00	
8	Misc.	$100.00	$100.00	$100.00	$100.00	
9						

PRESS ESC TO EXIT

Switching Between Modes

If you are using 386 enhanced mode, you can switch between the full-screen and windowed MS-DOS modes using one of two methods. You can use the shortcut keys ALT+ENTER. If the MS-DOS–based application is in the window mode, you can also use the Settings command from the Control menu to switch modes.

Toggle between modes

1 Press ALT+ENTER.

The screen shrinks to fit inside a window on the desktop. Note that Windows shrinks the size of the letters so you can see the same information in the smaller window.

2 Click the Maximize button.

The application window expands to the largest size possible.

3 Choose Settings from the Control menu.

The Settings menu appears.

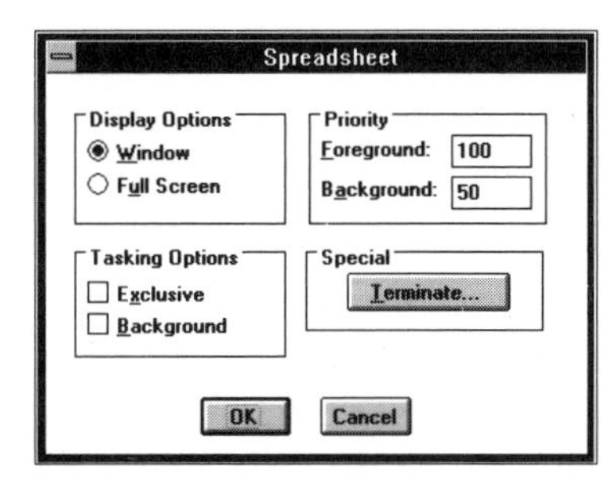

4 Click Full Screen under Display Options.

5 Click OK.

The screen switches to the full-screen MS-DOS mode. You can also use ALT+ENTER.

6 Press ALT+ENTER.

The screen returns to the windowed MS-DOS mode.

Start a second MS-DOS–based application

You can start a second MS-DOS–based application and run it at the same time as your first MS-DOS–based application. You can size this second window in the same way as the first window. You can stack the two windows, or size them to fit side by side.

1 Press ALT+TAB until the Program Manager appears.

2 Double-click the Database icon in the MS-DOS Based Applications group.

A second session of MS-DOS is started to run the program DB.EXE. This program represents a database program running in an MS-DOS window.

3 Press ALT+ENTER.

4 Use the mouse to move the database MS-DOS window so you can also see the title bar for the spreadsheet MS-DOS window.

5 Click the mouse in the partially hidden spreadsheet MS-DOS window.

This brings the spreadsheet MS-DOS window forward and makes it active.

Sharing Data Between MS-DOS– and Windows-Based Applications

You can copy and paste between MS-DOS–based applications and Windows-based applications. The MS-DOS–based application must be in a window for this feature to work.

Copy and paste

In this exercise you copy information from the spreadsheet MS-DOS window and paste it into a Notepad document.

1. Press ALT+TAB until the Program Manager appears.
2. Double-click Notepad in the Accessories group.
3. Type **This is text copied from my spreadsheet:** ENTER ENTER
4. Press ALT+TAB until the spreadsheet MS-DOS window appears.

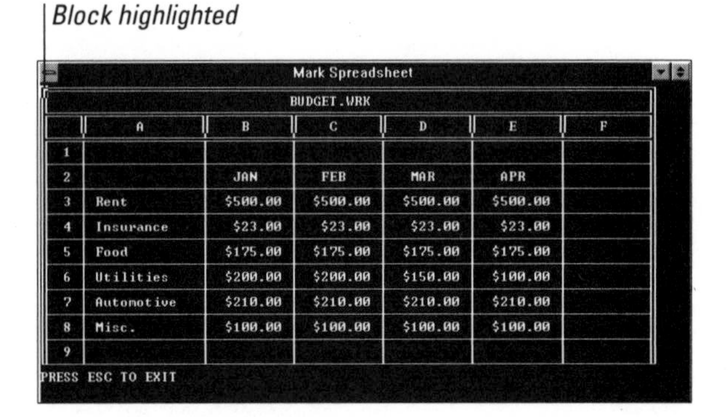

5. Click the Control-menu box, and from the Edit menu, choose Mark.

   A small block begins blinking in the top left corner of the window. This block represents the starting point of the information to be marked and copied onto the Clipboard.

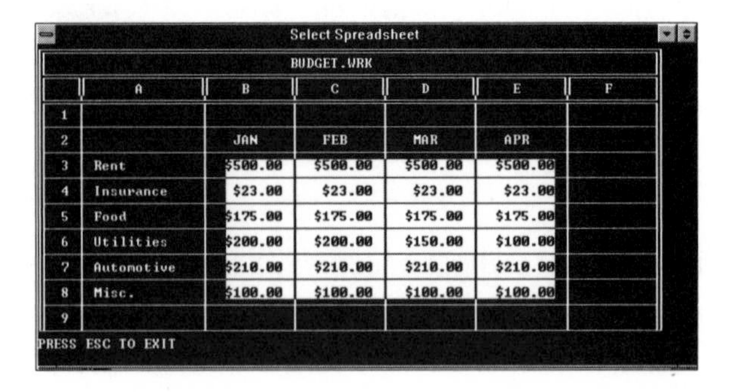

6. Click on the dollar sign in the first number (the *$500.00* under *JAN*) and drag down to the last zero in the table of numbers (the final *0* in *$100.00*).

   The highlight shows that you have selected the table of numbers.

7 Press ENTER.

The marked block is copied onto the Clipboard. You can also choose Copy from the Mark option in the Control menu.

8 Press ALT+TAB until Notepad appears.

9 Choose Paste from the Edit menu.

The data from the spreadsheet MS-DOS window is now pasted into the Notepad file.

Save and close the Notepad document

1 Choose Save from the File menu.

2 Type **MYBUDGET** in the File Name box.

3 Double-click the WIN31SBS folder icon.

4 Click OK.

5 Double-click the Control-menu box in the Notepad window.

Notepad closes.

Exiting an MS-DOS–Based Application

To shut down an MS-DOS–based application running under Windows, use the command provided within the MS-DOS–based application. Often this command is Quit or Exit. Other applications might use a special key, such as ESC. Most MS-DOS–based applications quit properly and return you to the Windows desktop or to another Windows-based application.

Exit normally from an MS-DOS–based application

1 Click in window running SHEET.EXE.

2 Press ESC.

The window closes.

Terminate an MS-DOS–based application

If an MS-DOS–based application stops responding to keystrokes or commands, a special Windows command, Terminate, allows you to close the MS-DOS–based application. Terminate stops the program without closing any other applications, Windows- or MS-DOS–based, that might still be running.

Although this command lets you resume working with your other applications, it also might corrupt the memory of your computer. As a safety procedure, switch to the other applications and save any files you have modified. After saving your work, exit Windows and reboot your computer.

1 Click the window running DB.EXE to select it.

2 Choose Settings from the Control menu.

3 Click Terminate.

A message box appears.

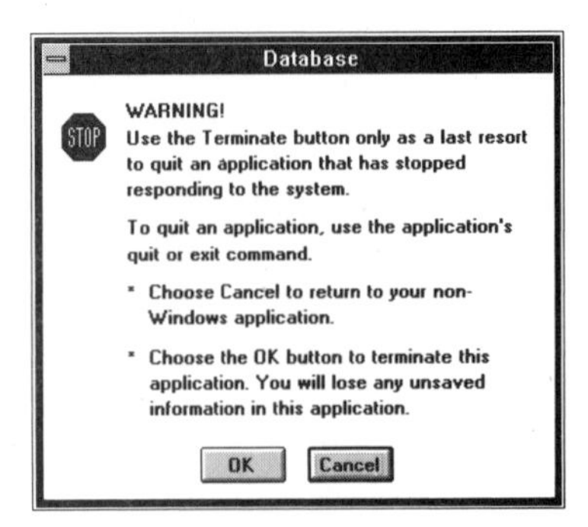

4 Click OK.

The window closes.

Close Windows and reboot

Always quit Windows and reboot your computer whenever you use the Terminate function to close an MS-DOS–based application.

1 Double-click the Control-menu box in the Program Manager window.

2 Click OK.

Your Windows session closes, and you return to the MS-DOS prompt.

3 Press CTRL+ALT+DEL.

Your computer reboots.

Restart Windows

▶ Type **WIN** ENTER.

Windows restarts.

When an Application Does Not Respond to Your Commands

You can close any application in Windows, whether it is a Windows-based or an MS-DOS–based application, using CTRL+ALT+DEL. This keystroke combination stops the operation of the active window, and it is useful whenever an application locks up your computer. Use this keystroke combination, however, *only* as a last resort. After you use this keystroke combination to close an application, immediately save and close any open files, close any open applications, exit Windows, and reboot.

Note Pressing CTRL+ALT+DEL from the MS-DOS prompt reboots your computer; pressing CTRL+ALT+DEL from Windows closes the active window without rebooting your computer.

One Step Further

In this exercise you use the Run command to start an MS-DOS–based application. You use the Browse command to find the MS-DOS–based application you want to run. You also open an MS-DOS window using the MS-DOS Prompt icon.

1. Switch to the Program Manager window.
2. Choose Run from the File menu.
3. Click the Browse button.
4. Double-click the WIN31SBS folder icon.
5. Double-click SHEET.EXE.

   This is the MS-DOS–based application you want to run.
6. Click OK.

   After a few moments, the application appears on the desktop.
7. Press ALT+TAB until the Program Manager window appears.

   When you press ALT+TAB (or choose any command to switch to another application), the MS-DOS–based application window is immediately reduced to an icon.
8. Double-click the MS-DOS Prompt icon in the Main group in the Program Manager.
9. An MS-DOS window opens.

   Press ALT+TAB until the window running SHEET.EXE reappears.
10. Press ESC.

    The spreadsheet MS-DOS window closes.
11. Press ALT+TAB until the MS-DOS window opens.
12. Type **EXIT** ENTER.

If you want to quit Windows for now

1. Double-click the Control-menu box in the Program Manager window.
2. When the message “This will end your Windows session” appears, click OK or press ENTER.

Lesson Summary

To	Do this
Start an MS-DOS–based application	Double-click its icon in Program Manager. *or* Choose Run from the File Manager, and type the name of the application. Press ENTER or click OK.
Toggle between the full screen and the window mode	Switch to the MS-DOS–based application window. Press ALT+ENTER. *or* Switch to the MS-DOS–based application window. If the application is in the window mode, choose Settings from the Control menu and click Full Screen or Window. If the application is in full screen mode, press ALT+ENTER.
Copy from an MS-DOS–based application	Toggle the MS-DOS–based application into a window. Click the Control menu, and choose Mark from the Edit menu. Use the mouse to highlight the area you want to mark and press ENTER.
Paste into an MS-DOS–based application	Switch to the MS-DOS–based application window. Toggle the MS-DOS–based application into a window. Click or use the cursor keys to move the insertion point to the desired location. From the Control menu, choose Edit. Click Paste.
Exit from an MS-DOS–based application	Switch to the MS-DOS–based application window. Type **EXIT** or **QUIT**, or choose the appropriate command from the MS-DOS–based application's menu to quit.
Terminate an MS-DOS–based application	Switch to the MS-DOS–based application window. If necessary, toggle the MS-DOS–based application into a window. Click the Control menu, and choose Settings. Click Terminate. At the message box, click OK.

Appendixes

Installing Windows 3.1

The installation of Microsoft Windows version 3.1 has been simplified. The process of setting up files on your hard disk takes approximately 20 to 30 minutes, and is largely automated. All you do is insert each Windows disk into your floppy disk drive and type on the keyboard in response to prompts that appear on the screen. This appendix helps you prepare for the options or choices you are likely to encounter as you go through the Windows 3.1 setup procedure. For more information about setting up Windows, see the booklet *Getting Started with Microsoft Windows* that comes in the Windows 3.1 package, particularly the *Welcome* section and *Chapter 1*.

Hardware and Software Requirements

To install and use Windows 3.1, your computer system must meet the following minimum requirements:

- *An MS-DOS–based computer with at least an 80286 microprocessor*. (An 80386- or 80486-based system is necessary to run Windows in *386 enhanced mode*.
- *At least 1 megabyte (MB) of memory* consisting of 640 kilobytes (K) conventional memory and 256K extended memory. (For 386 enhanced mode, you need at least 1024K of extended memory in addition to 640K conventional memory.)
- *A hard disk drive with at least 6 MB of free disk storage space* (8 MB for 386 enhanced mode). For best performance, 10 MB or more of free disk space is recommended.
- *At least one floppy disk drive*. To use the setup disks that are provided in the Windows 3.1 package, you need a high capacity drive (1.2 MB for 5.25-inch disks or 1.44 MB for 3.5-inch disks). If you have a low-capacity 3.5-inch drive (720K), you can order a set of low-density 3.5-inch disks from Microsoft at no extra charge.
- *A graphics display adapter that is supported by Windows,* along with a compatible monitor. A high resolution (VGA or better) color monitor is desirable but not necessary.
- *A mouse or other pointing device that is supported by Windows*. Although this is not an absolute requirement because the features of Windows can be controlled from the keyboard, a mouse is highly recommend to realize the full benefit of the graphical environment. The lessons in this book assume that your system includes a mouse.
- *MS-DOS version 3.1 or higher*. MS-DOS 5.0 is recommended for improved memory and disk handling features.

Setup Methods

You can use either of two methods to set up Windows 3.1—*Express Setup* or *Custom Setup*. Before you begin installing the program, you should decide which method to use. Early in the process you must select one of these methods.

Express Setup

Express Setup requires fewer decisions from you because it automatically checks most aspects of your system and uses many standard settings. If your system includes a printer, you should know the printer's type and the port to which is it connected (for example, parallel port LPT1, or serial port COM1). For most people, especially those with limited computer experience, Express Setup is recommended.

Custom Setup

Custom Setup gives you greater control over details of your Windows configuration. It also requires that you have more specific knowledge about your system as you set it up. At several points during the Custom Setup process, you are prompted to enter information about your hardware, software, and installation preferences.

You must specify such items as the following: the type of computer, display, mouse, keyboard, and printer you use; the directory in which you want to copy Windows files; any applications on your hard disk that you want to run with Windows; how to modify your AUTOEXEC.BAT and CONFIG.SYS files; and which optional parts of Windows you want to install. In many cases, the Setup program suggests a choice that you can either accept or modify. Custom Setup is recommended only if you have special installation needs *and* can provide the necessary information.

Upgrading from Windows 3.0

If your system already has Windows version 3.0 installed, you have two options—upgrade the Windows files to version 3.1 while preserving settings that you established while working in version 3.0, or install version 3.1 in a separate directory and leave version 3.0 files intact. Unless you have a special need to keep two independent versions of Windows available, you should choose to upgrade because it maintains your existing Program Manager groups, system settings, and device drivers (except drivers that are updated in version 3.1).

You can use either Express or Custom Setup to upgrade from Windows 3.0 to 3.1. Early in the installation process, the Setup program detects the existence of Windows in your system and suggests that you upgrade by installing the new version in the same directory. For more details about upgrading from Windows 3.1, see *Getting Started with Microsoft Windows,* Chapter 1, "Setting Up Windows."

Running the Setup Program

After you decide whether to use Express or Custom Setup and whether you want to upgrade from Windows 3.0, take the set of Windows 3.1 disks that match the size of your floppy drive and carry out the following steps.

Run Setup

1 Insert disk 1 into your disk drive and be sure it is locked in place.

2 At the MS-DOS prompt, type the letter of the floppy disk drive you are using, followed by a colon (:), and then press ENTER.

For example, if you are using drive A, type "A:".

3 Type **SETUP**, and then press ENTER.

After a few moments, your screen looks like the following:

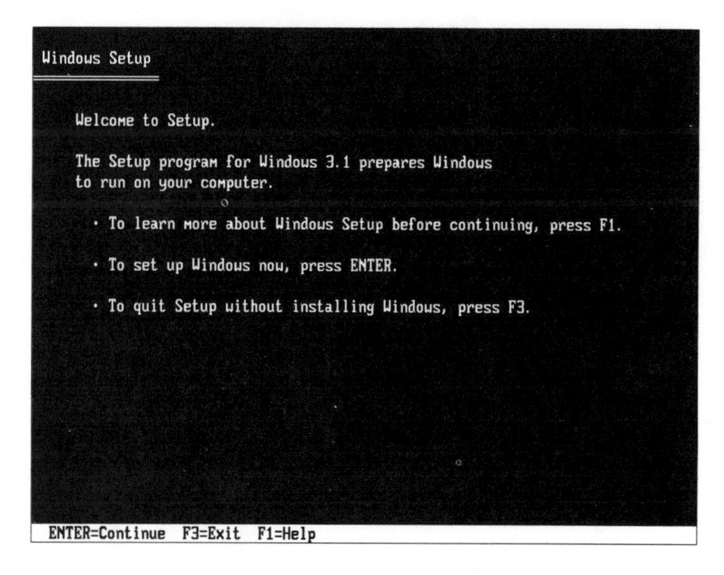

4 Press ENTER.

5 Follow the directions as they appear on screen.

Using OLE

Earlier versions of Windows provided two ways to copy information from one document to another: *pasting* and *linking*. Windows 3.1 adds another: *embedding*. The specifications used for linking and embedding are referred to by the acronym *OLE*, short for *Object Linking and Embedding*.

Often, when you copy information from one application and paste it into another, you may not be concerned about updating the information at a later date. The usual copy and paste procedure, using Clipboard, produces a *static copy* of the information, with no connection to its source. Linking with OLE lets you create a *live copy* which changes as corresponding information in its source document is changed.

Linking vs. Embedding

OLE gives Windows 3.1 two methods of importing live information from other documents: *linking* and *embedding*. Linking places a marker in the target document that identifies the source of the information. With this link in place, when you change the information in the source document, Windows updates the linked information in the target document. You can also link the same source to several target documents. Linked information is dependent on the presence of its source file.

While linking places only a marker in the target document, embedding places the actual data from the source document. No links are established, but when you select the embedded item and edit it, Windows starts the application that created the data. Files containing embedded data do not need to maintain a link to the data source, Embedded data is independent of its source document, which makes embedded data more easily portable than linked data.

Windows-based applications that support OLE are called *OLE-aware*. Windows 3.1 includes several OLE-aware accessories, such as Write, Paintbrush, and Cardfile.

An OLE-aware application can be an *OLE server,* an *OLE client,* or both. Paintbrush is an OLE server, because you can copy information *from* Paintbrush into other applications, using the Clipboard. Write, on the other hand, is an OLE client, because you can paste information from other applications *into* your Write document. Other Windows applications, such as Microsoft Word for Windows 2.0, Microsoft Excel for Windows 3.0, and Microsoft Excel for Windows 4.0, can act as either a client or server application, depending upon the OLE action you take.

Linking Files

Using the OLE process to link information from one application into another is similar to the common method of using Clipboard to copy and paste. When you use OLE to link information, you copy a piece of information from the server application onto the Clipboard, and then paste it into the client application using the Paste Link command. (This command can be reached through the Edit menu in OLE-aware applications.) Using an OLE link keeps your client file size small, because the information you see resides in the separate server file.

In order to update the linked information in the OLE client application, you must update the file used by the OLE server application . The information you see in the the OLE client application is only a copy of the data in the linked file. Because of the link, it will change as the linked file changes. For example, if you copy a picture in Paintbrush and paste it into Write using an OLE link, what you see in Write is only a copy of the information in the Paintbrush file.

To update the linked information in the Write file, you start Paintbrush and alter the information in the linked document. After you make your changes, Windows updates the information in the client application. (If the OLE server application is still open, you only need to switch to the application and make your changes.)

If you move or delete the linked file used by the OLE server application, Windows cannot make the changes, and displays an error message. That is, if you link a picture from Paintbrush into Write, you are linking a Paintbrush file on your disk into the Write document. You must not delete or move the Paintbrush OLE server file if you want to update the Write OLE client file.

In the following exercises you link a Paintbrush picture into a Write document.

Open Paintbrush and Write

1. Start Windows.
2. Double-click the Paintbrush icon.

   Paintbrush is in the Accessories group in the Program Manager window.
3. Press ALT+TAB until the Program Manager icon appears.
4. Double-click the Write icon.

   Write is in the Accessories group in the Program Manager window.
5. Press ALT+TAB until the Program Manager icon appears.
6. Click the Minimize button in the Program Manager window.

   The Program Manager window shrinks to an icon to reduce screen clutter.
7. Press CTRL+ESC.

   The Task List window appears.
8. Click the Tile button.

   Write and Paintbrush are tiled on the desktop.

Create the Write document

1 Click anywhere in the Write window.

This makes the Write window active.

2 Type **This is an example of an OLE link in action:** and press ENTER ENTER.

3 From the File menu in Write, choose Save.

The File Save As dialog box appears.

4 Type **OLE-TEST** in the Filename box.

5 Double-click the WIN31SBS folder in the Directories box.

This sets the default subdirectory to WIN31SBS.

6 Click OK.

Open the Paintbrush picture

1 Click anywhere in the Paintbrush window.

This makes the Paintbrush window active.

2 From the File menu, choose Open.

The File Open dialog box appears.

3 Double-click the WIN31SBS folder in the Directories box.

This sets the default subdirectory to WIN31SBS.

4 Double-click BALLOONS.BMP.

The file opens.

Note If you did not create the file BALLOONS.BMP, in Lesson 10 use the backup file BALLOONS.BMP from the C:\WINDOWS\WIN31SBS\FINAL subdirectory.

---

5 From the File menu, choose Save As.

The File Save As dialog box appears.

6 Type **OLE-LINK** in the Filename box.

7 Click OK.

The file is saved with a new name.

Link a Paintbrush picture into a Write document

In this exercise you link the Paintbrush file into the Write document.

1 Click the Scissors tool.

2 Drag the mouse to create a flexible box around the balloons.

3 Release the mouse button.

The balloons are selected.

4 From the Edit menu, choose Copy.

The balloons are pasted onto the Clipboard.

5 Click anywhere in the Write document.

This activates the Write window.

6 Press CTRL+END.

This moves the insertion point to the end of the document.

7 From the Edit menu, choose Paste Link.

Windows pastes a copy of the balloons from Paintbrush into the Write document and creates a link to the Paintbush picture.

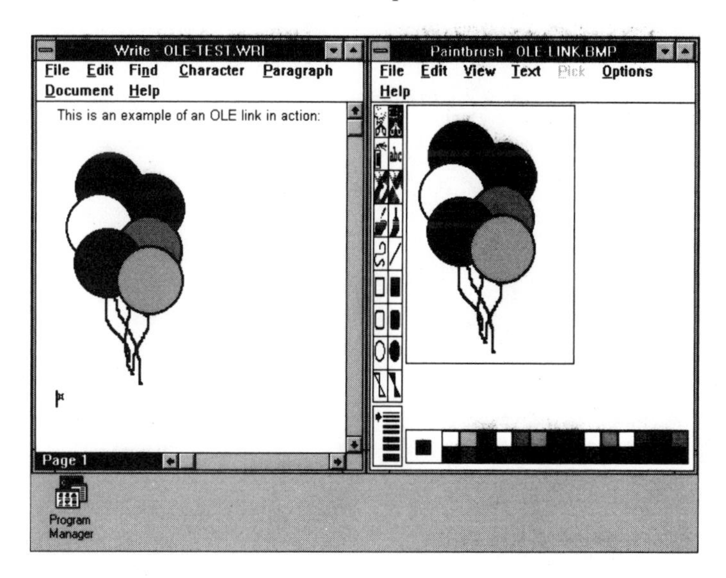

Save the file

▶ From the File menu, choose Save.

The Write document is saved.

Changing the linked information

When you change the information in your server application, Windows updates the information in the client application. If both the client and server applications are open, Windows performs the update in the client application as soon as you make it in the server application. If the client application is not open when you make the changes in the server application, Windows waits until you open the client application to update the information.

Modify the linked information

In this exercise you change the Paintbrush file, and watch Windows update the linked Write document.

1 Click anywhere in the Paintbrush window.

  This activates the window.

2 Click the Paint Roller tool.

3 Click the light gray color in the Color Palette box.

  This is the first gray color on the top row, immediately to the left of the red color in the Color Palette box.

4 Click in the background of the picture.

  The background color, white, changes to gray. The color in the background of the picture in the Write document also changes.

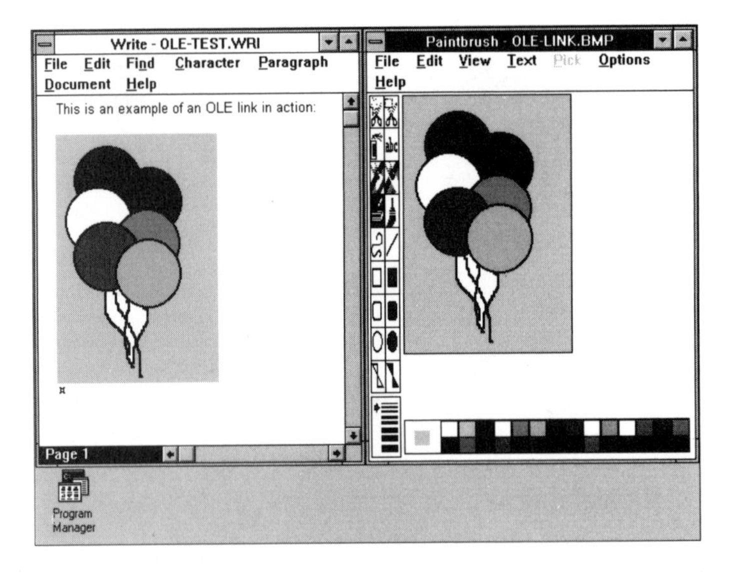

5 From the File menu in Paintbrush, choose Save.

  This saves the modified picture.

6 From the File menu in Write, choose Save.

  This saves the modified document.

Update information using OLE

In this exercise you close the document in the client application and make changes to the file in the server application. Then you reopen the document in the client application and use OLE to update the information from the file in the server application.

1. From the File menu in Write, choose New.

   This creates a new document, and closes the current document, OLE-TEST.WRI.
2. Click in the Paintbrush window to activate the window.
3. Click the blue color with the left mouse button in the Paintbrush color palette.

   This changes the foreground color to blue.
4. Click in the yellow balloon.

   This changes the yellow balloon to a blue balloon.
5. Click in the Write window to activate the window.
6. From the File menu, choose Open.

   The File Open dialog box appears.
7. Double-click OLE-TEST.WRI in the File box.

   The file opens, but a dialog box appears asking you if you want to update the linked object.

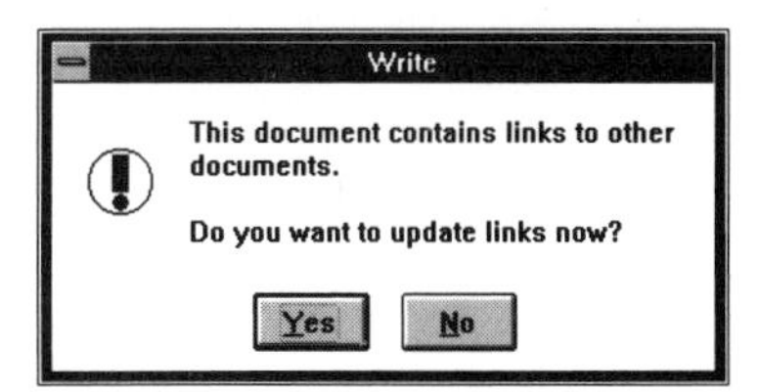

8. Click Yes.

   Write opens the document and Windows updates the link.

Restart the OLE server for a linked object

When you modify the linked object in your document, the server application does not have to be open; it will be started automatically. You activate the OLE link in several ways. You can use the Activate or Edit button in the Links dialog box, which starts the server application and loads the server document. (Double-clicking the linked object does the same thing.)

If you have not closed the server application and the server document, you can switch to the server application and make changes in the document. After you make changes in the server application, Windows updates the linked information in the client application.

Close the OLE server

▶ Double-click the Control-menu box in the Paintbrush window, and save changes.

Paintbrush closes.

Restart the OLE server

1 From the Edit menu in the Write window, choose Links.

The Links dialog box appears. Note that OLE-LINK.BMP is linked, and that the link displays as a set of coordinates. These coordinates tell OLE what section of the picture is to be linked from the OLE server application into the OLE client application.

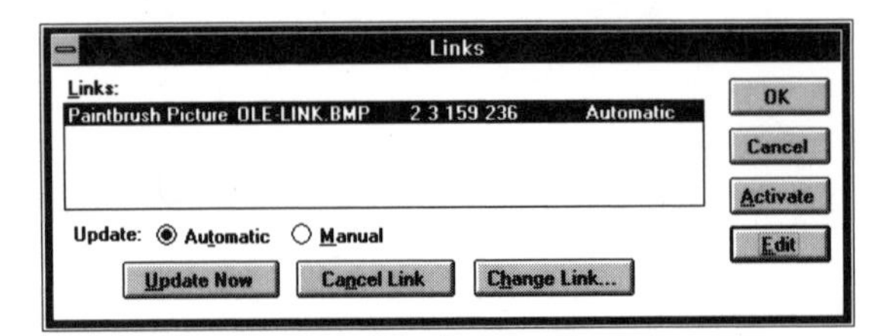

2 Click the Activate button.

After a few moments, the OLE server (Paintbrush) opens and becomes the active window.

3 Click the yellow color in the Color Palette box with the left mouse button.

4 Click the Paint Roller tool.

5 Click one of the blue balloons to change the color to yellow.

The picture in Paintbrush changes. After a few moments, Windows updates the picture in Write.

6 From the File menu, choose Save.

7 From the File menu, choose Exit.

Paintbrush closes.

Embedding Information

The other method of using OLE is to *embed* the information from the server application into a client document. This method, although slightly more complex than creating an OLE link, is often easier to maintain. Embedding the information inserts the actual information into the client document as compared to the marker placed by linking. You only use the OLE server application to change the information in the *client* document rather than changing the server document as you do with a linked file. Embedding an object into a file makes that file larger, because the embedded information is placed into the client document.

Unlike linking, embedding an object does not require you to have a separate file containing the information. When you want to update the information, Windows starts the server application, but loads the information *from the client document.*

When you edit the embedded picture, Windows starts Paintbrush for you to make your changes. Rather than loading a file from your hard disk, Paintbrush uses the information embedded in your client document. After you save your changes and exit Paintbrush, the picture in your Write document is updated. You can move the OLE client file wherever you want on your hard disk, and the picture can always be updated, because there is no physical OLE server file.

To embed an object for the first time or to update an existing object, you use the Update command. This command is found on the File menu in the server application.

Embed an object into Write

In this exercise you embed an OLE object into your Write document.

1. Click the Maximize button in the Write window.
2. Press CTRL+END to move to the end of the document and press ENTER ENTER.
3. Type **This is an embedded OLE object:** and press ENTER ENTER.
4. From the Edit menu, choose Insert Object.

   The Insert Object dialog box appears.
5. Double-click Paintbrush Picture in the list of OLE server applications.

   After a brief pause, Paintbrush opens. The title bar displays the text "Paintbrush - Paintbrush Picture in OLE-TEST.WRI."

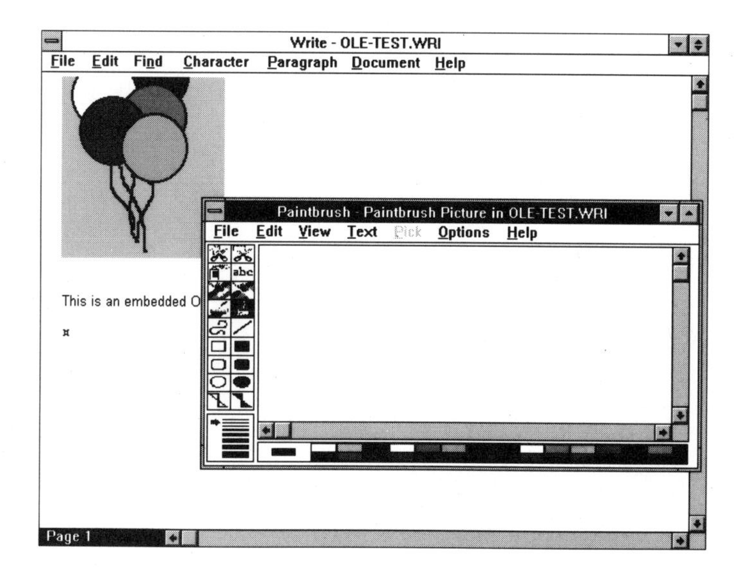

6 Click the red color with the left mouse button.

This sets the foreground color to red.

7 Click the Filled Circle/Ellipse tool and drag the mouse from the top left corner toward the bottom right corner to create a circle about 2 inches in diameter.

8 From the File menu, choose Update.

The object is embedded in the Write document.

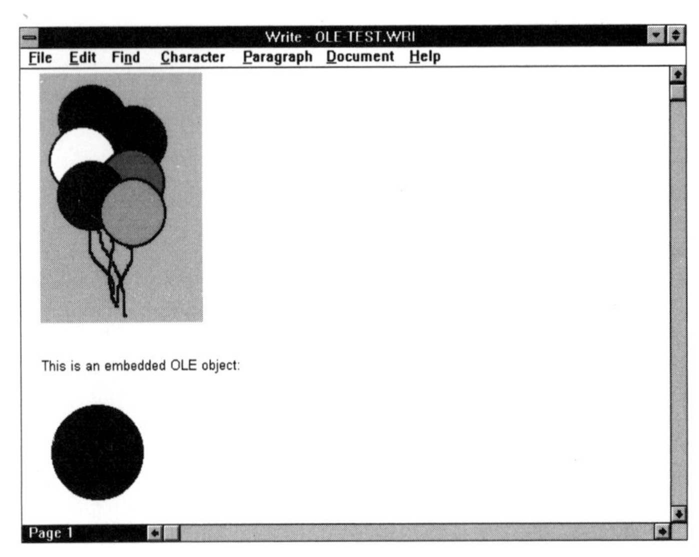

9 From the File menu, choose Exit & Return to OLE-TEST.WRI.

Paintbrush closes, and Windows returns you to the Write document.

Modifying the embedded object

You modify the embedded object using the OLE server application that created it. However, unlike linking, the server application uses the information *in the client application* instead of using a separate linked file. Unlike the procedure you use when you edit a linked object, you select the embedded object to edit it.

Once the embedded object is selected, you edit it using the command Edit Paintbrush Picture Object command on the Edit menu. (The actual command may be slightly different depending upon the OLE client and server applications you use.)

This menu command starts the OLE server application, and loads the information you selected in the OLE client application. (You can also double-click the object to start the OLE server application.)

Change an embedded object

1. Click the circle to select it.
2. From the Edit menu, choose Edit Paintbrush Picture Object.

   After a few moments, Paintbrush opens and puts the red circle in the drawing area.
3. Click the green color with the left mouse button.
4. Click the Filled Rectangle tool.
5. Drag in the middle of the red circle to create a green square.
6. From the File menu, choose Update.

   Paintbrush updates the embedded object in Write.
7. From the File menu, choose Exit.

   Paintbrush closes.
8. From the File menu in Write, choose Save.

   Write saves the file.
9. From the File menu, choose Exit.

   Write closes.

Close Windows

1. Double-click the Program Manager icon.

   Windows restores the Program Manager window.
2. Double-click the Control-menu box in the Program Manager window.
3. At the dialog box, press ENTER or click OK.

   Windows closes.

Summary of OLE

- You use OLE to link or embed information from one application into another.
- The OLE server sends, and the OLE client receives information.
- When you change information in the server document, OLE changes the linked information in the client document.
- When you embed information using OLE, you edit it using the program that created it.
- An OLE-aware application can only link or embed with other OLE-aware applications.

Glossary

386 enhanced mode A mode for Windows that uses the virtual memory capacities of an 80386 processor. This mode allows multitasking of non-Windows-based applications. *See also* multitasking.

accessory One of several application programs included with Windows, initially found in a group called Accessories.

active A window, file, icon or document that is immediately available to respond to user input. If several items are open, only one can be active at a time. For example, you can only have one active window at a time. The active window appears in front of all other windows, and its title bar has a different color.

application A program designed to perform a task for the user, such as word processing, numeric calculation, picture design, or database management.

application window A window containing an open application. The title bar of the window displays the name of the application. There may be one or more document windows within an application window.

associate In File Manager, to identify a file with the application that created it. Double-clicking an associated file starts the application and the file within it.

attribute A characteristic of a file. For example, different attributes determine whether the file is modifiable by the user, hidden, or part of the operating system.

bit mapped font *See* screen font.

border The frame around the four sides of a window. Dragging any part of a border can change a window's size or shape.

branch Part of a directory tree, consisting of a specific directory plus all lower-level subdirectories and files contained in that directory.

capacity *See* disk capacity.

cascade Window arrangement in which multiple windows overlap so that all of their title bars are visible.

Character Map An accessory that contains all characters available in a selected font. You can choose special characters that are not found on standard keyboards and copy them into documents. For example, ½ and ¢ are characters in the Character Map.

check box A dialog box control consisting of a small square next to a description of an option. Clicking the square causes an X to appear or disappear, instructing the program to enable or disable that option.

choose To activate a command or command button through either a mouse or keyboard action.

click To move the mouse pointer to a specific spot on the screen and press a mouse button.

Clipboard An area in computer memory where items that have been cut or copied are temporarily stored. You can copy information from one application to the Clipboard and then paste the information from the Clipboard to another application.

close To quit an application and remove its window or remove a document window from an application window.

collapse To eliminate the display of an entire branch in a directory tree. You collapse a branch by either double-clicking a directory or choosing the Collapse Branch command from the Tree menu.

COM port *See* serial port.

combo box A dialog box control consisting of a text box combined with a list box.

command button A dialog box control consisting of a rectangular button labeled with a command. You click the button to activate the command.

command A word or phrase that, when chosen, executes an action in a program. A list of commands appears in a menu, or a single command appears on a command button.

confirmation An additional step in certain program operations that makes you actively affirm your intention to carry out the operation. In File Manager, for example, you may have to respond to a confirmation dialog box when you attempt to copy or delete a file.

contents list In File Manager, the right side of a directory window showing the directories and files contained in the current directory.

Control menu A menu of window control commands, opened using the Control-menu box.

Control Panel An application found in the Main group of Program Manager. The Control Panel allows you to modify such basic Windows and computer functions as screen appearance, printing, fonts, and date/time settings.

Control-menu box A small box in the upper-left corner of a window, containing a horizontal line. When you click this box, the control menu drops down. When you double-click this box, the window closes.

copy To duplicate a program item, file, or selection.

current directory In File Manager, the active directory in a directory window. You change the current directory by selecting a different one in the directory tree.

current drive In File Manager, the disk drive whose directory tree is displayed in an active directory window. You change the current drive by clicking a different one in the disk drive area near the top of a directory window.

data file A file that contains information created using an application program.

default printer The printer that is automatically used when you choose Print from a File menu. You can select any printer to be the default printer using the Print Manager.

default The settings and parameters in an application program when you first start it.

description A name assigned to a group icon or program-item icon in Program Manager.

desktop The screen background that appears when you run Windows. Screen objects such as windows and icons all appear on the desktop.

destination The target location in a *move* or *copy* operation. For example, you copy a file from a source directory to a destination directory.

dialog box A special type of window that pops up in response to a user action. Before the program can continue, you may be required to select among one or more types of options. You close a dialog box by choosing a command button.

directory A named group of files. Each directory can contain both individual files and additional directories.

directory path A string of directories that connect a given directory to the root directory.

directory tree A symbolic representation of the interconnecting structure of directories on a disk. In File Manager, a directory tree is usually shown on the left side of a directory window.

directory window A window within File Manager that can display both the directory tree of a specified disk and the contents of a selected directory.

disk capacity The maximum amount of data that can be stored on a disk. Disk capacity depends on the disk's physical size and density.

disk drive A device that stores and retrieves information from disks.

document window A window within an application's window that you use to create or modify a document. In many applications, you can open more than one document window within the main application window.

double-click To click the primary mouse button twice. You double-click to perform tasks like choosing an option, opening a window or document, or selecting text or a graphic.

double-density disk A floppy disk that holds 360K of data.

drag To hold down a mouse button, move the mouse to a different location, and release the button. Dragging allows you to perform tasks such as moving text or graphics to a different location in a document.

drive *See* disk drive.

dynamic link A link that allows you to exchange data automatically between applications. For example, if you alter a graphic that is linked with a word processor document, the graphic is automatically updated in the word processor document.

embed To store an item created by one application, whether text or graphics, into a file from another application. If you embed a graphic in a word processor file, you do not have to open the original graphic file in order to edit it—Windows loads the application you used to create the item to allow you to edit it.

expand To show more levels of a directory tree in File Manager. Expanding a branch allows you to see subdirectories that are hidden. You can expand one branch, one directory, or an entire tree.

extension Three characters that can identify a file as a particular kind of file or associated with a particular application. For example, an EXE file is an executable file, usually an application, while a WRI file contains text and was created in Write.

file Information that has been collected into a unit, named, and stored on a disk. Windows stores all applications and documents as files.

file size The length of a file, generally expressed in bytes.

filename The name of an electronic file consisting of up to eight characters, followed by an optional extension of a period and up to three additional characters.

floppy disk A magnetic disk used to store data. Depending on their size and density, floppy disks can hold from 360K to 1.44 MB of information.

font A set of characters that are formatted in the same typeface, style, and size. For example, Courier, Arial, and Times New Roman are fonts.

format To initialize and prepare a disk to store data. Formatting erases all data previously on a disk.

full screen mode A mode in which MS-DOS–based applications run under Windows. In full screen mode, the application behaves as if it were running without Windows and fills the entire screen.

group icon An icon representing a minimized window containing a group of program items.

group window A window containing one or more program items. Group windows display applications or data files associated with the applications. You can create new group windows or alter the contents of existing group windows with Program Manager.

high-density disk A disk that can hold more data than a double-density disk. A 5.25-inch high-density disk can hold 1.2 MB of information. A 3.5-inch high density disk can hold 1.44 MB.

icon A graphic element that represents various objects in Windows. Icons can represent many elements in Windows, including disk drives, applications, and documents.

landscape An orientation for printing. Choosing landscape prints images sideways on the page. *Also known as* Wide.

LCD Liquid crystal display. A type of monitor primarily used in laptop computers.

link To set files up so that you can exchange data automatically between applications. For example, if you alter a graphic that is linked with a word processor document, the graphic is automatically updated in the word processor document.

list box A box containing a list of items that you can select by clicking. List boxes are often found in dialog boxes.

LPT port *See* parallel port.

macro A set of actions recorded and saved using Recorder. Recorder performs the actions when you play back the macro. You can assign a shortcut key code or a name to a macro as a timesaving way to play back the macro.

Maximize button The small box with an upward arrow in the upper-right corner of a window. Clicking the maximize button enlarges the window so that it takes up the entire screen.

maximize To enlarge a window so that it fills the entire screen.

menu A list of commands that can be executed at the click of a mouse or with the keyboard. Menu commands carry out commands in Windows-based applications.

menu bar The horizontal bar that appears just below the title bar in applications. The menu bar contains the names of all the menus available in the application.

microfloppy disk A 3.5-inch disk used to store data. Depending on their density, microfloppy disks can store 720K or 1.44 MB of information.

Minimize button The small box with a downward arrow in the upper-right corner of a window. Clicking the minimize button reduces the window to an icon.

minimize To reduce a window to an icon.

move To transfer information from one place to another. For example, you can move text from one place to another in a document or from one document to another. In File Manager, you can move a file from one directory to another.

MS-DOS Acronym for Microsoft Disk Operating System.

MS-DOS–based application A non-Windows-based application that runs under MS-DOS. MS-DOS–based applications can be run in either full screen mode or window mode, depending on the processor in your computer.

multitasking Running more than one application at a time. In Windows, you can switch between open applications and work with different programs without closing any of them.

non-Windows-based application An application that does not require Windows to run. Often an MS-DOS–based application.

open To start an application, access a data file, or enlarge a minimized window.

option button A round button, usually found in a dialog box, that you click to choose an option. Only one option button in a set can be selected at a time.

parallel port The connection on a computer for a parallel device. Printers are often connected by cables to parallel ports.

paste To insert text or graphics into a document from the Clipboard.

path The complete name of a file, including its name and extension plus all the directories and subdirectories under which it resides.

pel *See* pixel.

PIF Program Information File. A file that holds information that Windows needs in order to run non-Windows-based applications.

pixel A small spot, the smallest single unit that a computer can display. Sometimes called pel or picture element.

plotter font A font used to display text on a screen Plotter fonts can be scaled to any size without distortion, but their display quality is not as high as a TrueType font. Also known as Vector fonts or Stroke fonts.

point size The height of a character measured in units called points. One point equals approximately 1/72 of an inch. *Also known as* font size.

pointer The arrow-shaped cursor that Windows displays on the screen and that you control with the mouse.

port The location for connecting cables attached to other devices such as printers or modems to your computer. Ports can be parallel or serial.

portrait An orientation for printing. A page printed in a portrait orientation is longer than wide. Portrait orientation is the standard orientation for most pages. *Also known as* Tall.

PostScript A page description language from Adobe Systems that describes the elements of a page to printers or displays.

PostScript printer A printer that can interpret and print PostScript files.

primary button The button used for most mouse actions. The left mouse button is usually the primary button.

print queue The list of files that you have sent to be printed. You can look at and change the order of files in the print queue using the Print Manager.

printer resolution The degree of clarity that a printer can attain in an image. Expressed in dots per inch (dpi), some common resolutions are 125 dpi for a low-quality dot-matrix printer and 300 dpi for a laser printer. The more dots per inch, the higher the resolutions, and the better the image quality.

program file An executable file that you run to perform a task, as opposed to a data file that simply contains information like a letter or a report. Files with the extension EXE are usually program files.

Program Information File A file that holds information that Windows needs in order to run non-Windows-based applications. *See also* PIF.

program item An application or accessory in Windows, such as Paintbrush, Write, or File Manager.

program-item icon The graphic element that represents a program item when that application or accessory is closed or minimized. For example, the picture of a filing cabinet is the program-item icon for File Manager.

queue *See* print queue.

quick format A faster way of reformatting a disk that has been previously formatted. Quick formatting does not check the entire disk surface for defects like normal formatting does.

raster font *See* screen font.

resolution The degree of clarity that a monitor or printer can attain in an image. Printer resolution is expressed in dots per inch (dpi) while screen resolution is expressed in pixels. Some common resolutions are 125 dpi for a low-quality dot-matrix printer and 300 dpi for a laser printer. Common screen or monitor resolutions are 640 pixels across by 350 pixels down for EGA and 720 pixels across by 480 pixels down for VGA.

Restore button The small box in the upper-right corner of a window with both an upward and a downward facing arrow. Clicking this button restores the window to its previous size, whether larger or smaller.

restore To change the window size so that it matches the previous size, whether larger or smaller than the current size. Click the Restore button or choose Restore in the Control menu to restore a window.

root directory The main or highest directory level on a disk. When you format a disk, the root directory is automatically created.

scale To enlarge or reduce an image. You can scale graphics or fonts.

screen font A font used for displaying text on the screen. Screen fonts closely approximate printer fonts so that the documents on the screen look the same as printed documents. *Also known as* raster font or bit mapped font.

scroll arrow The arrow at the top and bottom of the scroll bar that allows you to scroll the contents of a screen up or down the window.

scroll bar The band that appears at the right edge of a window for vertical scrolling or at the bottom edge of the window for horizontal scrolling.

scroll box The small square in a scroll bar that indicates the position of the visible contents relative to the total contents of the window.

scroll To move horizontally or vertically through a window that is too small to display all of its contents at one time.

select To highlight text, graphics, or another item with the mouse or keyboard, usually done prior to performing some action.

serial port The connection on a computer for a serial device. Modems are often connected by cables to serial ports.

source The disk or directory that contains information that you want to copy to another disk or directory.

StartUp A specific group window that contains program items that run automatically when you start up Windows.

status bar A band of information along the bottom edge of an application window. In File Manager, for example, the status bar gives data about the capacity of the current disk and the size of the files in the current directory.

subdirectory A directory contained in another directory.

system disk A disk containing copies of the system files necessary to start MS-DOS.

task list A list of the various applications currently running under Windows. The task list appears in a window and allows you to switch between the applications.

terminate A command for MS-DOS–based applications that allows you to exit applications that have stopped responding to keystrokes or commands. Do not use Terminate unless the application has stopped responding; use the program's quit command instead.

text box A rectangular box in which you can enter text from the keyboard. Text boxes are usually found in dialog boxes.

text file A file that contains only text, versus a file that contains non-text items such as a program file.

tile To arrange open windows so that they do not overlap, but are all visible. Each tiled window takes up a portion of the Program Manager's window.

title bar The band that appears at the top edge of a window showing the window's name.

toggle To switch between on and off. For example, you can toggle the display of the ruler in Write.

toolbox An element in Paint containing the various tools needed to create and edit graphics and text.

tree structure A data structure that is organized hierarchically, with branches. For example, MS-DOS–based directories employ a tree structure that includes a root directory, several subdirectories or branches, and files.

TrueType font A scalable font that can be changed to virtually any size. TrueType fonts look the same whether displayed on the screen or printed.

vector font *See* plotter font.

wallpaper An image or pattern that displays on the desktop. You can choose different wallpaper using Control Panel.

wildcard character A character that takes the place of one or more characters in a filename. The question mark represents a single character and the asterisk represents multiple characters. For example, if you need all files with the extension EXE in a directory, you would use the asterisk wildcard *.EXE to generate the list.

window A rectangular area of the screen that can display a document or an application.

window mode A mode in which MS-DOS–based applications run under Windows. In window mode, the application runs in a resizable window. This mode in only available on 80386-based or higher computers.

Windows-based application An application designed to run with Windows which has standard features, such as dialog boxes and menu bars. Windows-based applications cannot run without Windows.

wordwrap A feature that automatically breaks a line of text near the right margin and moves it down to the next line. Write uses wordwrap, Notepad does not.

Index

Note: Italicized page numbers refer to illustrations.

D

E

F

G

Q

R

S

T

Catapult, Inc.

Catapult is a national software training company dedicated to providing the highest quality application software training. Years of PC and Macintosh instruction for major corporations and government institutions provide the models used in building Catapult's exclusive Performance-Based Training program. Based on the principles of adult learning, Performance-Based Training materials ensure that training participants leave the classroom reliably able to accomplish every class performance objective.

Catapult's Curriculum Development Group is pleased to share their training skill with a wider audience through the Step by Step series. This book should help you develop the confidence necessary to achieve increased productivity with Windows 3.1.

Catapult's corporate headquarters are in Bellevue, Washington.

Great Resources for Windows™ 3.1 Users

RUNNING WINDOWS™ 3.1, 3rd ed.

Craig Stinson

Build your confidence and enhance your productivity with Microsoft Windows, quickly and easily, using this hands-on introduction. This Microsoft-authorized edition—for new as well as experienced Windows users—is completely updated and expanded to cover all the new exciting features of version 3.1. You'll find a successful combination of step-by-step tutorials, helpful screen illustrations, expert tips, and real-world examples. Learn how to install and start using Windows 3.1, use applications with Windows, and maximize Windows performance.

560 pages, softcover $27.95 ($37.95 Canada)

WINDOWS™ 3.1 COMPANION

The Cobb Group:

Lori L. Lorenz and R. Michael O'Mara with Russell Borland

This bestseller is now completely updated to cover the important new features of version 3.1. Both a step-by-step tutorial and a comprehensive reference, this book is specifically designed to help you quickly find the information you need—moving from the basics to more advanced information. Learn to take advantage of all the extraordinary improvements and added features of version 3.1, including the new, *faster* File Manager; TrueType font; support for multimedia; the improved Program Manager; the faster Printer Manager; automatic network reconnections; the new "drag and drop" feature. The authors include a wealth of expert tips and tricks and great examples to show you how to use Windows more efficiently.

550 pages, softcover $27.95 ($37.95 Canada)

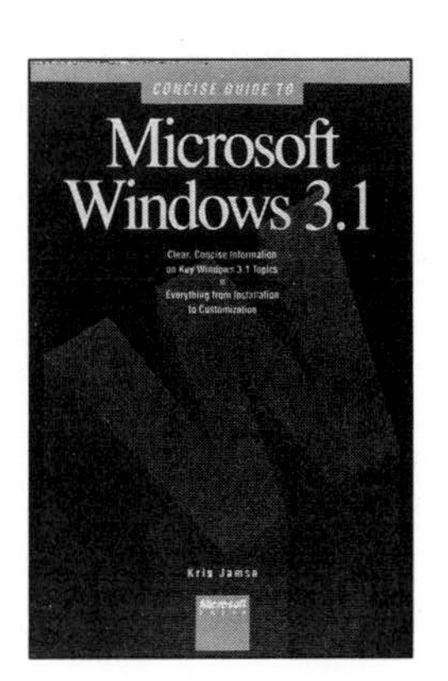

CONCISE GUIDE TO MICROSOFT® WINDOWS™ 3.1

Kris Jamsa

Instant answers to your Windows 3.1 questions! Clear, concise information on all the key Microsoft Windows 3.1 features. For beginning to intermediate users. A great complement to *Windows 3.1 Companion.*

192 pages, softcover $12.95 ($17.95 Canada)

Microsoft Press books are available wherever quality computer books are sold. Or call 1-800-MSPRESS for ordering information or placing credit card orders.* Please refer to BBK when placing your order. Prices subject to change.

*In Canada, contact Macmillan Canada, Attn: Microsoft Press Dept., 164 Commander Blvd., Agincourt, Ontario, Canada M1S 3C7, or call (416) 293-8141.

In the U.K., contact Microsoft Press, 27 Wrights Lane, London W8 5TZ.

STEP BY STEP SERIES

The Official Microsoft® Courseware

Tried-and-tested, these book-and-disk packages are Microsoft's official courseware. Complete with follow-along lessons and disk-based practice files, they are ideal self-study training guides for business, classroom and home use. Scores of real-world business examples make the instruction relevant and useful; "One Step Further" sections for each chapter cover advanced uses. These courseware products are the perfect training guide for business, classroom, or home use.

MICROSOFT® WORD FOR WINDOWS™ STEP BY STEP
Version 2

Microsoft Corporation

Learn to produce professional-quality documents with ease. Covers Microsoft Word for Windows version 2.

296 pages, softcover with one 5.25-inch disk
$29.95 ($39.95 Canada)

MICROSOFT® POWERPOINT® FOR WINDOWS™ STEP BY STEP

Steven M. Johnson

The fastest way to get up and running with Microsoft PowerPoint! Covers Microsoft PowerPoint version 3.

300 pages, softcover with one 3.5-inch disk
$29.95 ($39.95 Canada)
Available August 1992

MICROSOFT® EXCEL FOR WINDOWS™ STEP BY STEP, 2nd ed.
Version 4

Microsoft Corporation

Become a spreadsheet expert the easy way!

325 pages, softcover with one 3.5-inch disk
$29.95 ($39.95 Canada)

MICROSOFT® EXCEL MACROS STEP BY STEP For Windows™ and the Macintosh®
Version 4

Steve Wexler and Julianne Sharer

The ideal way for proficient Microsoft Excel users to learn how to use macros to save time and simplify their work. Scores of examples.

272 pages, softcover with one 720-KB 3.5-inch PC disk and one 800-KB 3.5-inch Macintosh disk
$34.95 ($47.95 Canada)

Microsoft Press books are available wherever quality computer books are sold. Or call 1-800-MSPRESS for ordering information or placing credit card orders.* Please refer to BBK when placing your order. Prices subject to change.

*In Canada, contact Macmillan Canada, Attn: Microsoft Press Dept., 164 Commander Blvd., Agincourt, Ontario, Canada M1S 3C7, or call (416) 293-8141.

In the U.K., contact Microsoft Press, 27 Wrights Lane, London W8 5TZ.

IMPORTANT — READ CAREFULLY BEFORE OPENING SOFTWARE PACKET(S).
By opening the sealed packet(s) containing the software, you indicate your acceptance of the following Microsoft License Agreement.

Microsoft License Agreement

MICROSOFT LICENSE AGREEMENT
(Single User Products)

This is a legal agreement between you (either an individual or an entity) and Microsoft Corporation. By opening the sealed software packet(s) you are agreeing to be bound by the terms of this agreement. If you do not agree to the terms of this agreement, promptly return the book, incuding the unopened software packet(s), to the place you obtained it for a full refund.

MICROSOFT SOFTWARE LICENSE

1. GRANT OF LICENSE. Microsoft grants to you the right to use one copy of the Microsoft software program included with this book (the "SOFTWARE") on a single terminal connected to a single computer. The SOFTWARE is in "use" on a computer when it is loaded into temporary memory (i.e. RAM) or installed into permanent memory (e.g., hard disk, CD-ROM, or other storage device) of that computer. You may not network the SOFTWARE or otherwise use it on more than one computer or computer terminal at the same time.

2. COPYRIGHT. The SOFTWARE is owned by Microsoft or its suppliers and is protected by United States copyright laws and international treaty provisions. Therefore, you must treat the SOFTWARE like any other copyrighted material (e.g., a book or musical recording) except that you may either (a) make one copy of the SOFTWARE solely for backup or archival purposes, or (b) transfer the SOFTWARE to a single hard disk provided you keep the original solely for backup or archival purposes. You may not copy the written materials accompanying the SOFTWARE.

3. OTHER RESTRICTIONS. You may not rent or lease the SOFTWARE, but you may transfer the SOFTWARE and accompanying written materials on a permanent basis provided you retain no copies and the recipient agrees to the terms of this Agreement. You may not reverse engineer, decompile, or disassemble the SOFTWARE. If the SOFTWARE is an update or has been updated, any transfer must include the most recent update and all prior versions.

4. DUAL MEDIA SOFTWARE. If the SOFTWARE package contains both 3.5" and 5.25" disks, then you may use only the disks appropriate for your single-user computer. You may not use the other disks on another computer or loan, rent, lease, or transfer them to another user except as part of the permanent transfer (as provided above) of all SOFTWARE and written materials.

5. LANGUAGE SOFTWARE. If the SOFTWARE is a Microsoft language product, then you have a royalty-free right to reproduce and distribute executable files created using the SOFTWARE. If the language product is a Basic or COBOL product, then Microsoft grants you a royalty-free right to reproduce and distribute the run-time modules of the SOFTWARE provided that you: (a) distribute the run-time modules only in conjunction with and as a part of your software product; (b) do not use Microsoft's name, logo, or trademarks to market your software product; (c) include a valid copyright notice on your software product; and (d) agree to indemnify, hold harmless, and defend Microsoft and its suppliers from and against any claims or lawsuits, including attorneys' fees, that arise or result from the use or distribution of your software product. The "run-time modules" are those files in the SOFTWARE that are identified in the accompanying written materials as required during execution of your software program. The run-time modules are limited to run-time files, install files, and ISAM and REBUILD files. If required in the SOFTWARE documentation, you agree to display the designated patent notices on the packaging and in the README file of your software product.

LIMITED WARRANTY

LIMITED WARRANTY. Microsoft warrants that (a) the SOFTWARE will perform substantially in accordance with the accompanying written materials for a period of ninety (90) days from the date of receipt, and (b) any hardware accompanying the SOFTWARE will be free from defects in materials and workmanship under normal use and service for a period of one (1) year from the date of receipt. Any implied warranties on the SOFTWARE and hardware are limited to ninety (90) days and one (1) year, respectively. Some states/countries do not allow limitations on duration of an implied warranty, so the above limitation may not apply to you.

CUSTOMER REMEDIES. Microsoft's and its suppliers' entire liability and your exclusive remedy shall be, at Microsoft's option, either (a) return of the price paid, or (b) repair or replacement of the SOFTWARE or hardware that does not meet Microsoft's Limited Warranty and which is returned to Microsoft with a copy of your receipt. This Limited Warranty is void if failure of the SOFTWARE or hardware has resulted from accident, abuse, or misapplication. Any replacement SOFTWARE or hardware will be warranted for the remainder of the original warranty period or thirty (30) days, whichever is longer. Outside the United States, these remedies are not available without proof of purchase from an authorized non-U.S. source.

NO OTHER WARRANTIES. Microsoft and its suppliers disclaim all other warranties, either express or implied, including, but not limited to implied warranties of merchantability and fitness for a particular purpose, with regard to the SOFTWARE, the accompanying written materials, and any accompanying hardware. This limited warranty gives you specific legal rights. You may have others which vary from state/country to state/country.

NO LIABILITY FOR CONSEQUENTIAL DAMAGES. In no event shall Microsoft or its suppliers be liable for any damages whatsoever (including without limitation, damages for loss of business profits, business interruption, loss of business information, or any other pecuniary loss) arising out of the use of or inability to use this Microsoft product, even if Microsoft has been advised of the possibility of such damages. Because some states/countries do not allow the exclusion or limitation of liability for consequential or incidental damages, the above limitation may not apply to you.

U.S. GOVERNMENT RESTRICTED RIGHTS

The SOFTWARE and documentation are provided with RESTRICTED RIGHTS. Use, duplication, or disclosure by the Government is subject to restrictions as set forth in subparagraph (c)(1)(ii) of The Rights in Technical Data and Computer Software clause at DFARS 252.227-7013 or subparagraphs (c)(1) and (2) of the Commercial Computer Software — Restricted Rights 48 CFR 52.227-19, as applicable. Manufacturer is Microsoft Corporation/One Microsoft Way/Redmond, WA 98052-6399.

This Agreement is governed by the laws of the State of Washington.

Should you have any questions concerning this Agreement, or if you desire to contact Microsoft for any reason, please write: Microsoft Sales and Service/One Microsoft Way/ Redmond, WA 98052-6399.